Mandala Seductive Shapes

One Of A Kind Adult Coloring Book For Women And Men With 50 Stress-Relieving Designs

Coloring Book For Adults

Copyright © 2018 Michael Weiner

Copyright © 2018 by Michael Weiner

All rights reserved. No part of this publication may be reproduced, distributed, or transmitted in any form or by any means, including photocopying, recording, or other electronic or mechanical methods, without the prior written permission of the publisher, except in the case of brief quotations embodied in critical reviews and certain other noncommercial uses permitted by copyright law. For permission requests, write to the publisher, addressed "Attention: Permissions Coordinator," at the address below.

Glass By Michael, LLC
michael@liveasuperchargedlife.com
liveasuperchargedlife.com

Ordering Information:
Quantity sales. Special discounts are available on quantity purchases by corporations, associations, and others. For details, contact the publisher at the address above.

Orders by U.S. trade bookstores and wholesalers. Please contact Live A Supercharged Life
michael@liveasuperchargedlife.com
liveasuperchargedlife.com
First Edition

Copyright © 2018 Michael Weiner

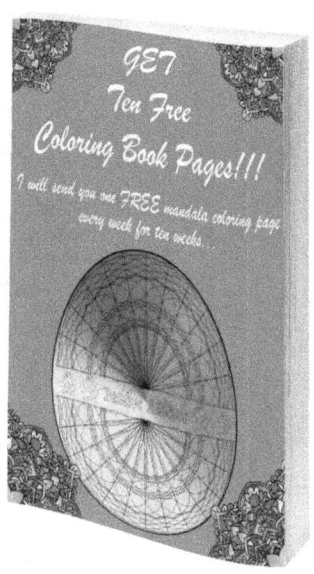

Sign Up For Your 10
FREE
Printable Mandala Coloring Book Pages Now!
http://www.liveasuperchargedlife.com/free-mandala-coloring-pages/

Check Us Out on Social Media

Email: michael@liveasuperchargedlife.com
https://www.facebook.com/liveasuperchargedlife/
https://www.instagram.com/liveasuperchargedlife/
https://www.youtube.com/channel/UCwfgl-GmDbQf5C0m7bLEiUQ
https://www.pinterest.com/liveasupercharg/
https://twitter.com/Superchargedway

Check Out Our Other Books

http://www.liveasuperchargedlife.com/books-by-michael/

Copyright © 2018 Michael Weiner

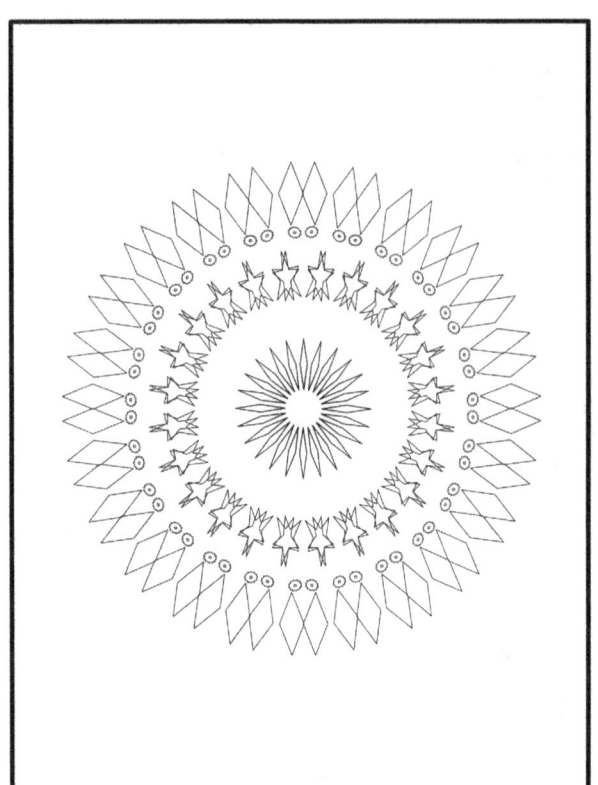
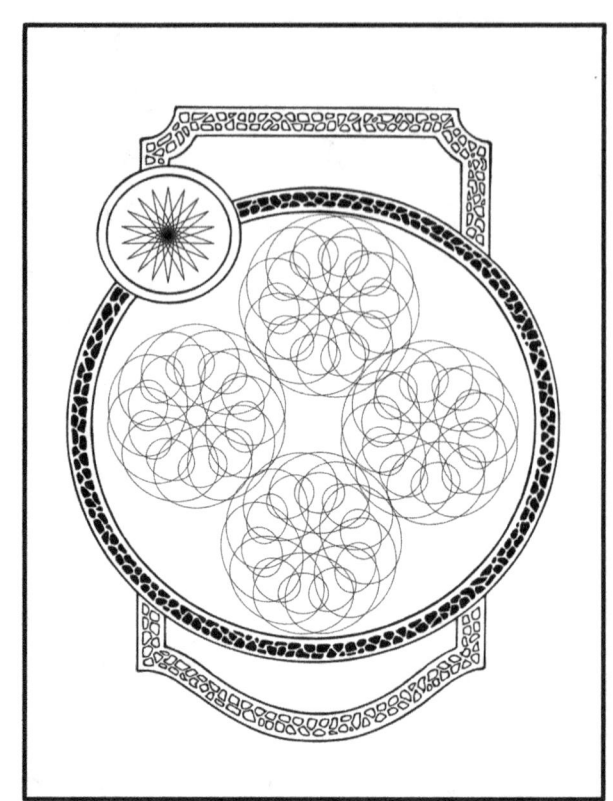

Coloring Book Sample Pages

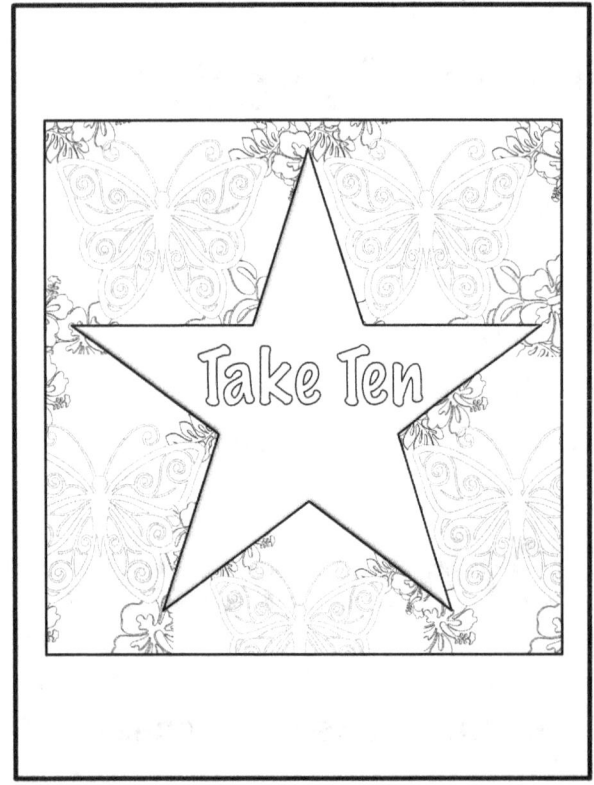
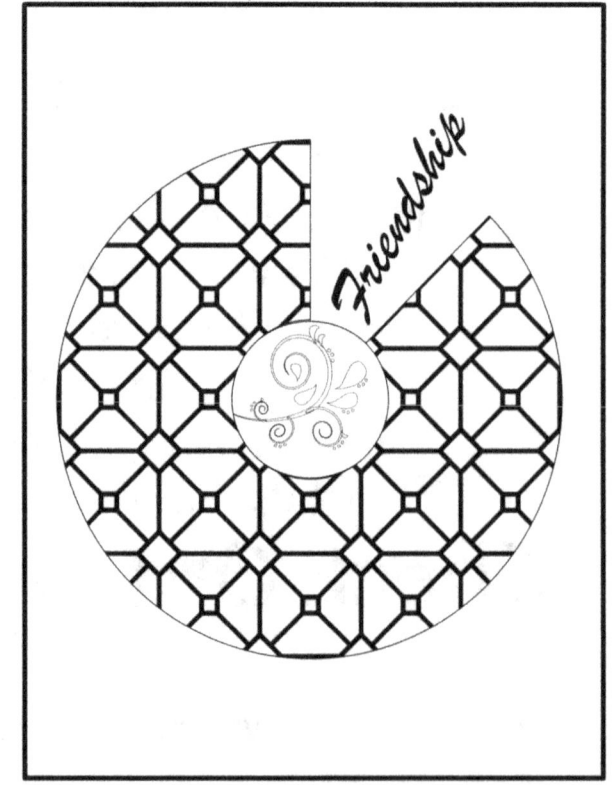

This Book Belongs To

Copyright © 2018 Michael Weiner

Test your color palette

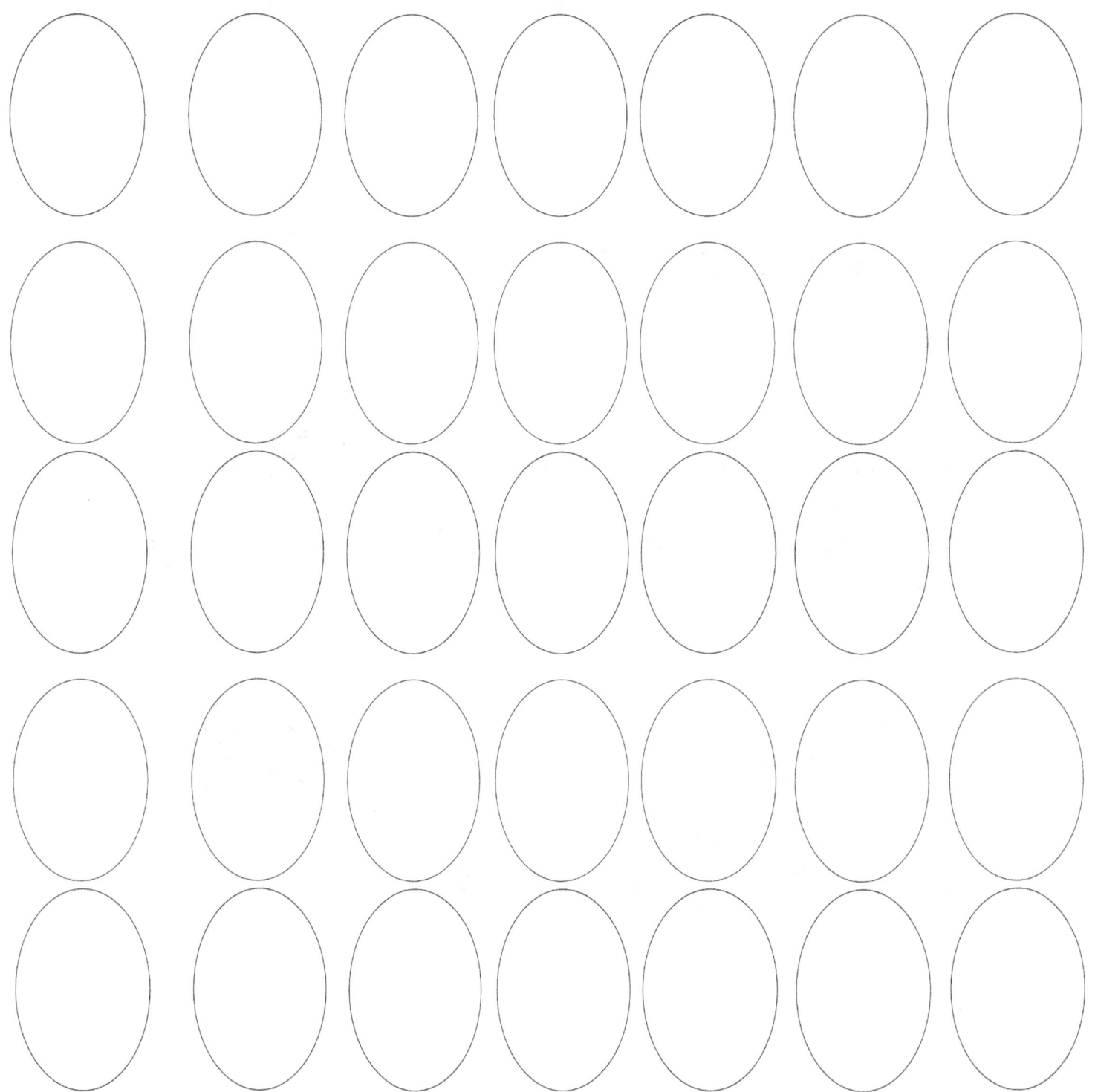

Copyright © 2018 Michael Weiner

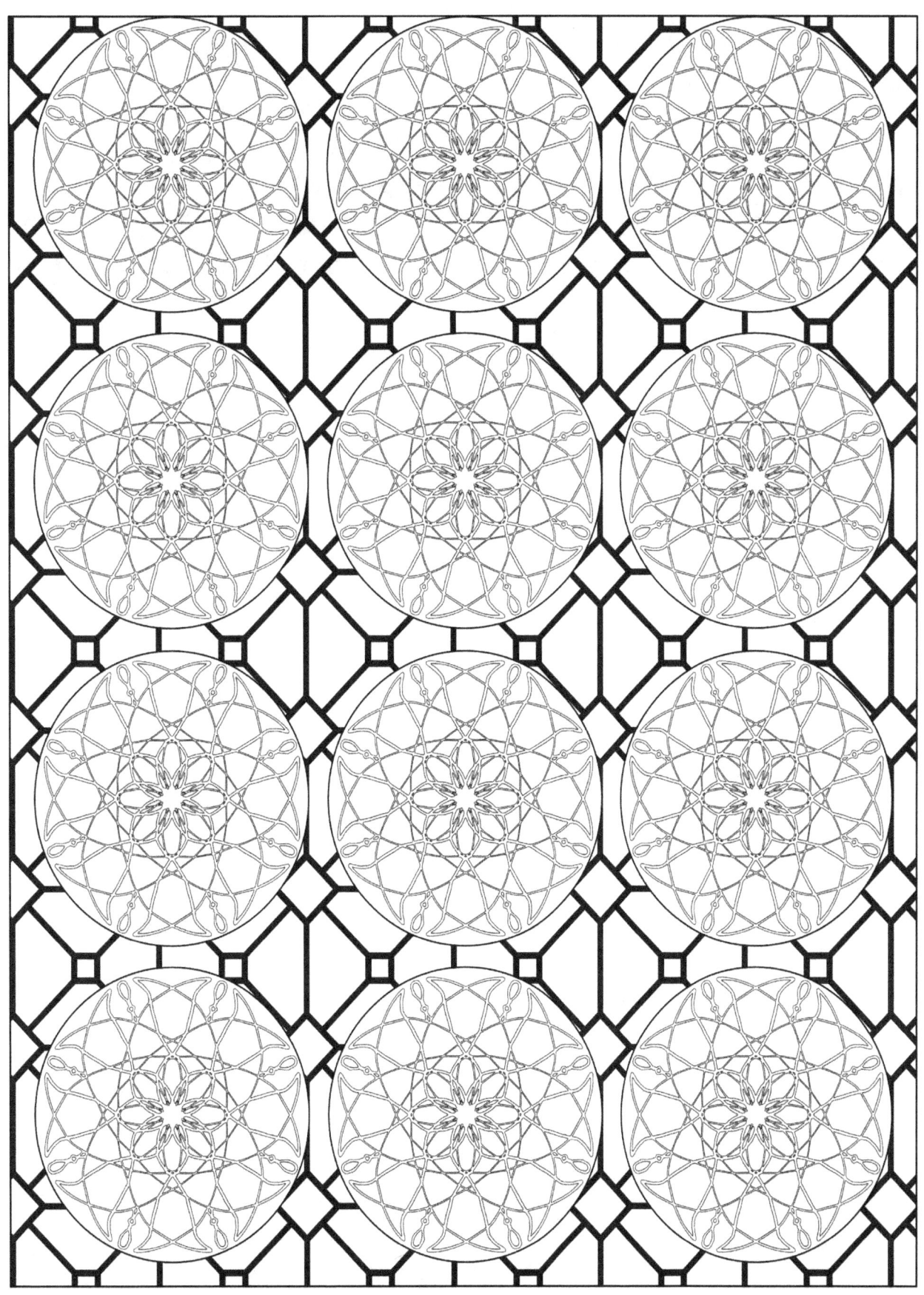

Copyright © 2018 Michael Weiner

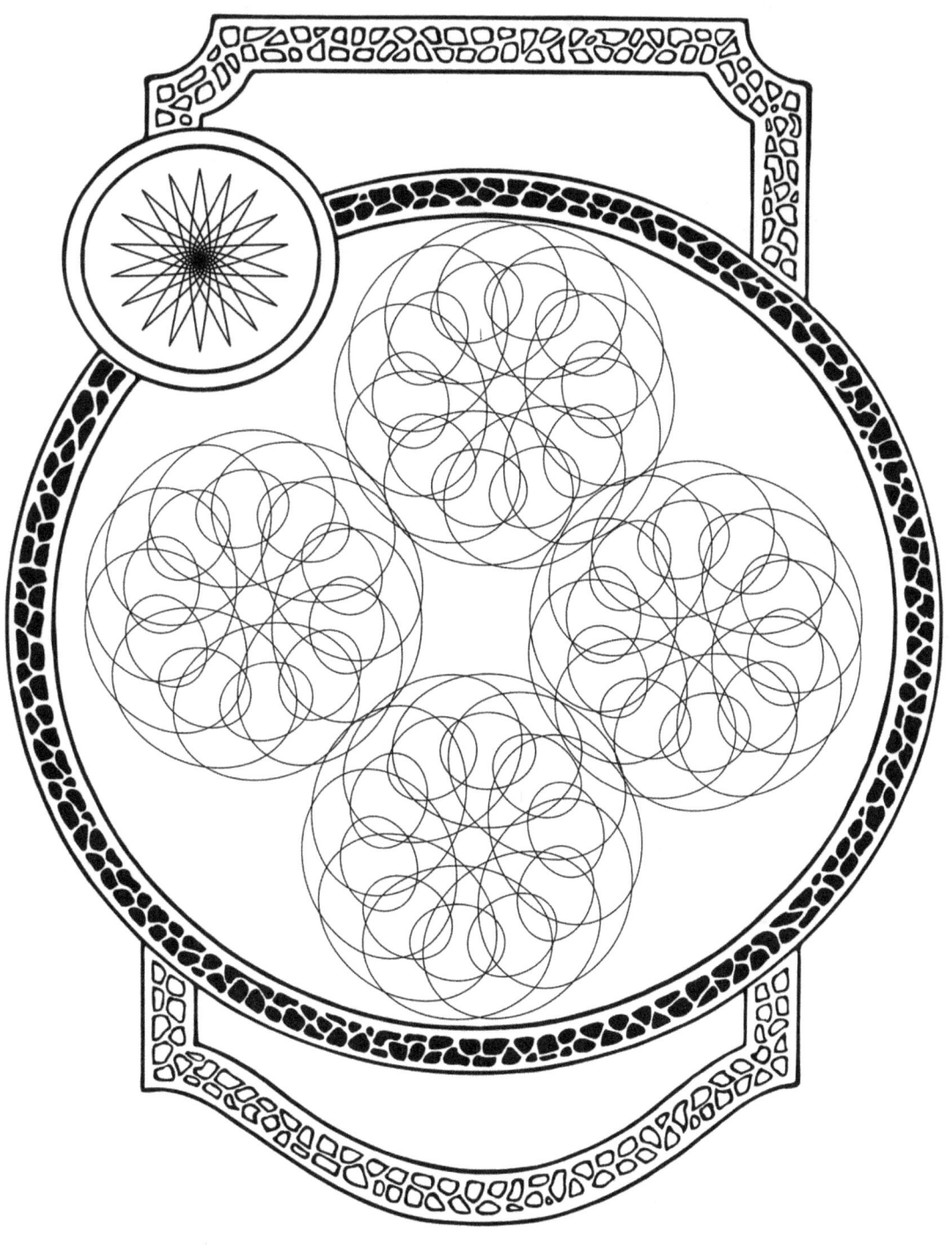

Copyright © 2018 Michael Weiner

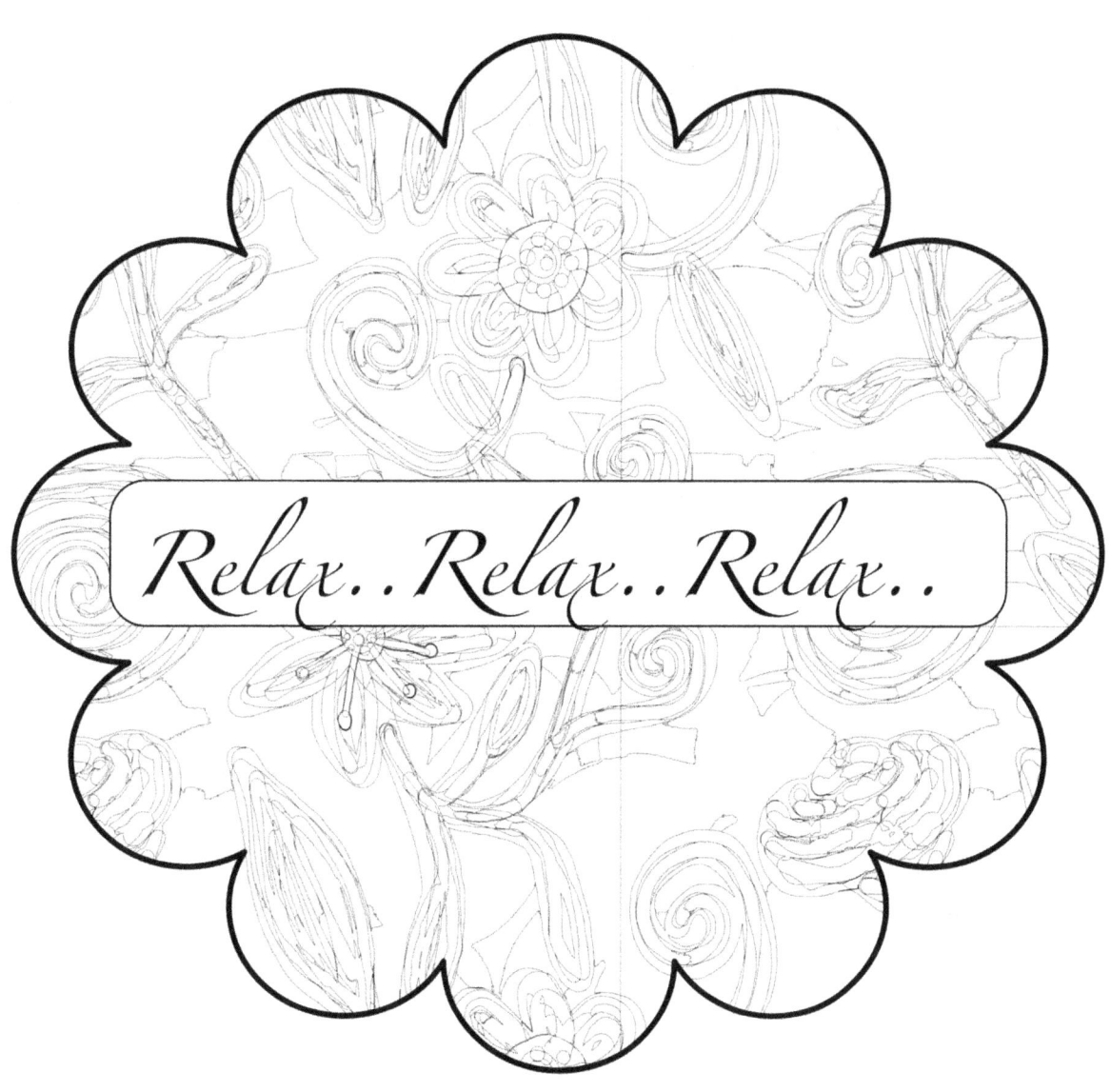

Copyright © 2018 Michael Weiner

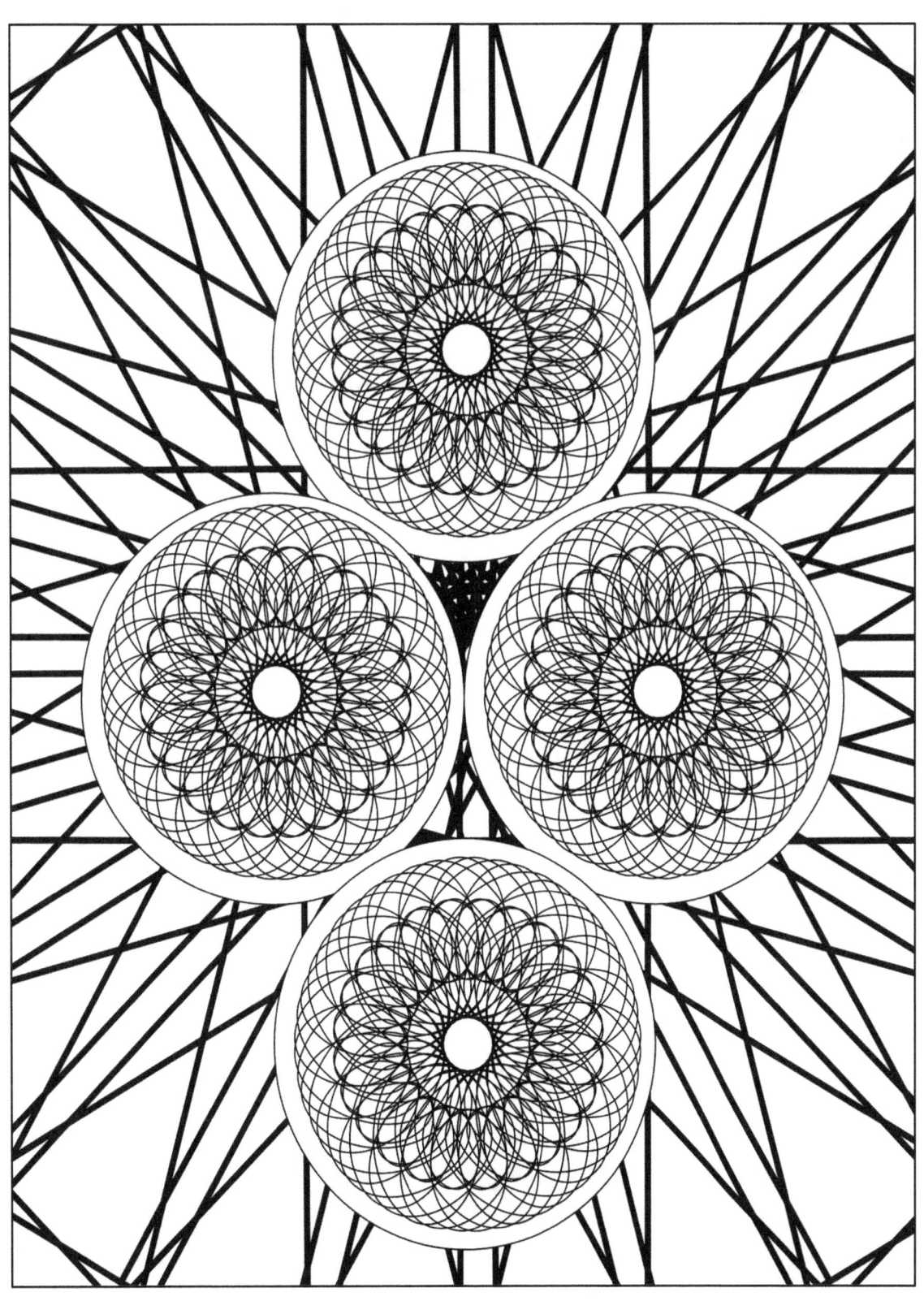

Copyright © 2018 Michael Weiner

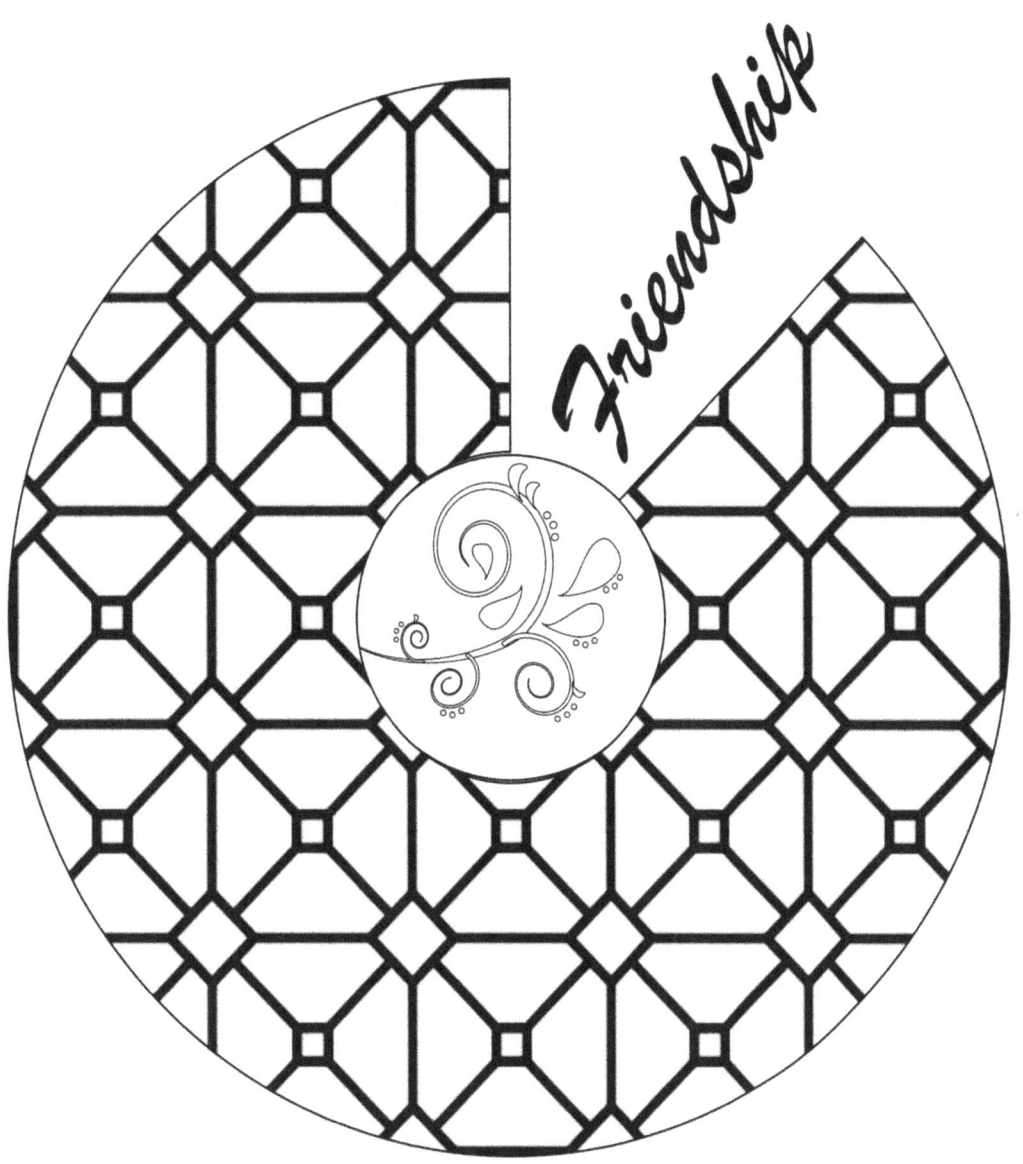

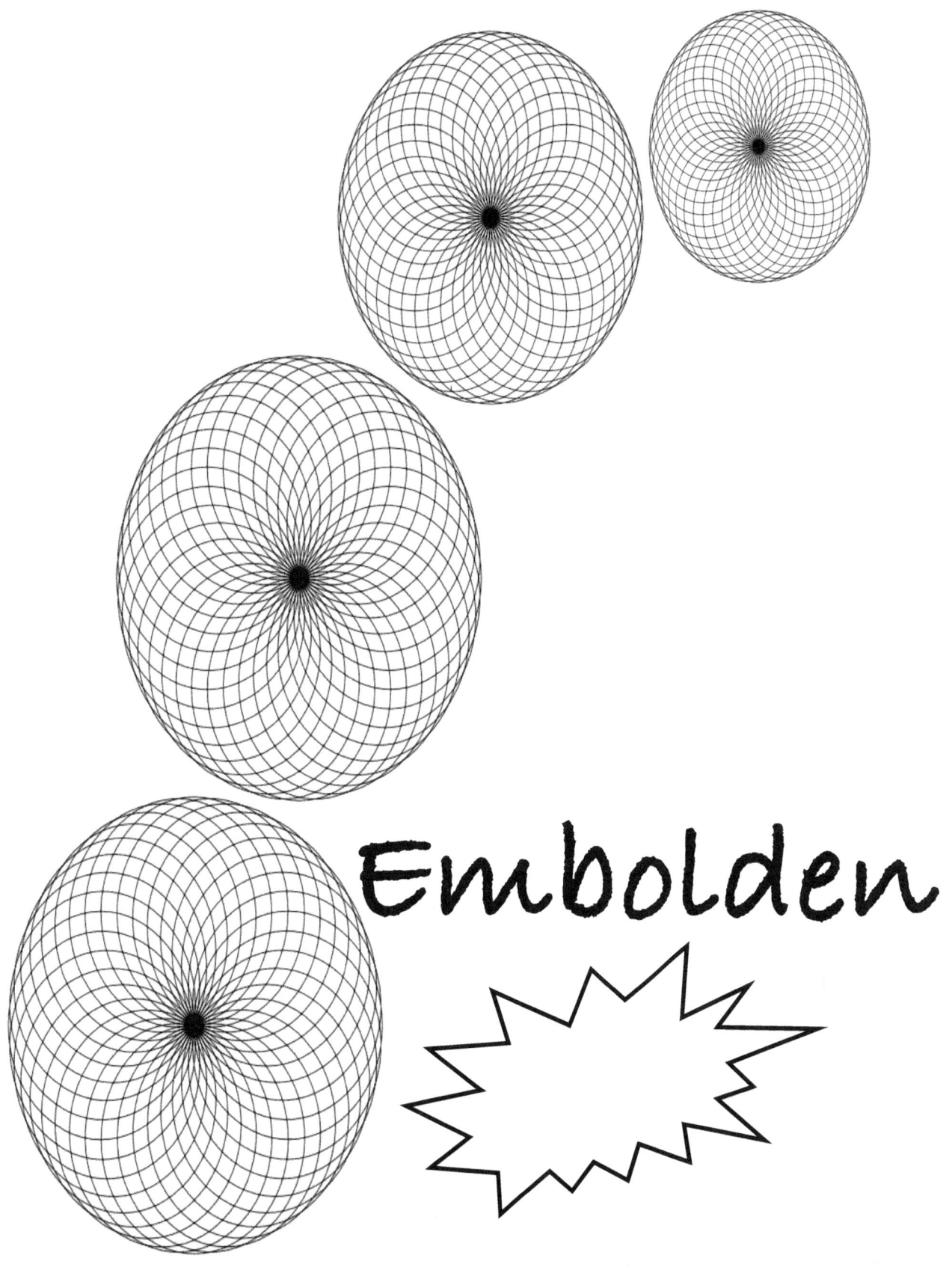

Copyright © 2018 Michael Weiner

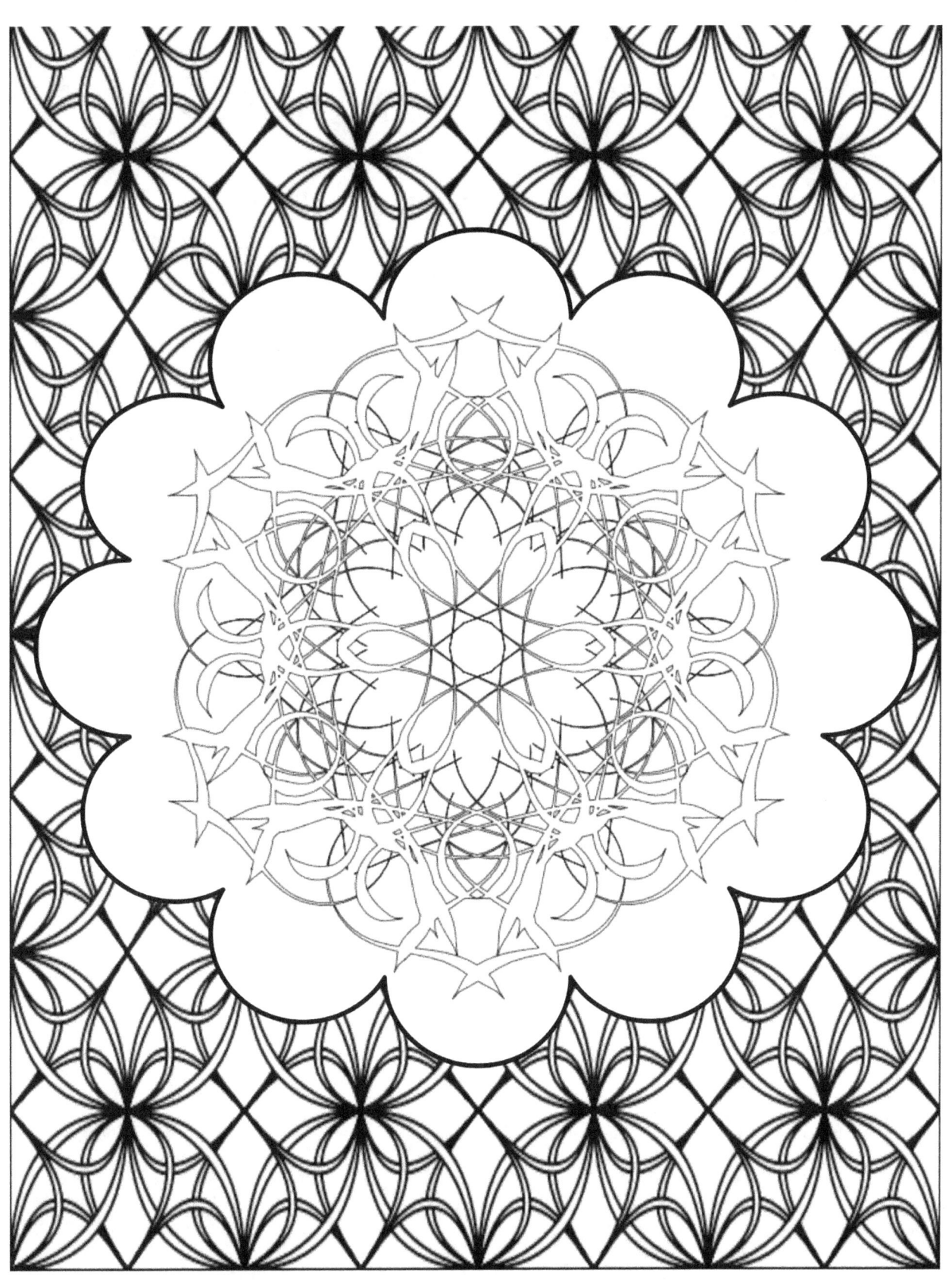

Copyright © 2018 Michael Weiner

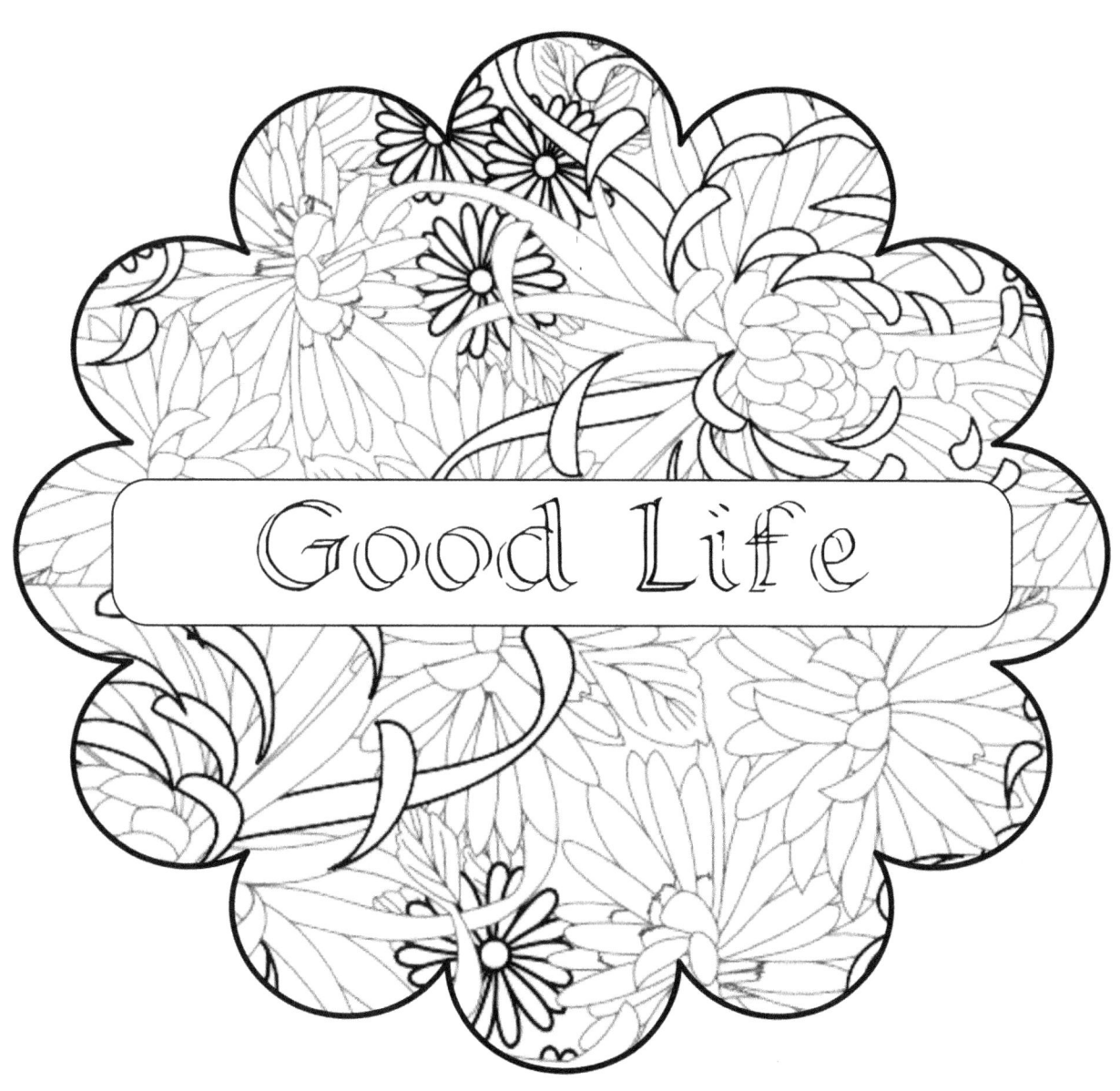

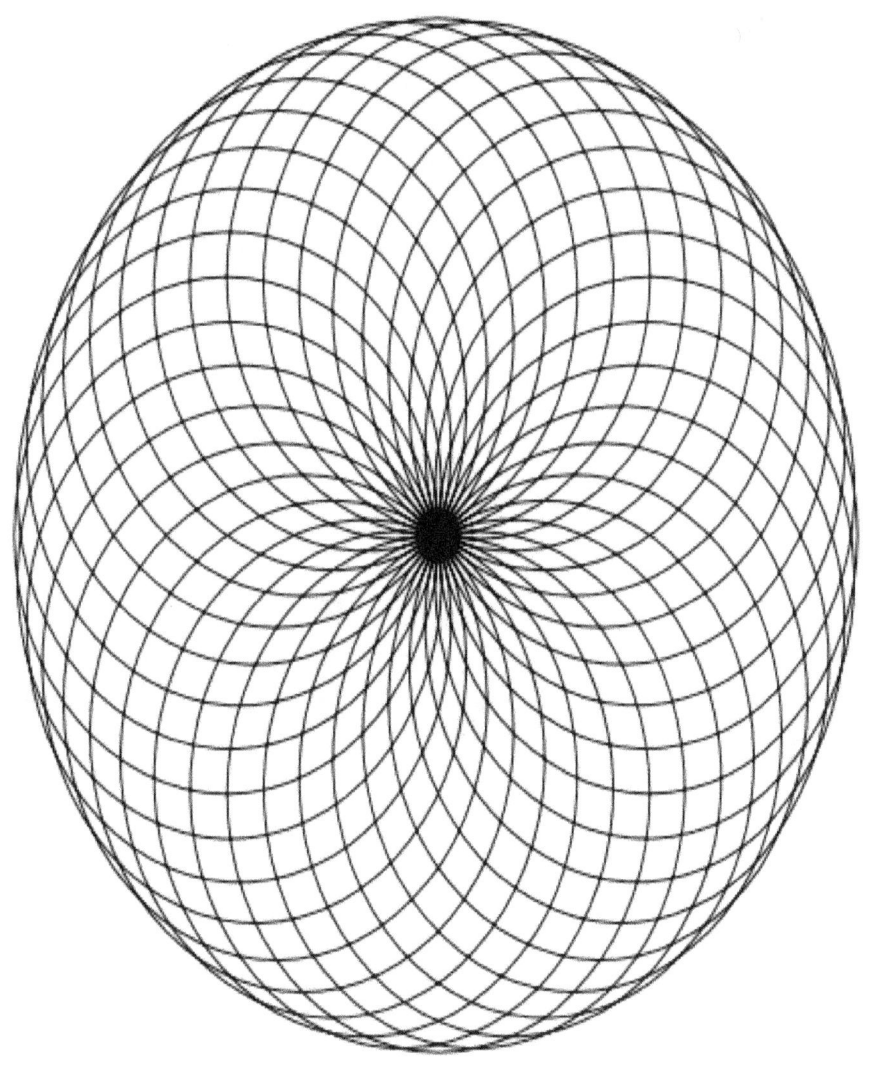

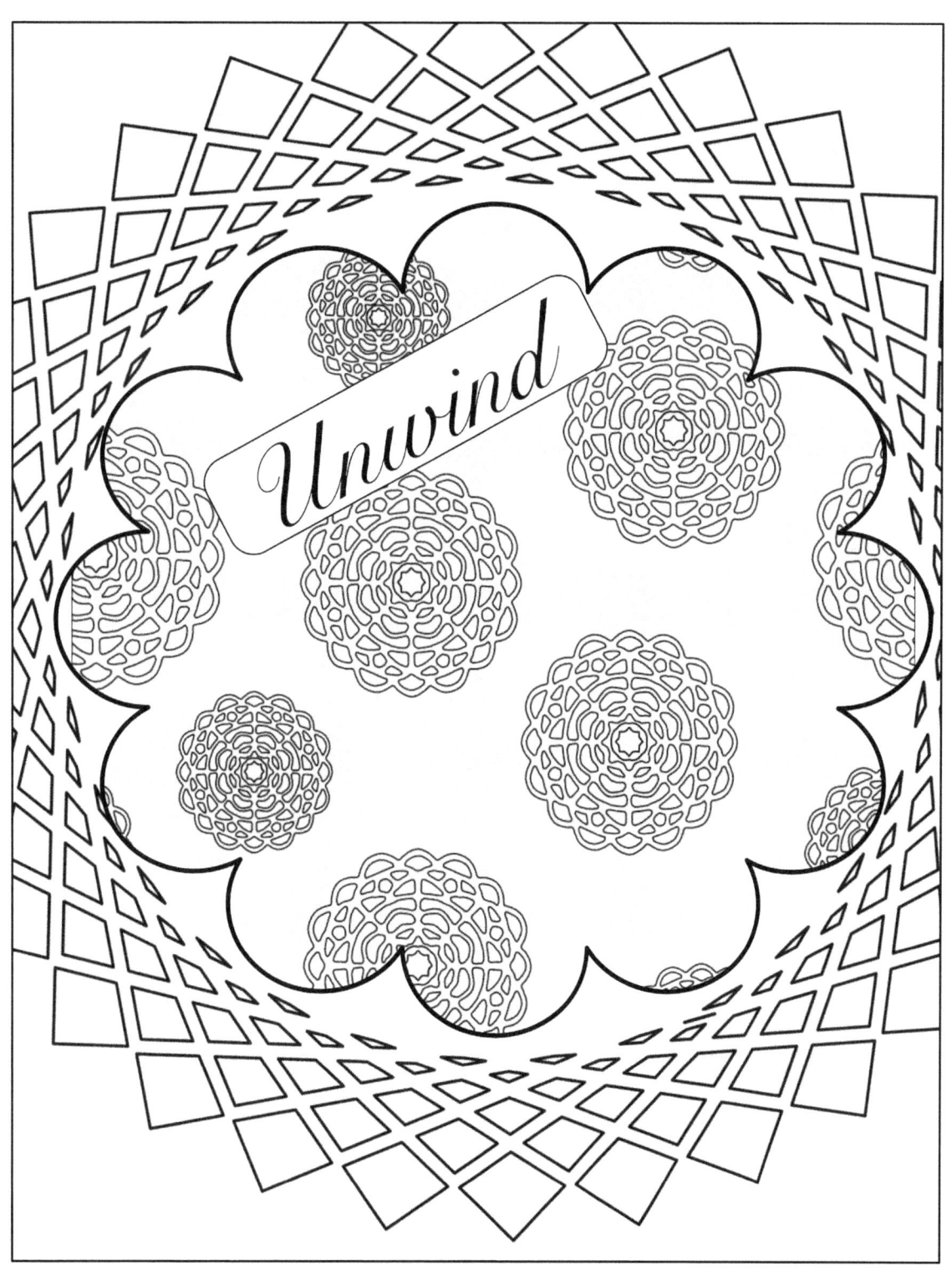

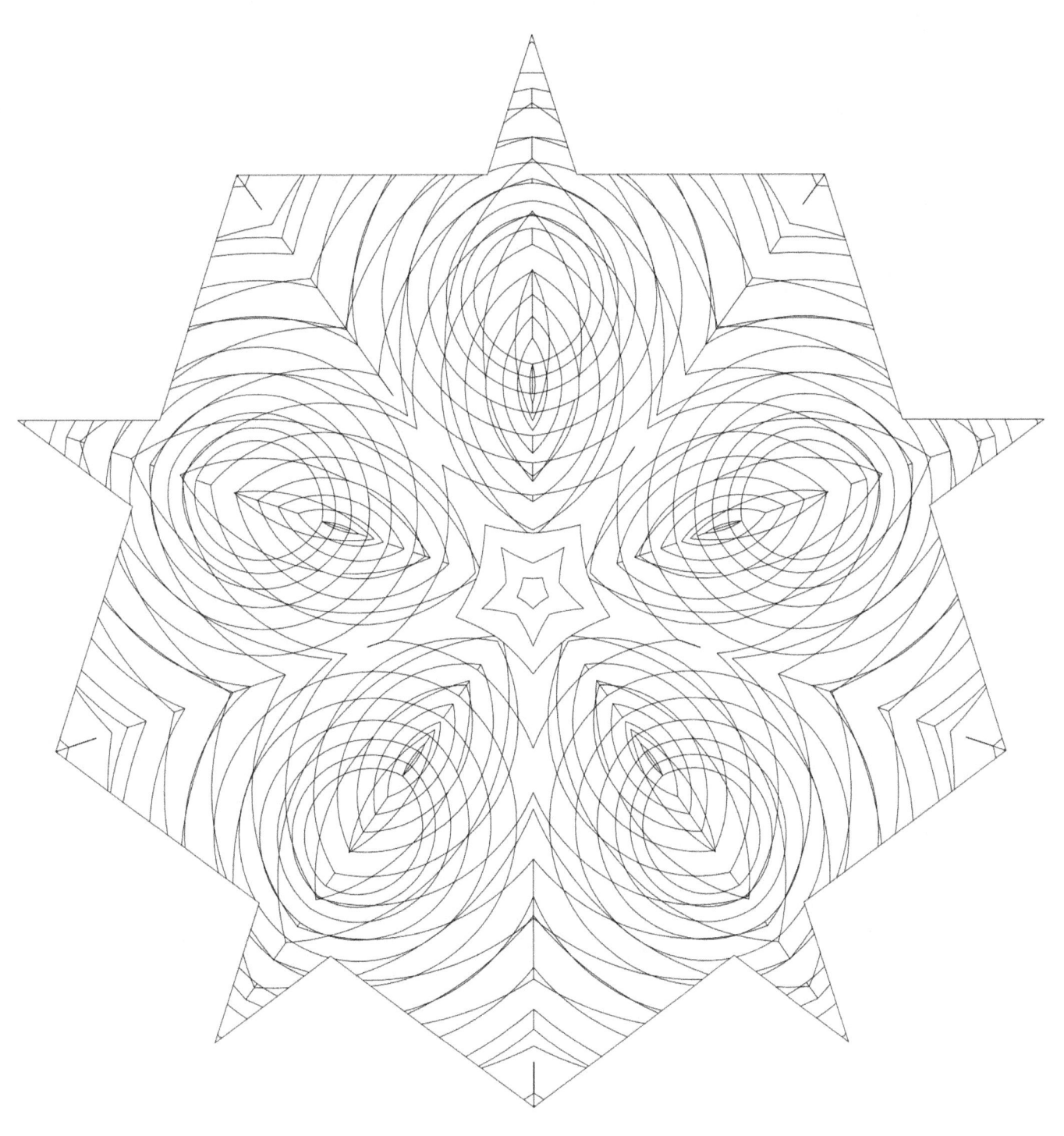

Copyright © 2018 Michael Weiner

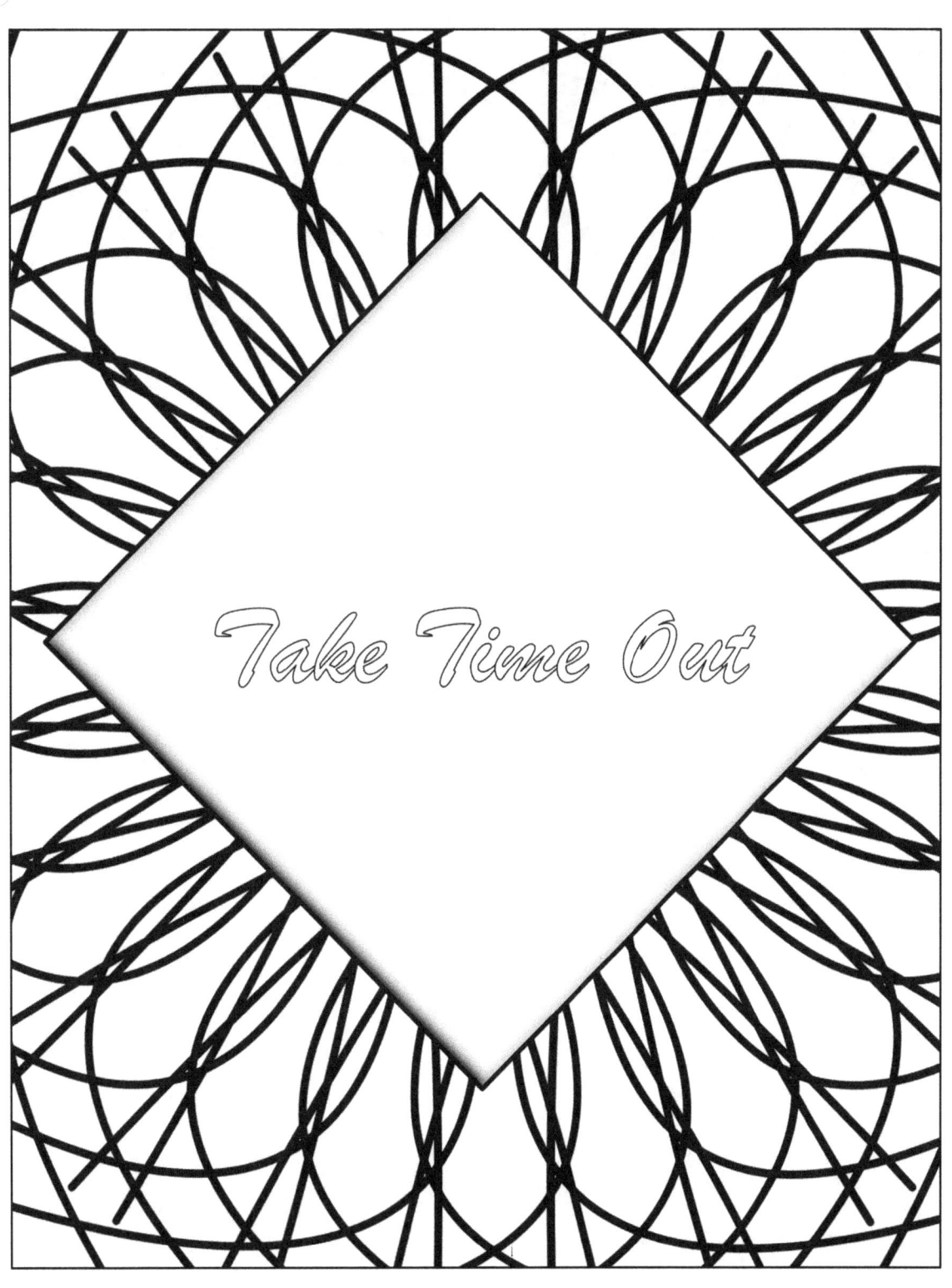

Copyright © 2018 Michael Weiner

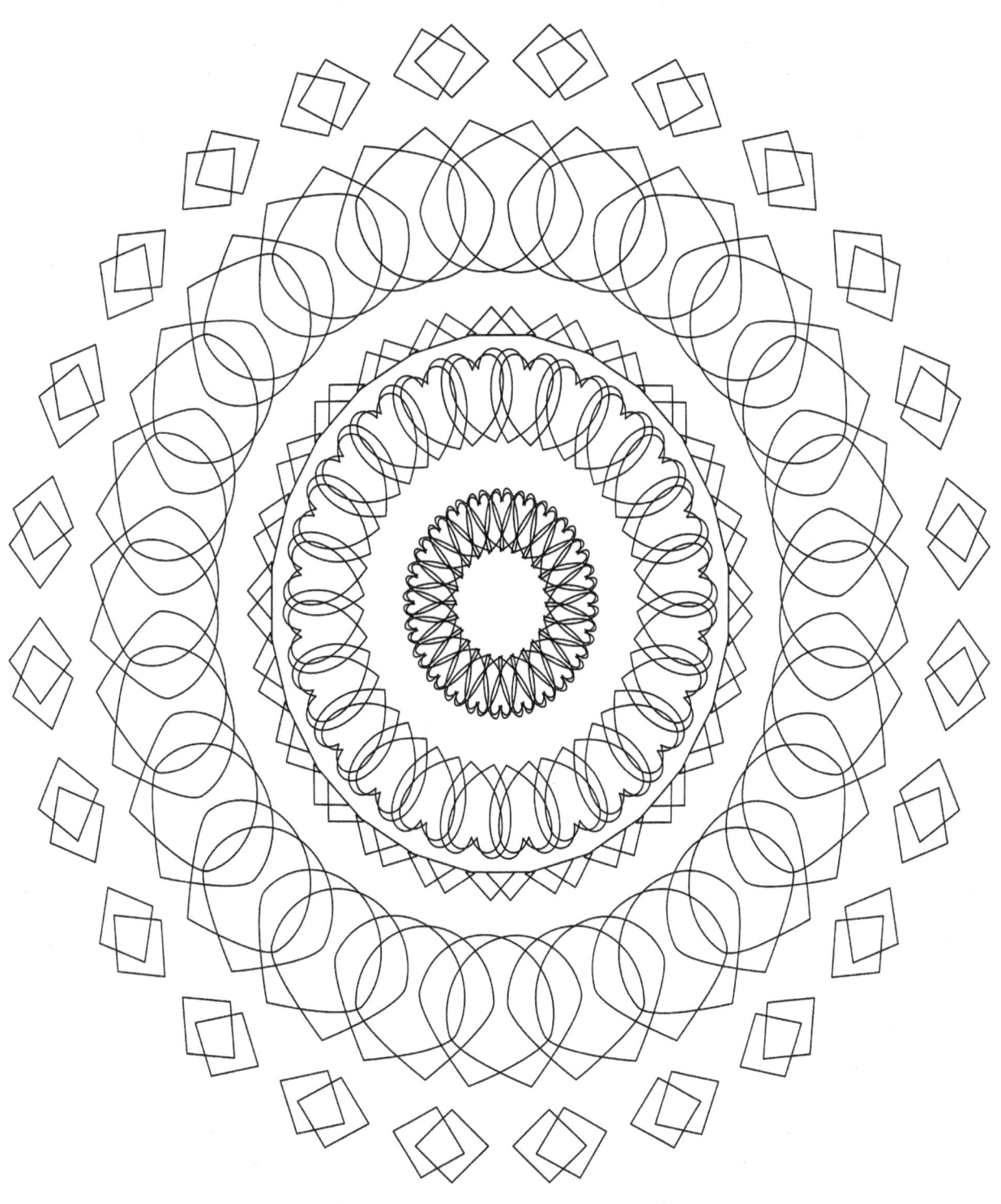

Copyright © 2018 Michael Weiner

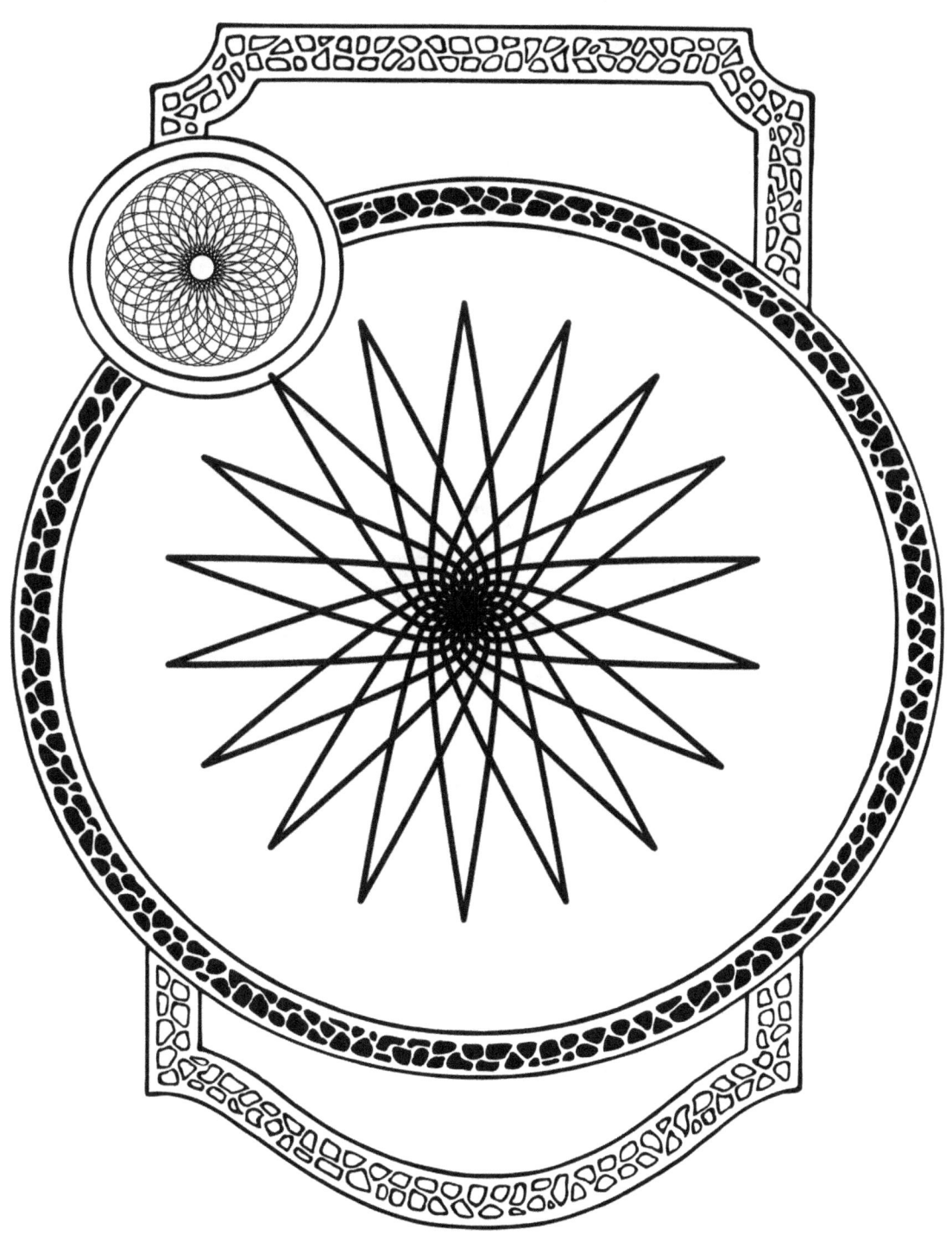

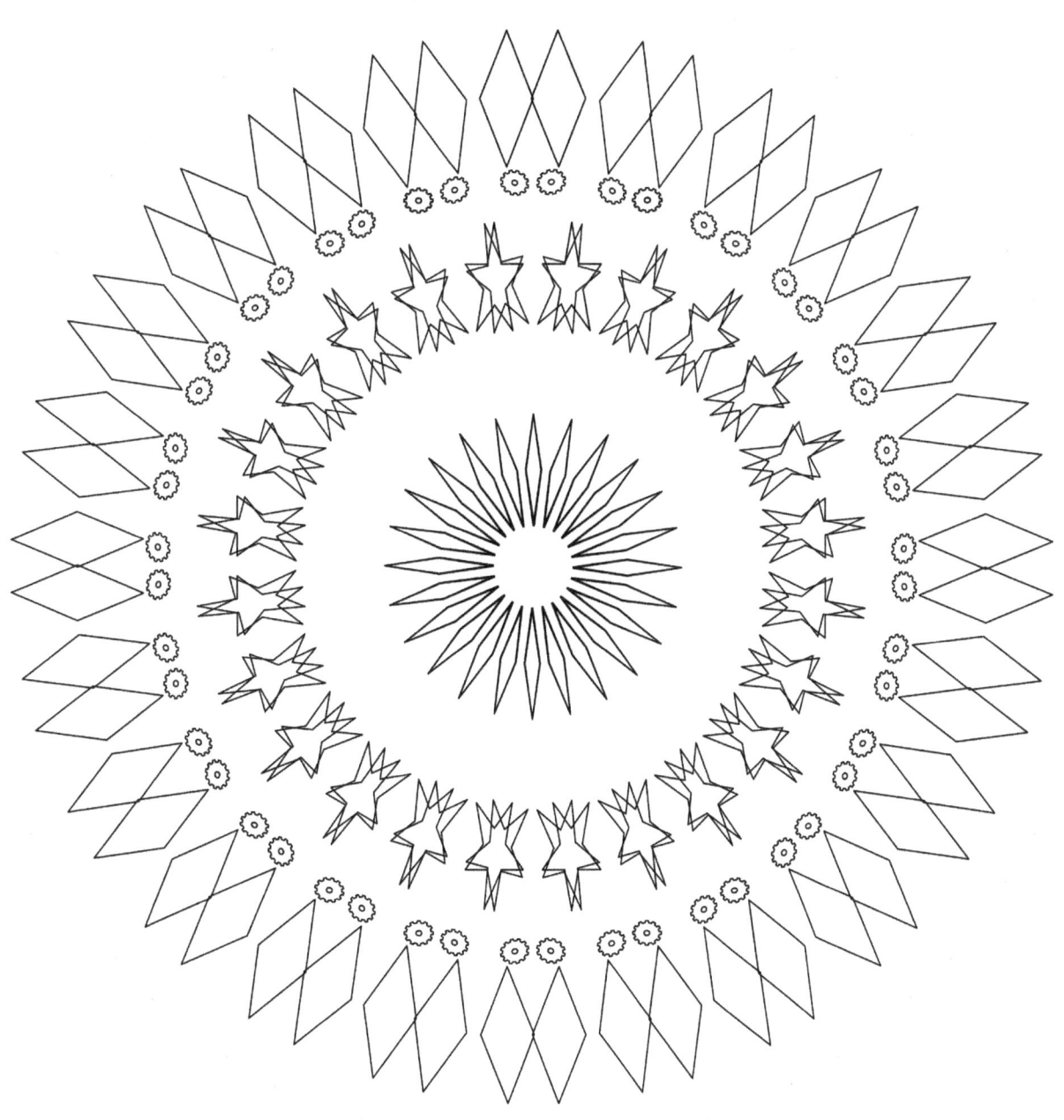

Copyright © 2018 Michael Weiner

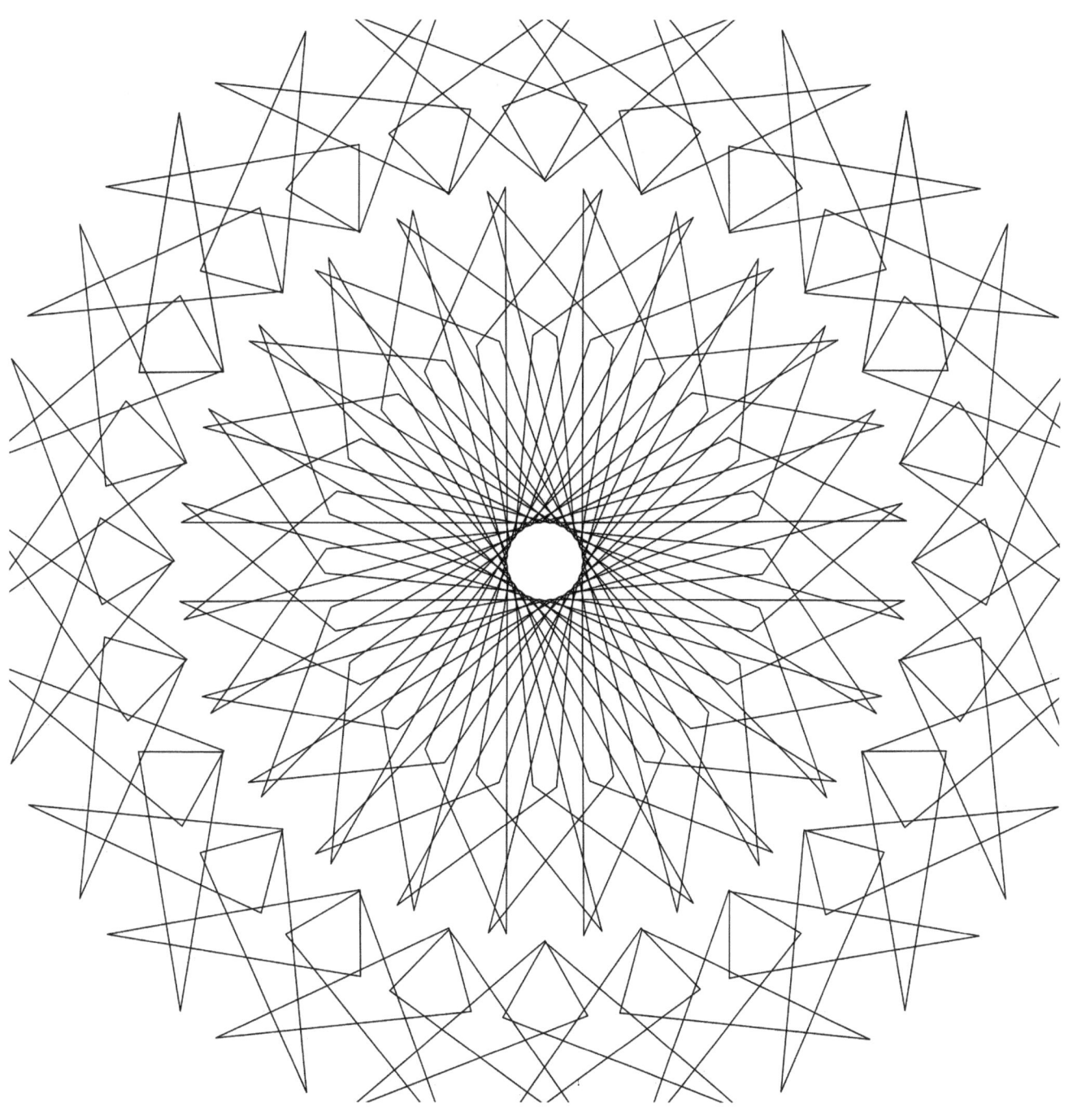

Copyright © 2018 Michael Weiner

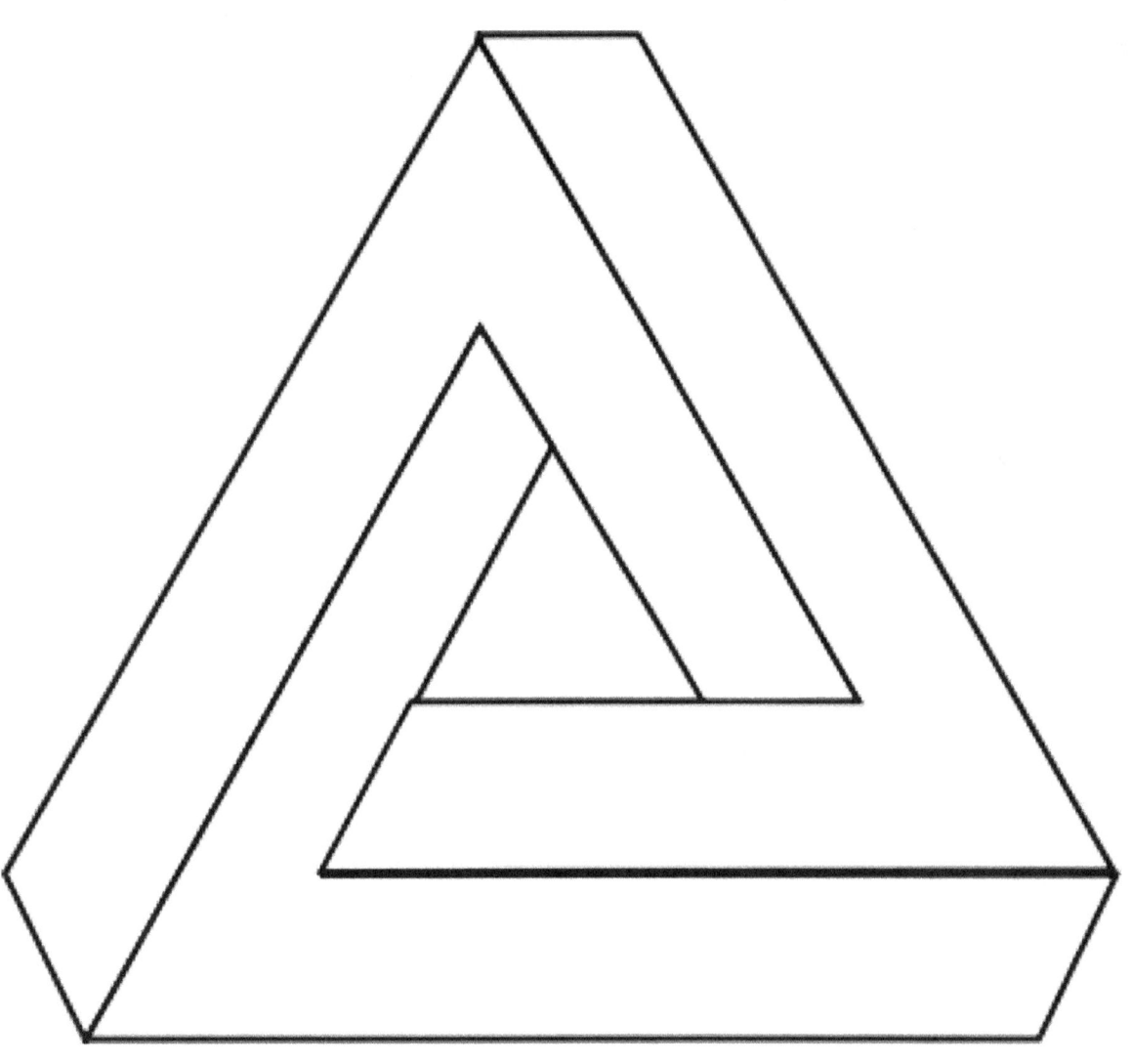

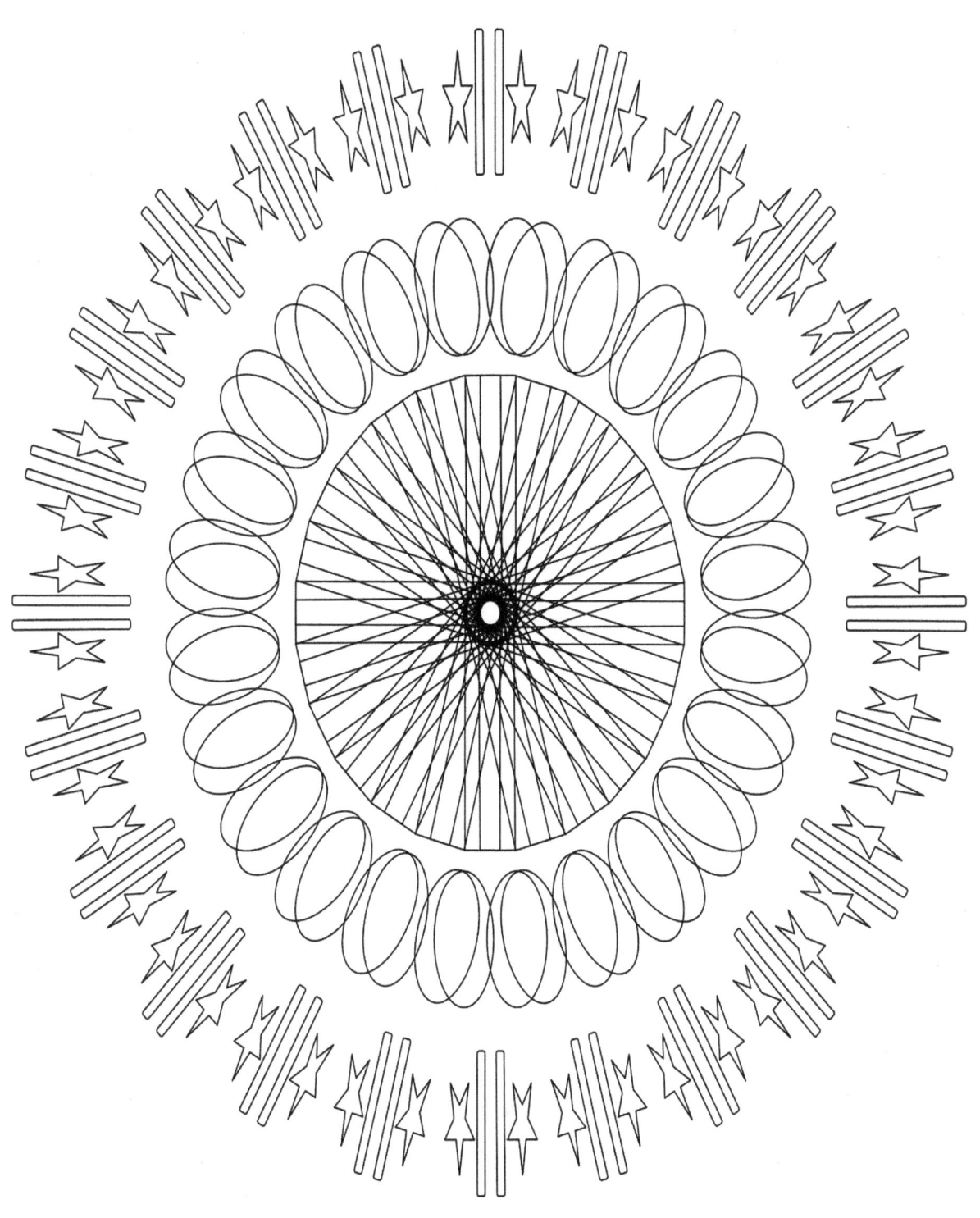

Copyright © 2018 Michael Weiner

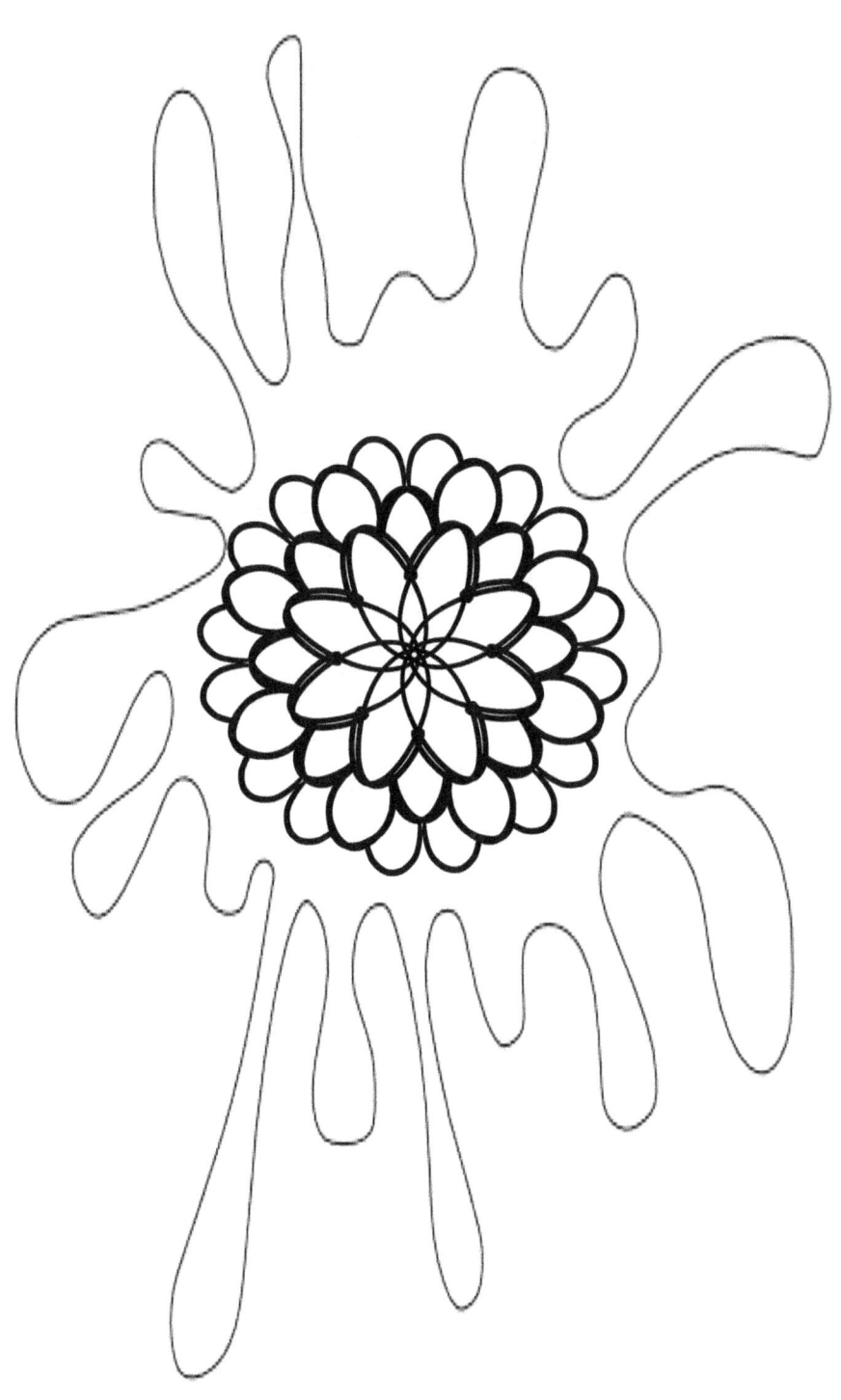

Copyright © 2018 Michael Weiner

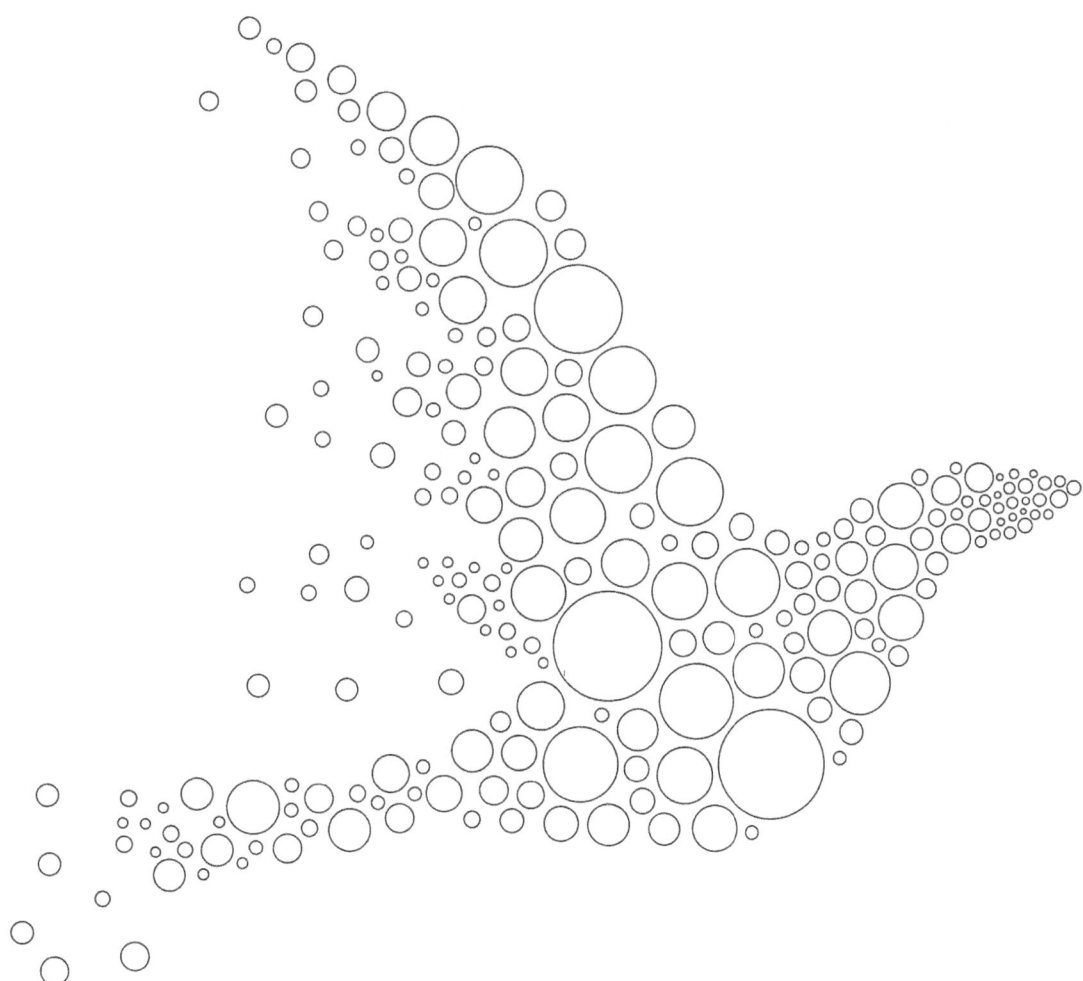

Copyright © 2018 Michael Weiner

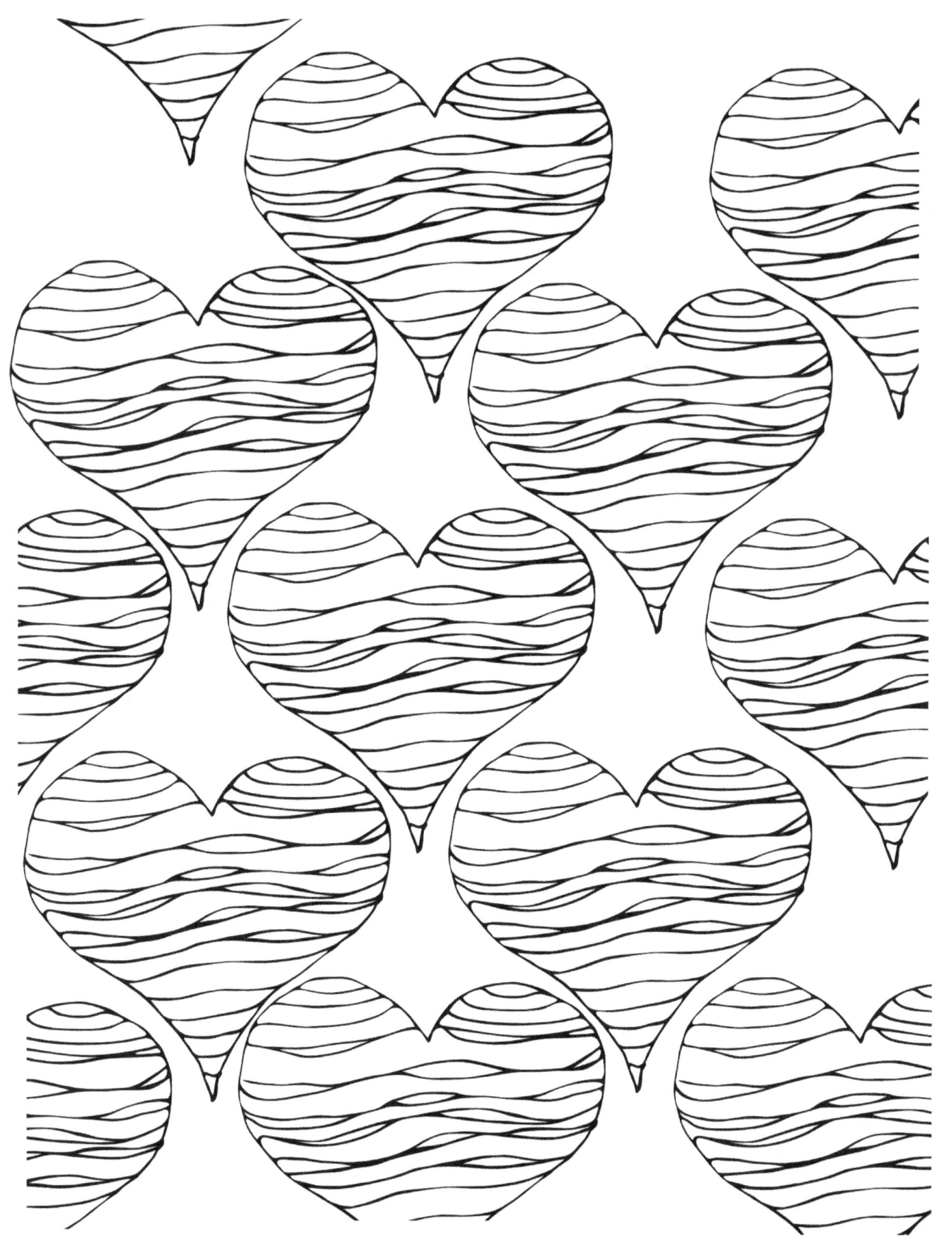
Copyright © 2018 Michael Weiner

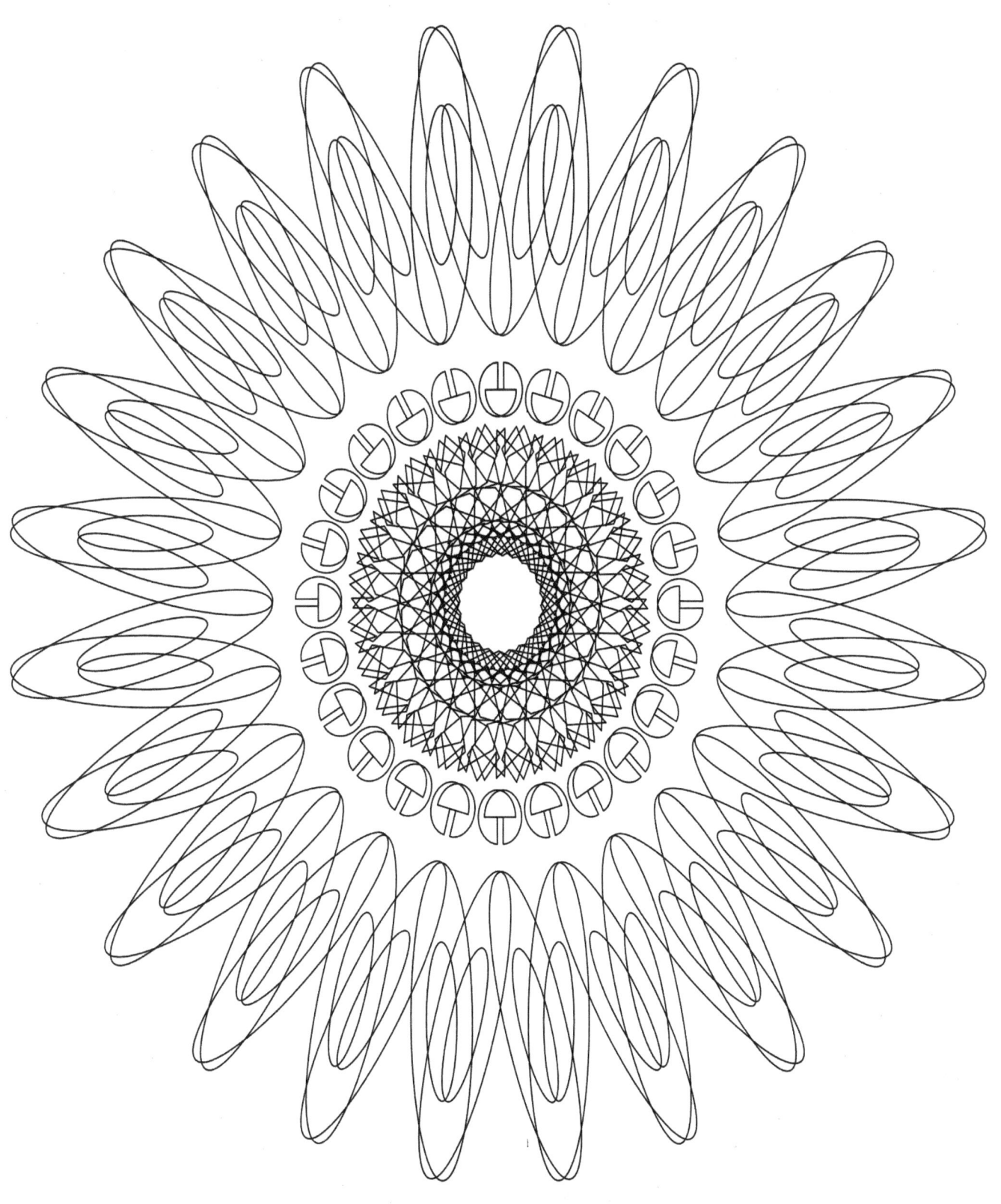

Copyright © 2018 Michael Weiner

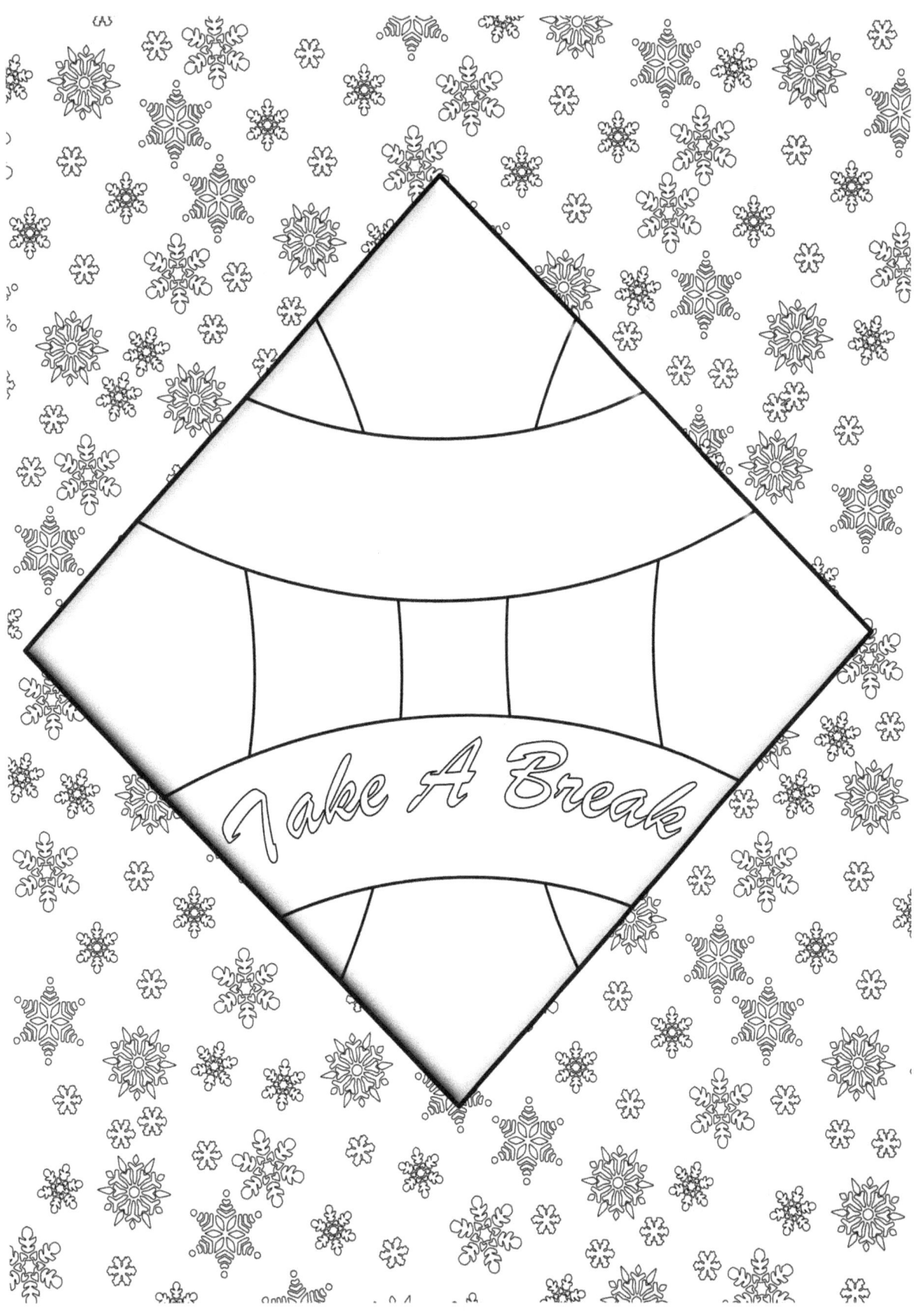

Copyright © 2018 Michael Weiner

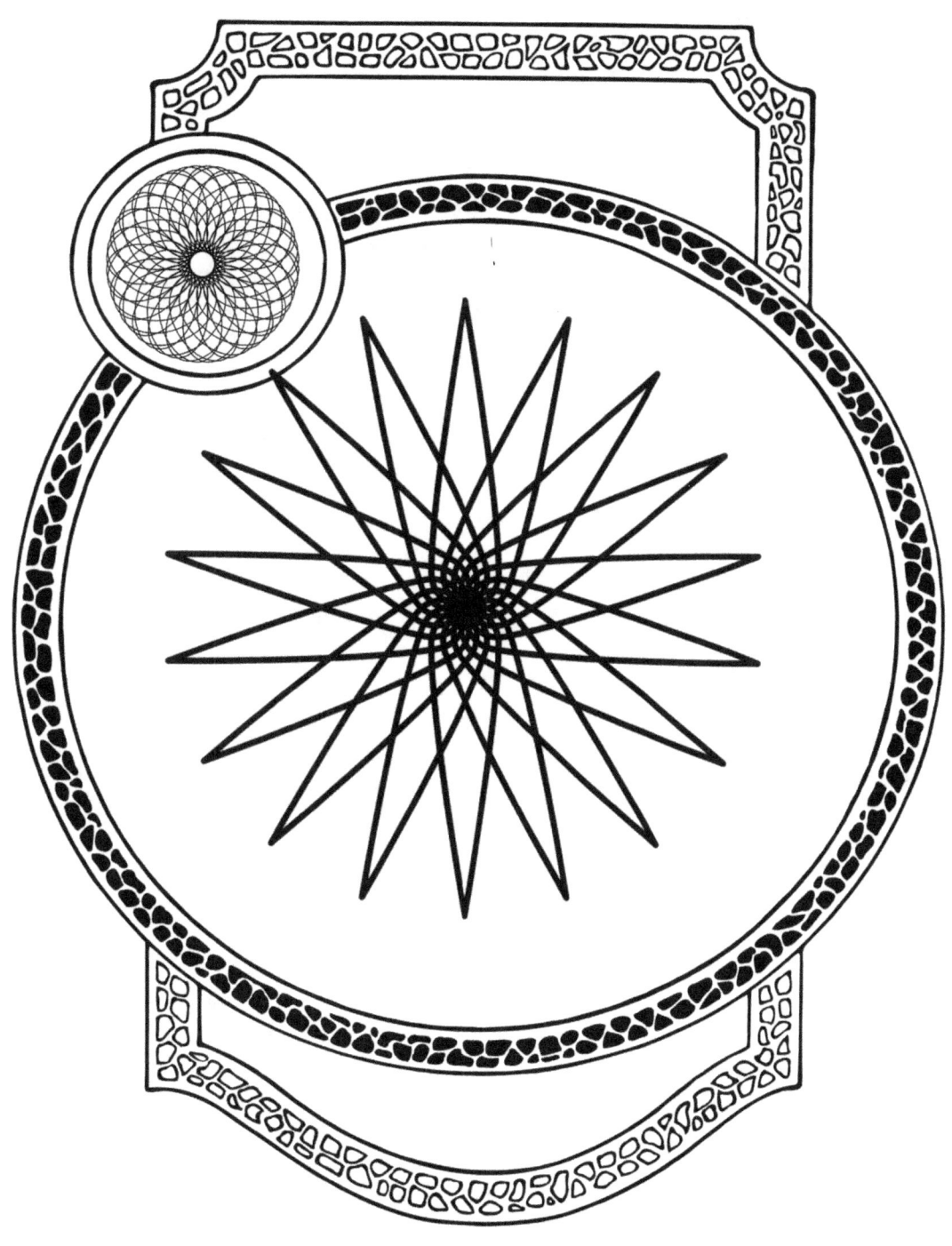

Copyright © 2018 Michael Weiner

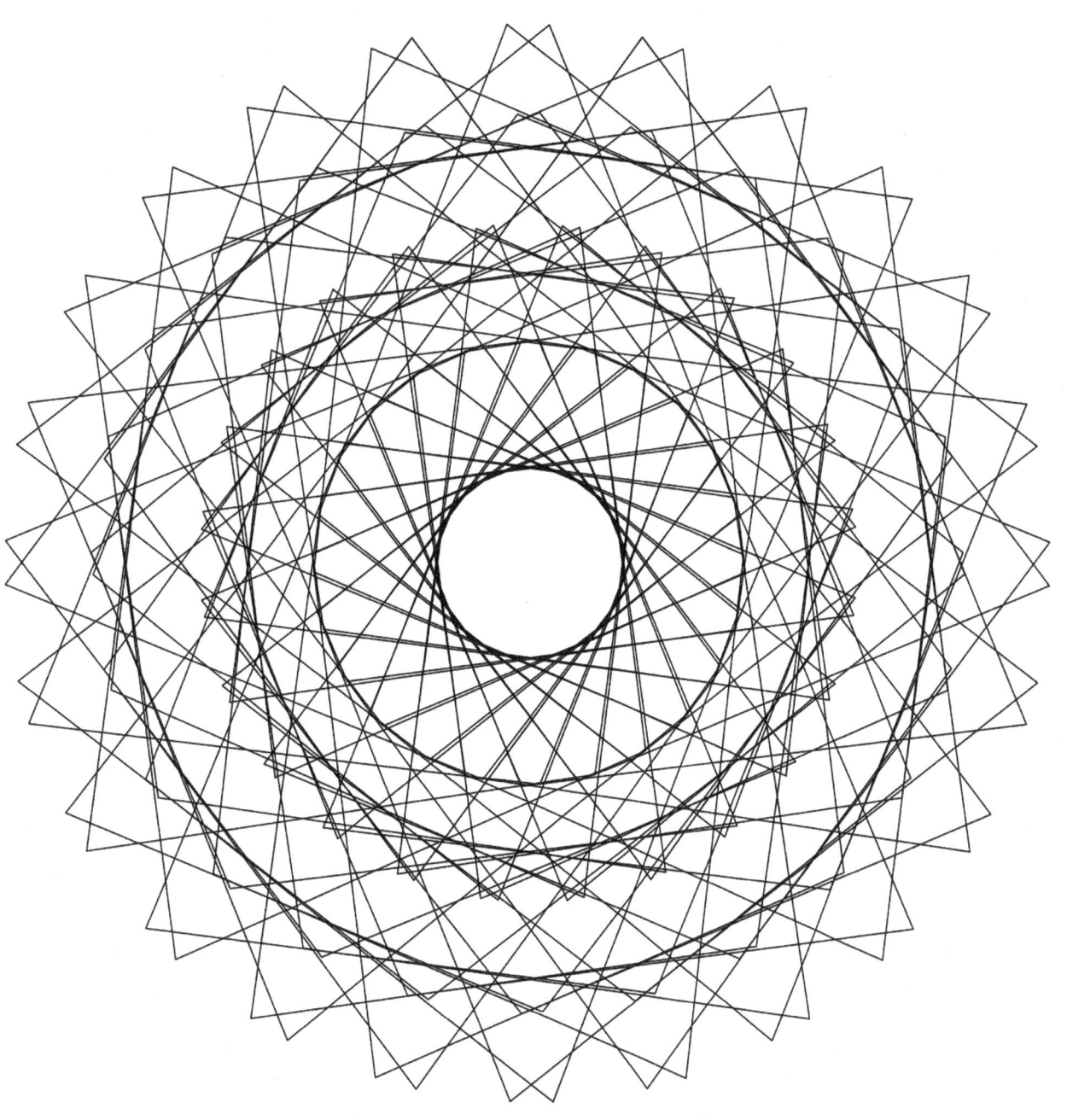

Copyright © 2018 Michael Weiner

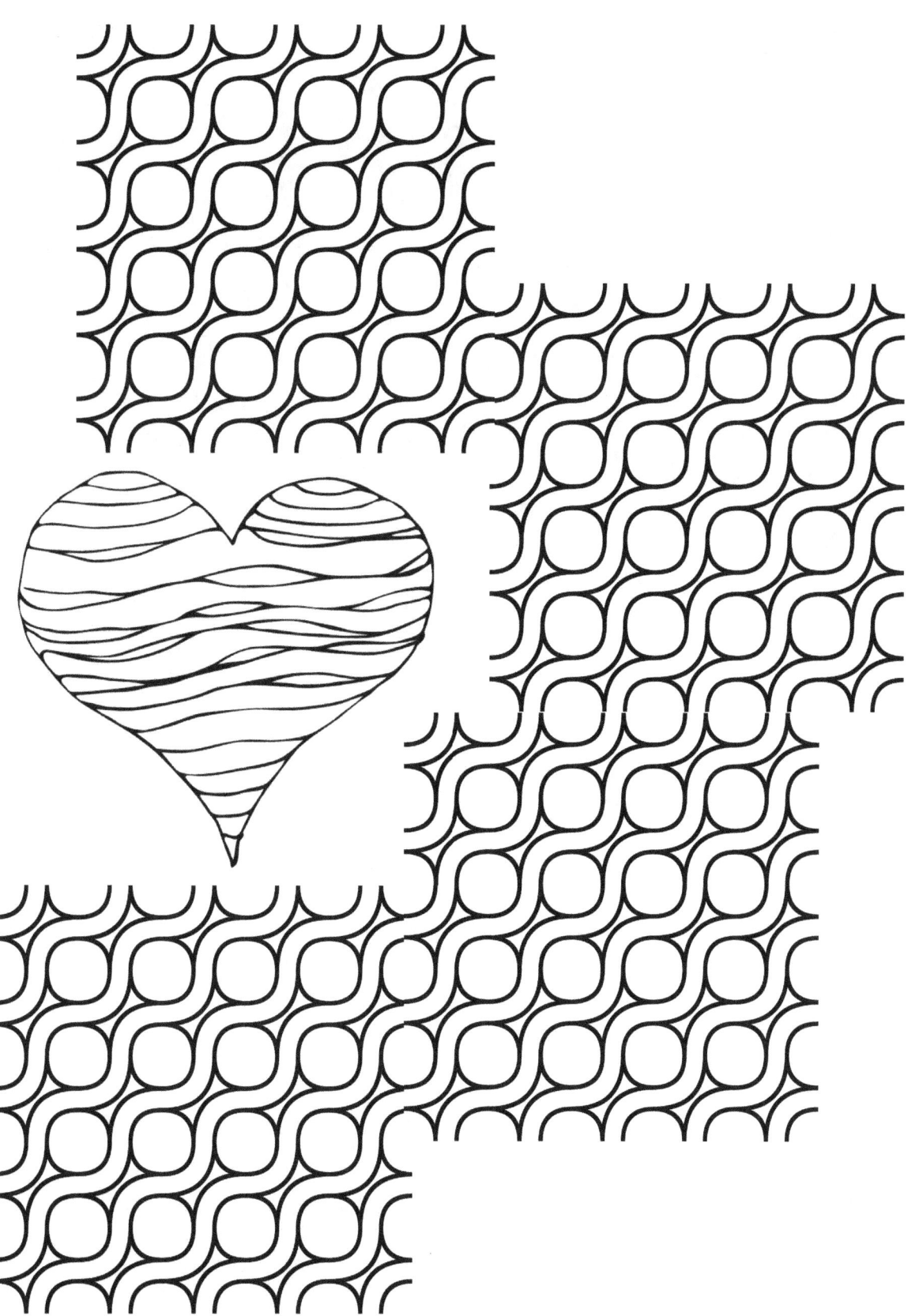

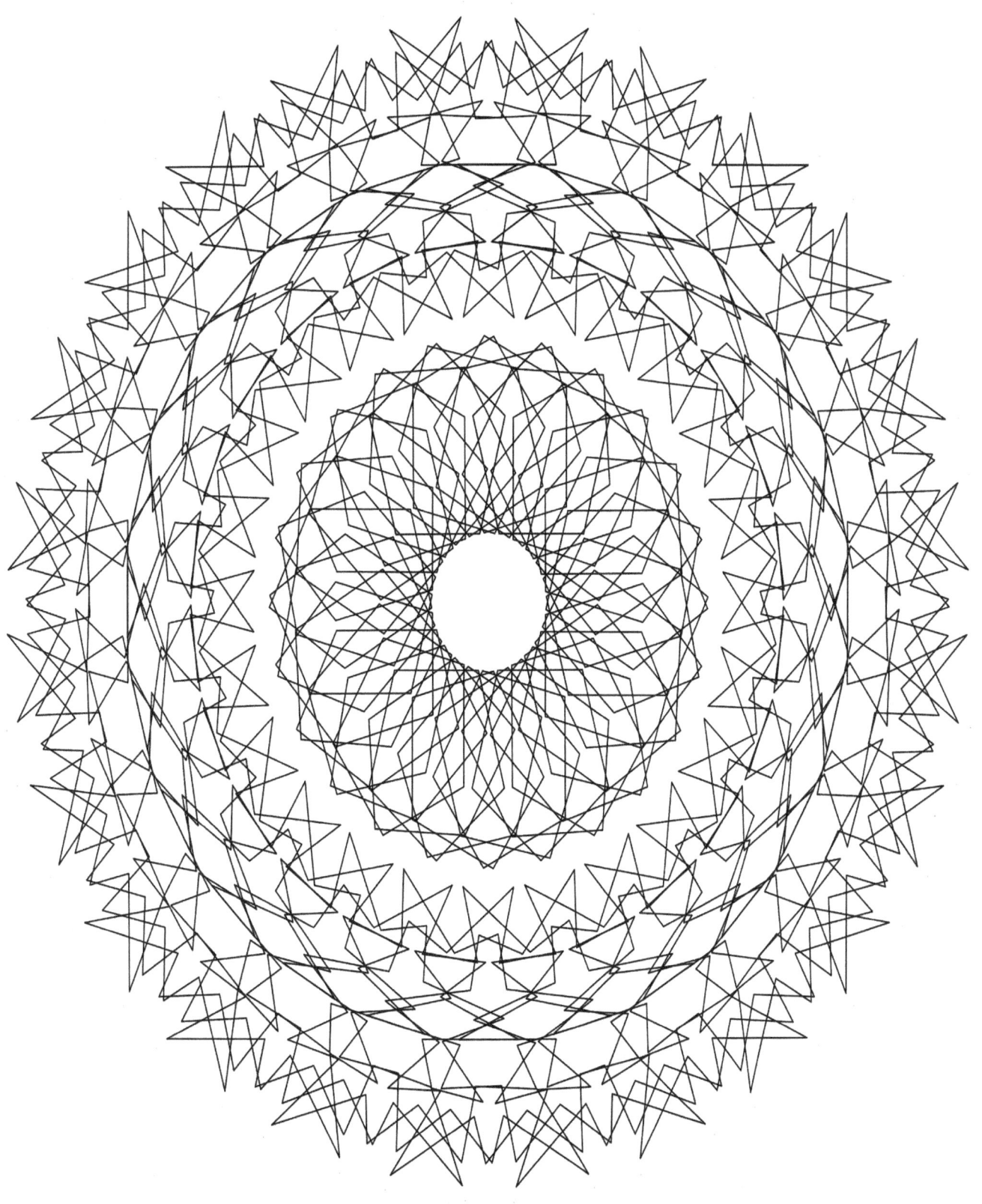

Copyright © 2018 Michael Weiner

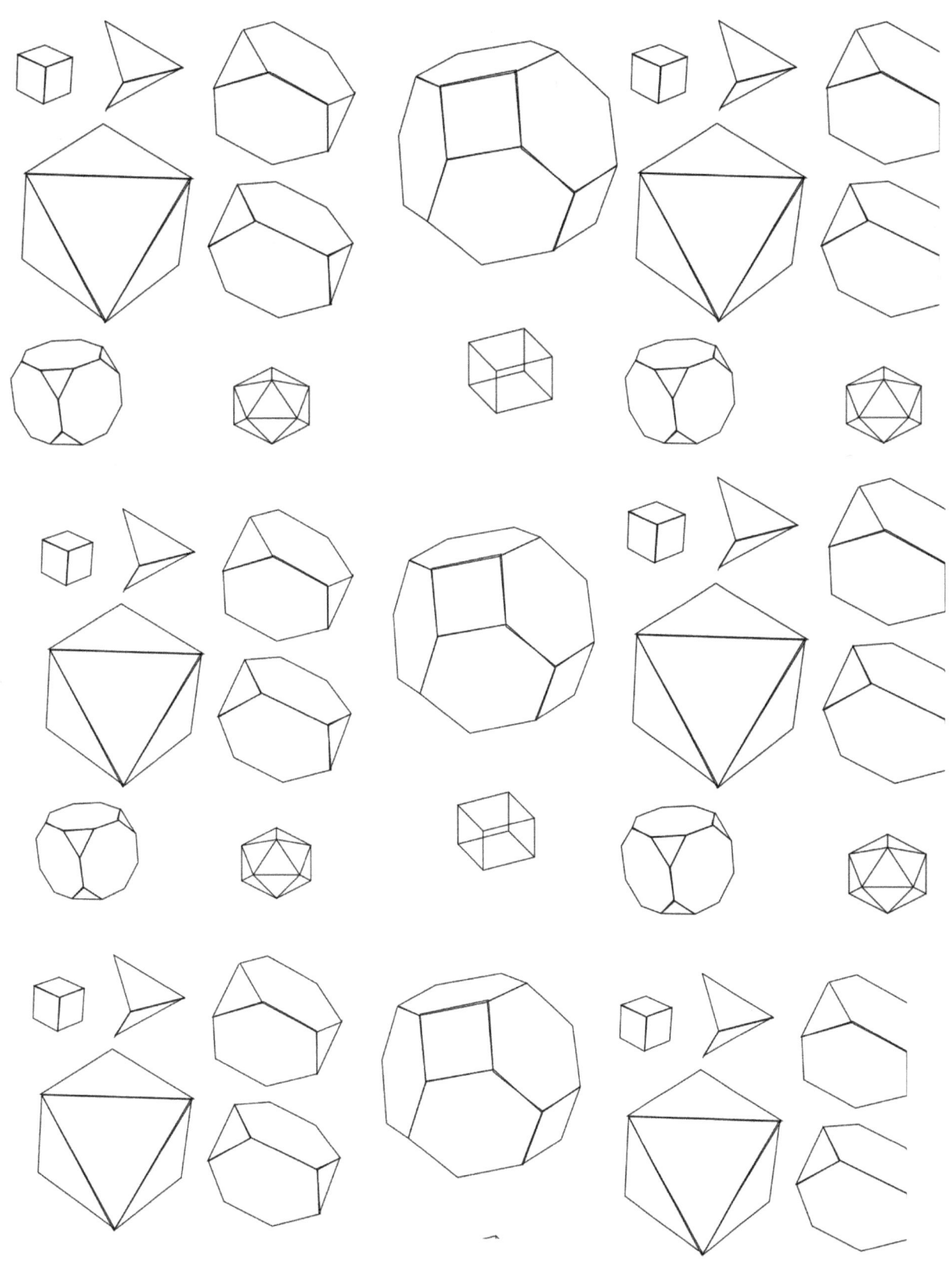

Copyright © 2018 Michael Weiner

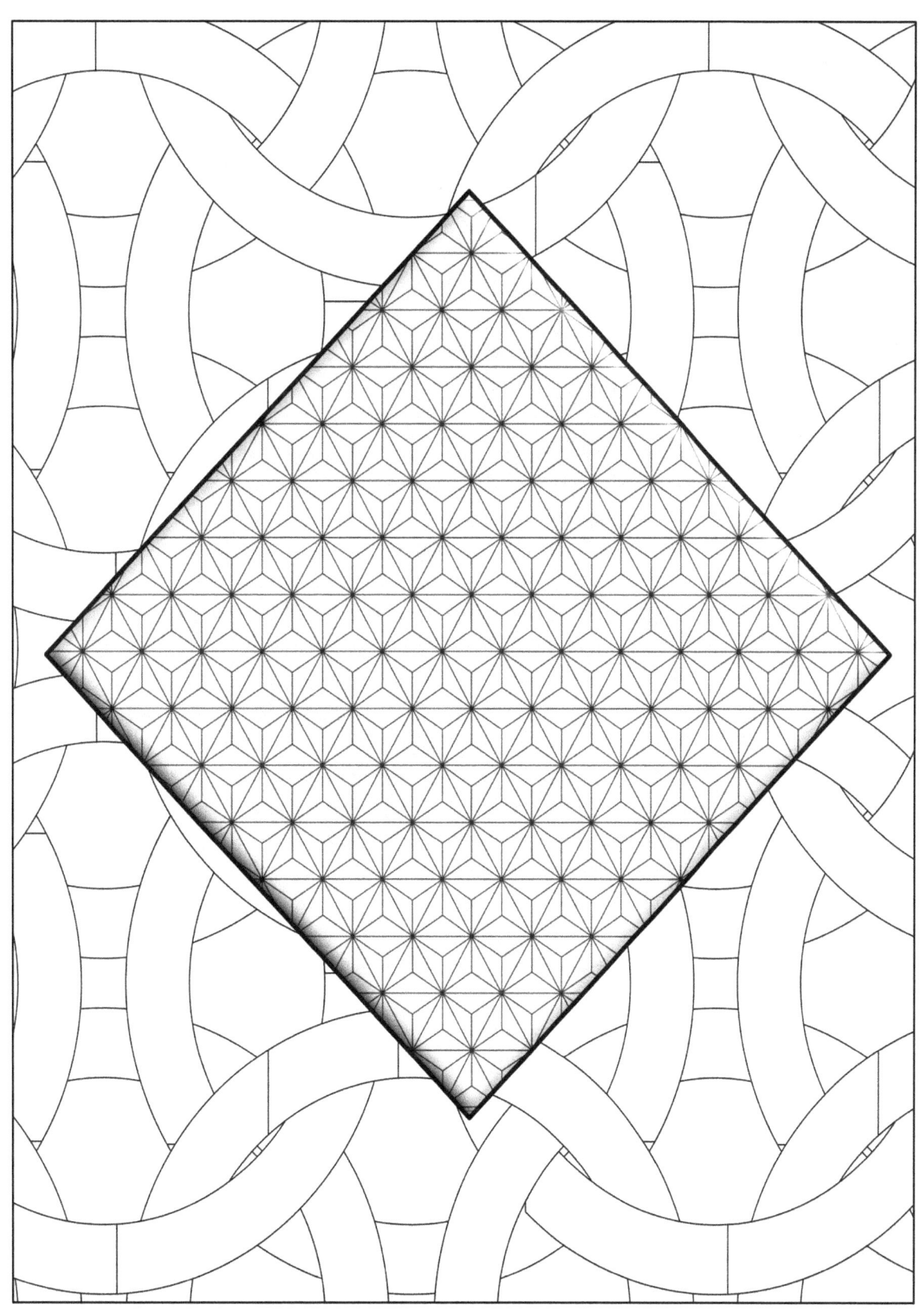

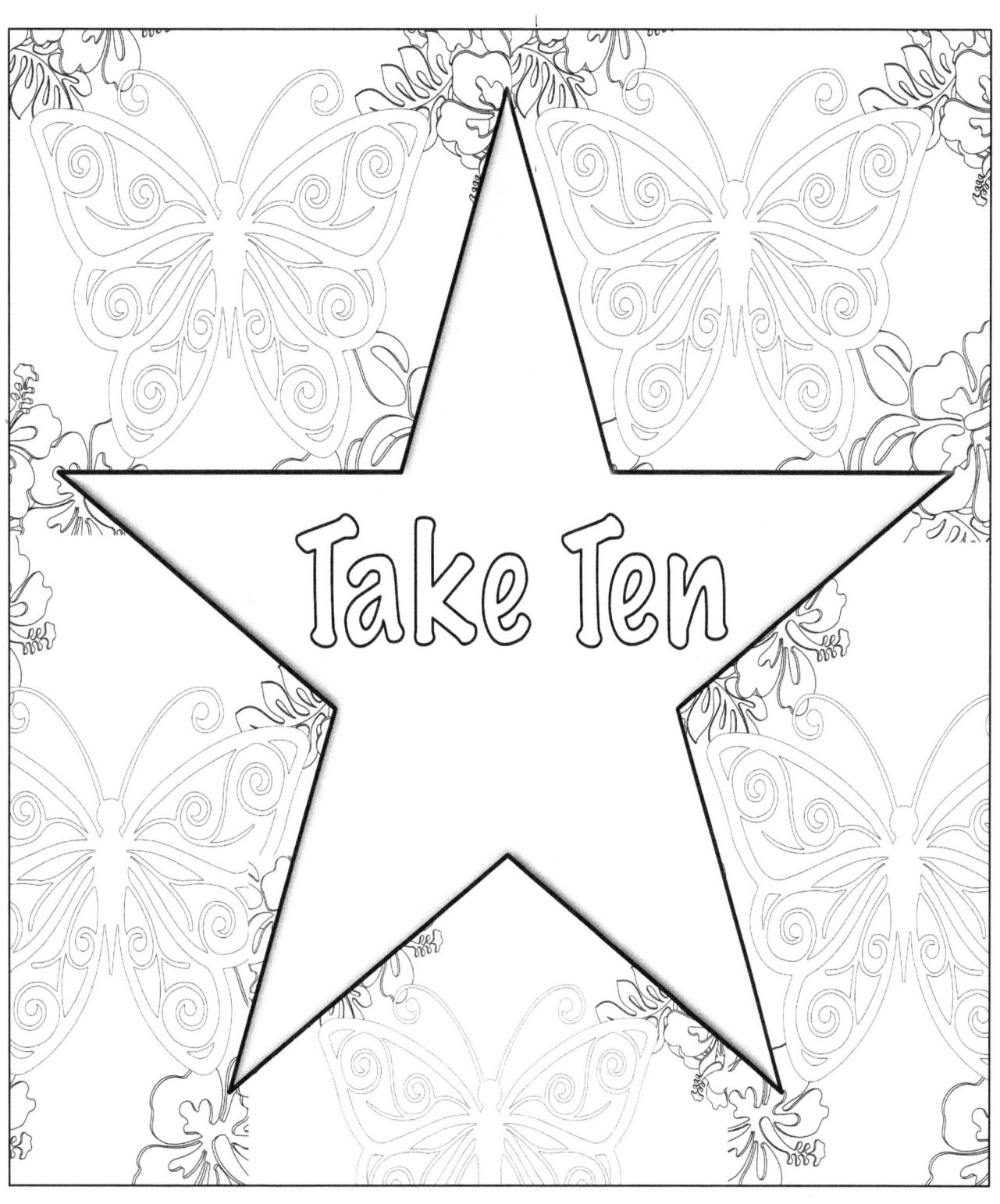

Copyright © 2018 Michael Weiner

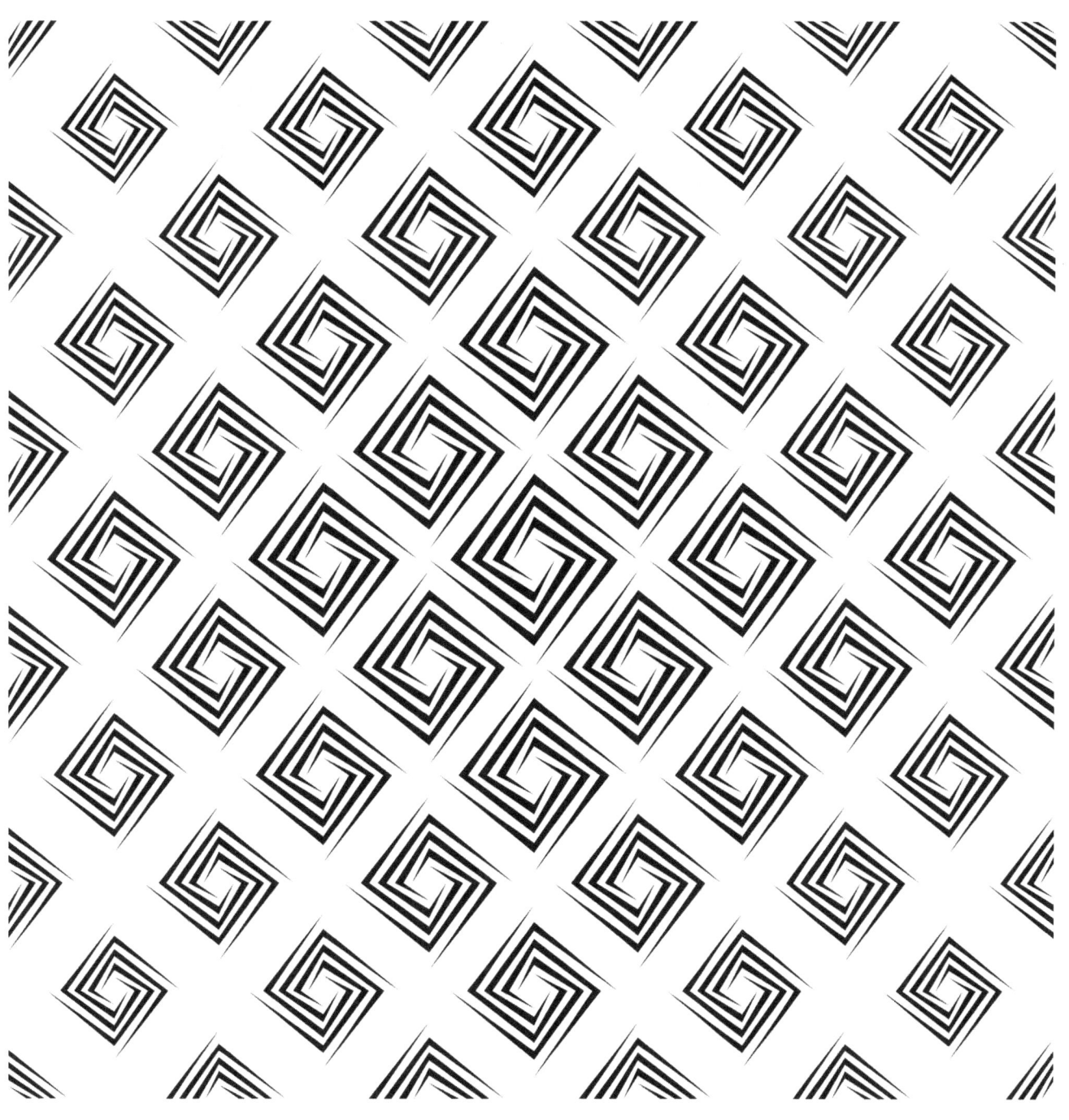

Copyright © 2018 Michael Weiner

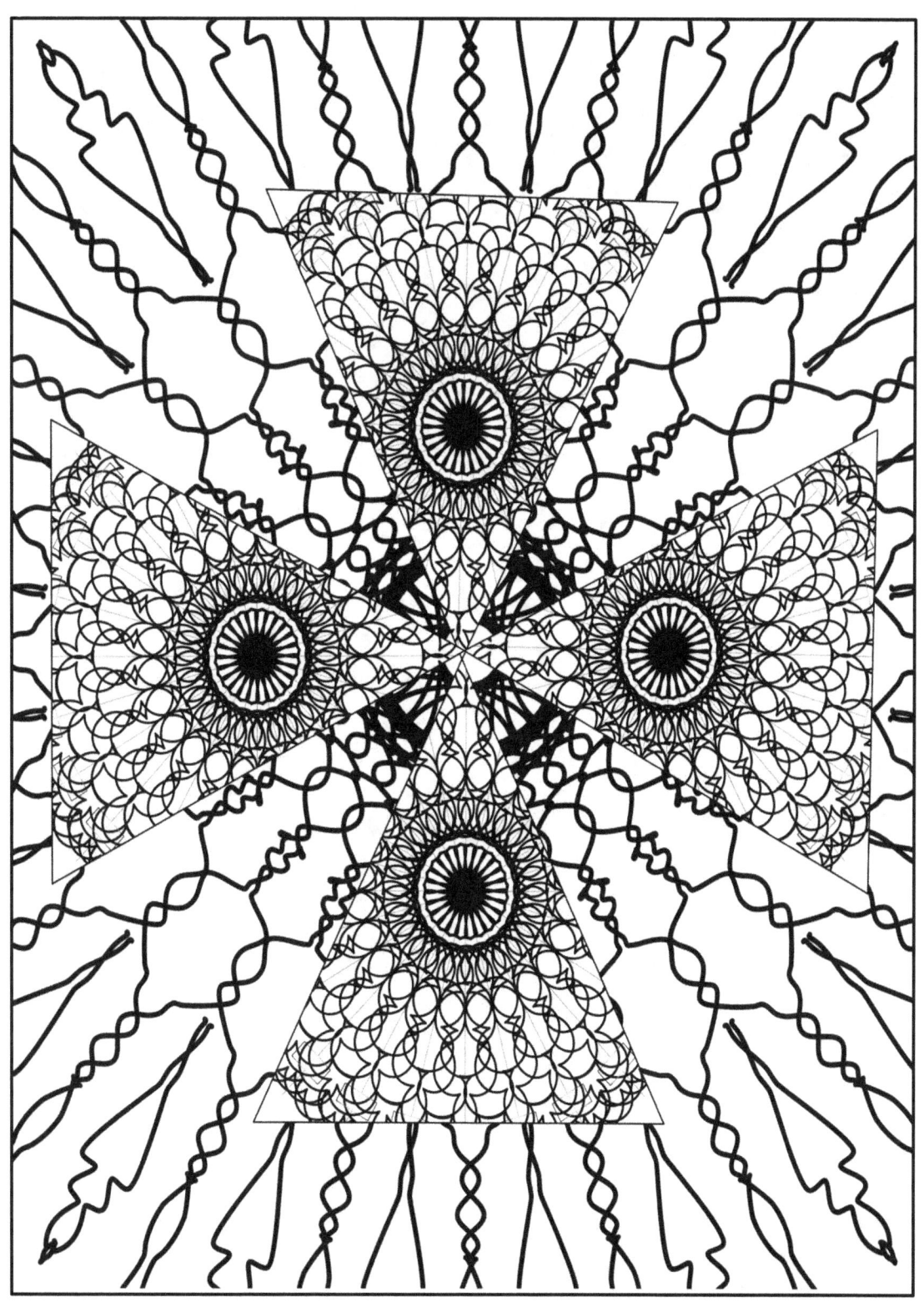

Copyright © 2018 Michael Weiner

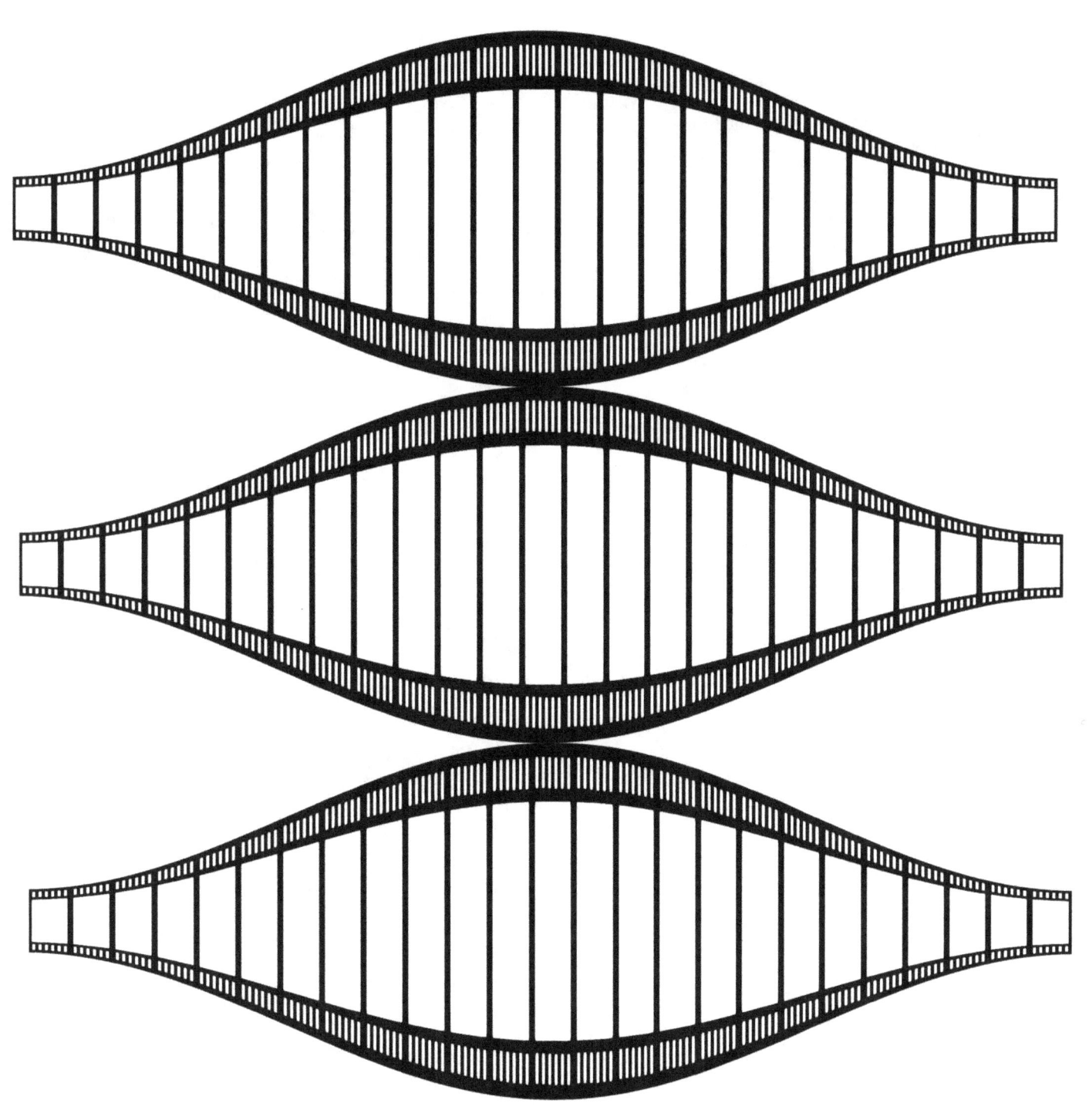

Copyright © 2018 Michael Weiner

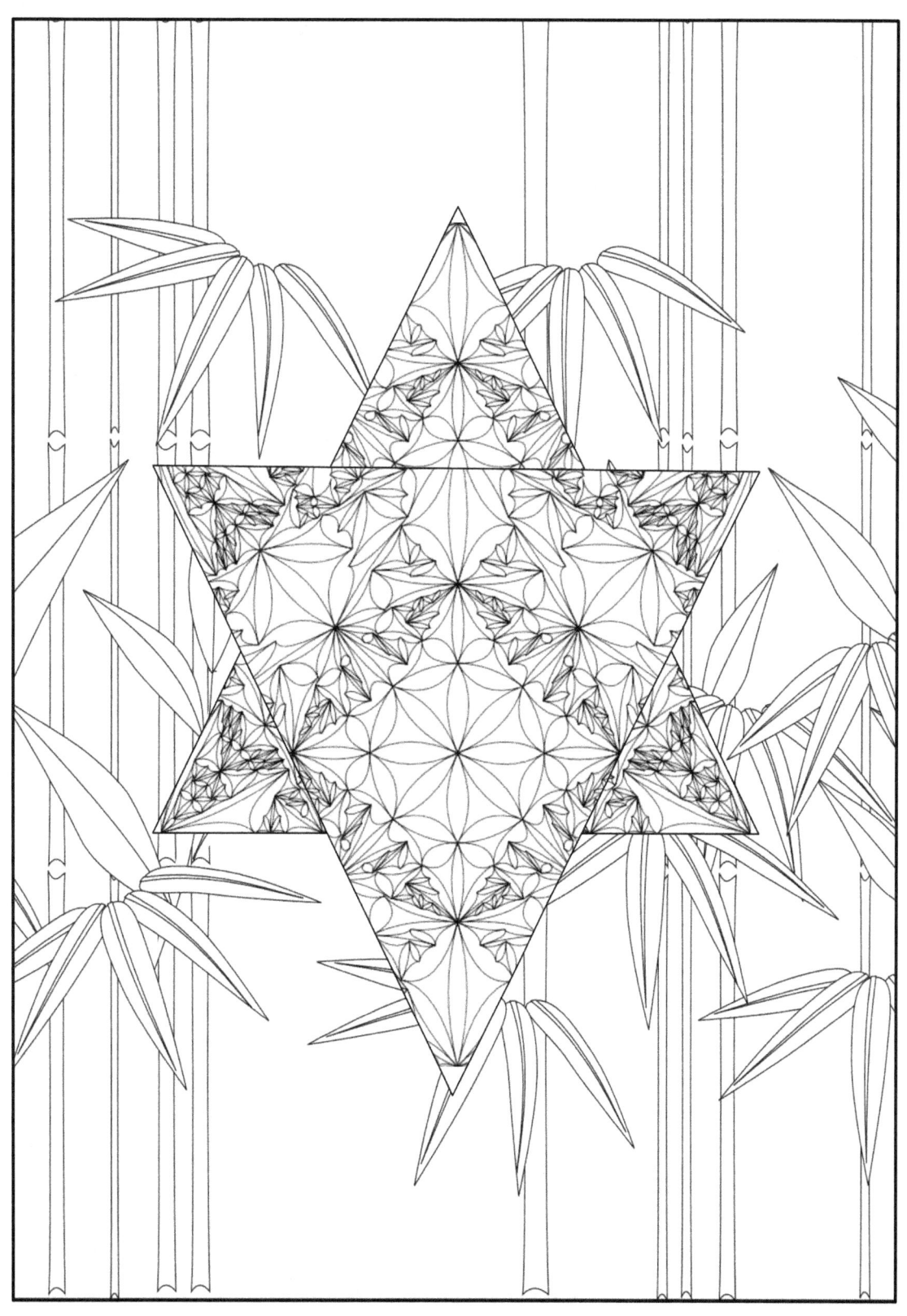

Copyright © 2018 Michael Weiner

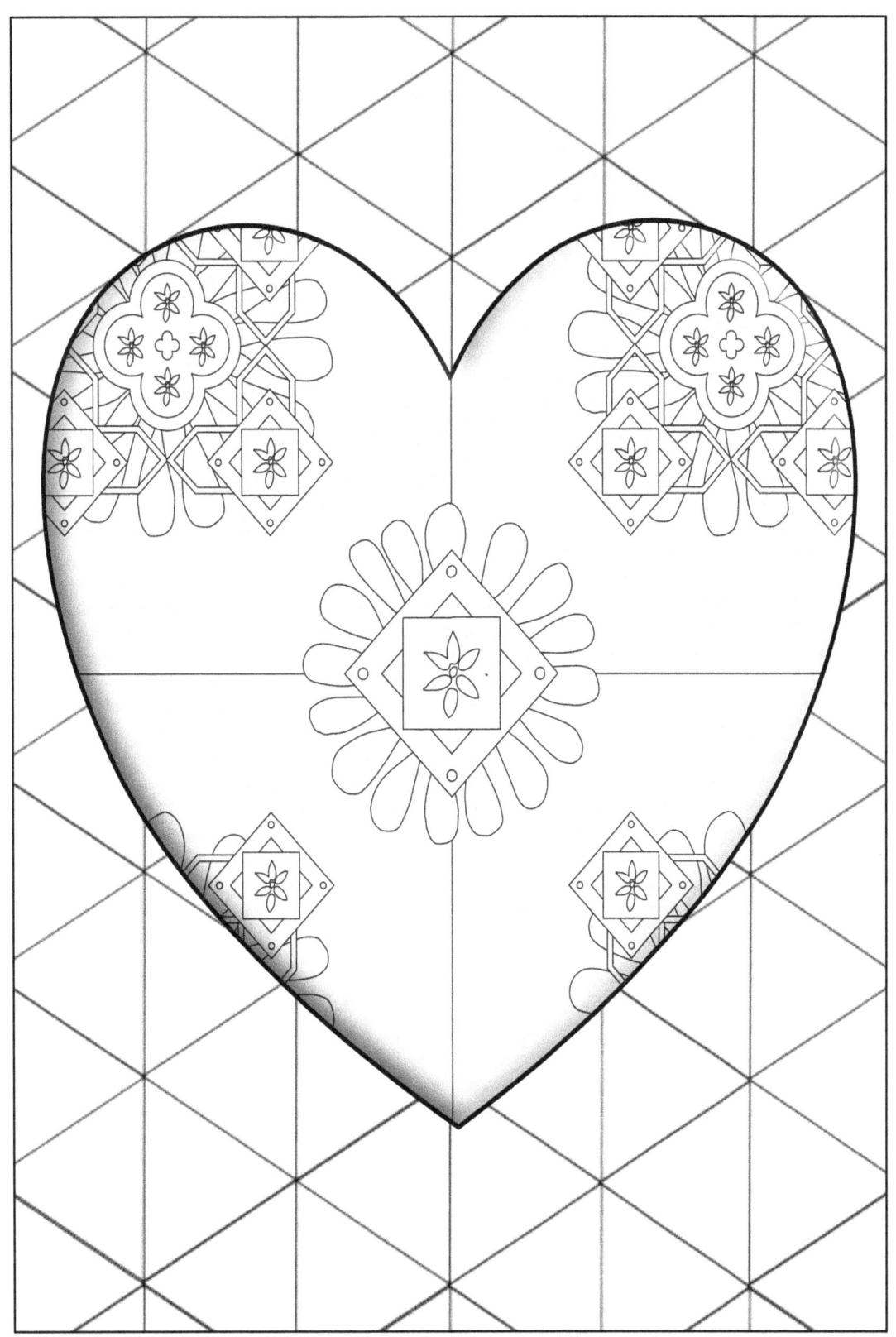

Copyright © 2018 Michael Weiner

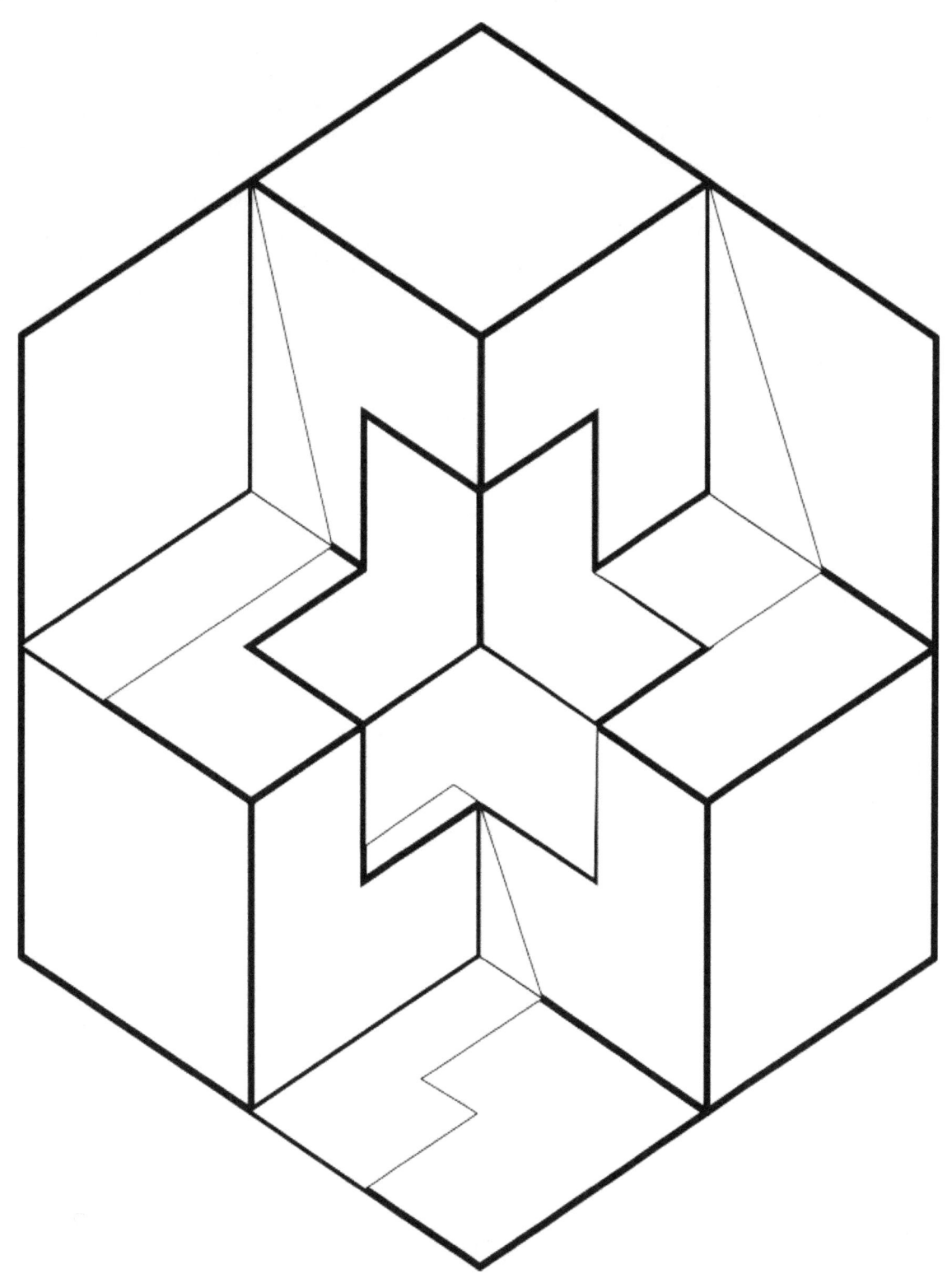

Copyright © 2018 Michael Weiner

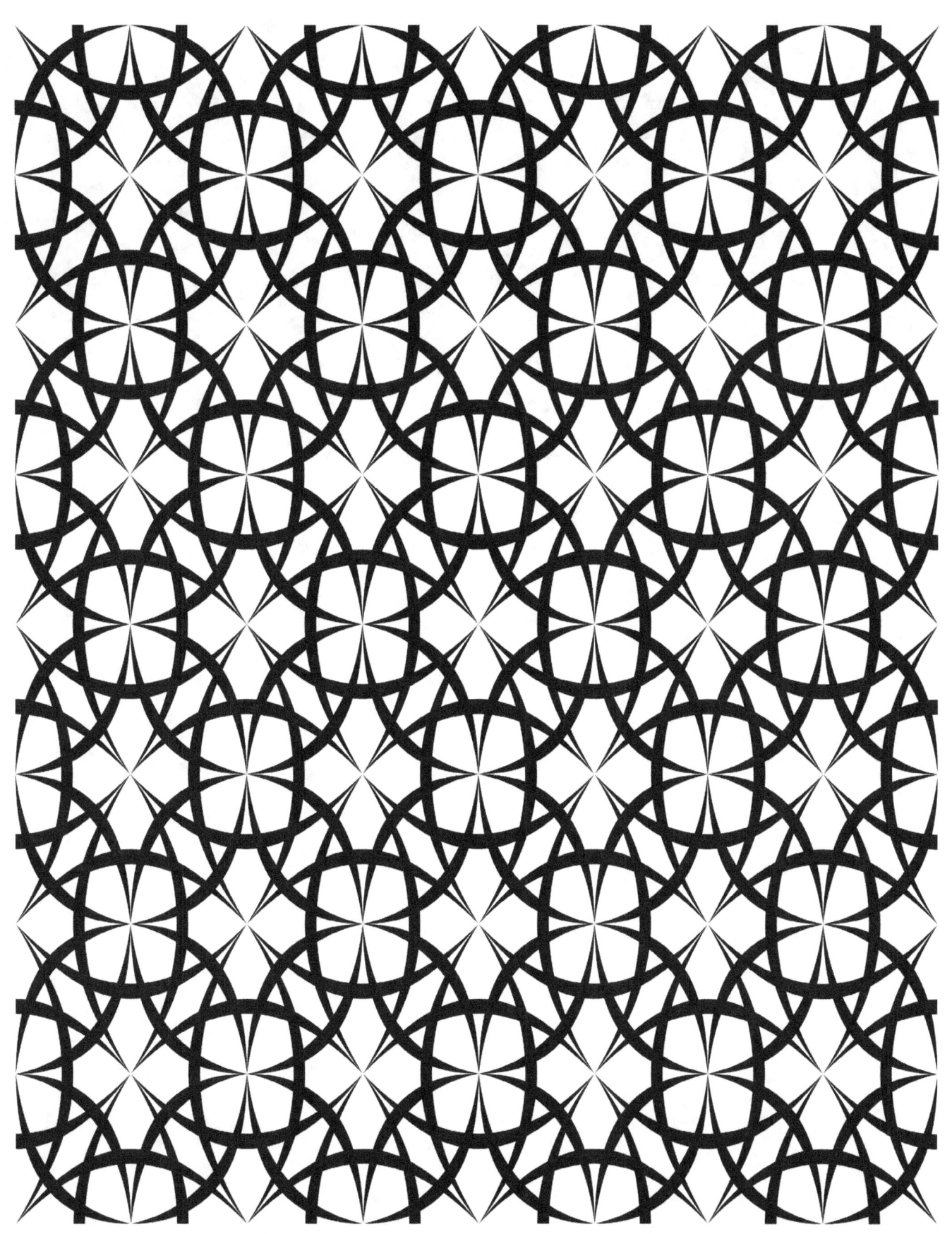

Copyright © 2018 Michael Weiner

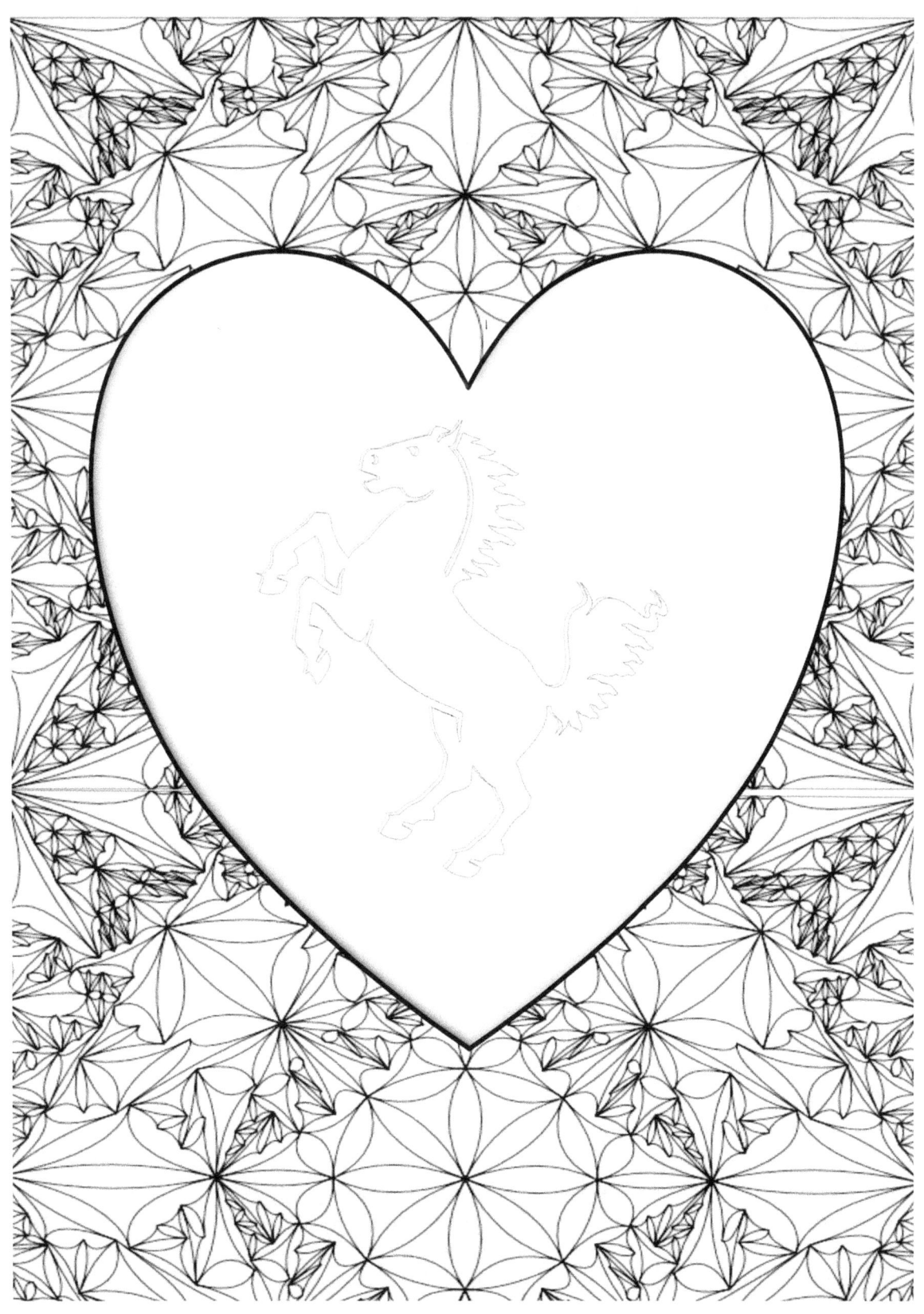

Copyright © 2018 Michael Weiner

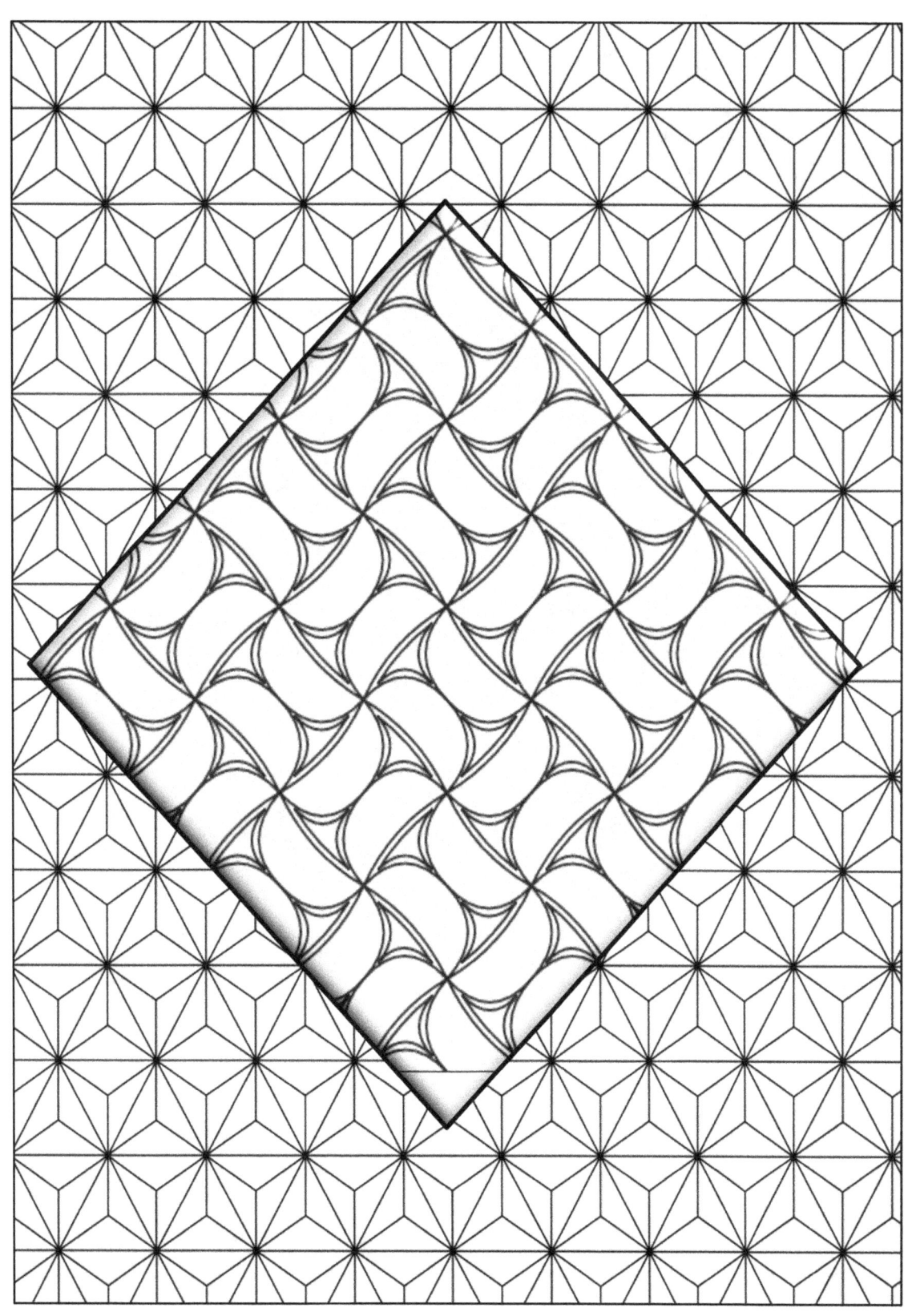

Copyright © 2018 Michael Weiner

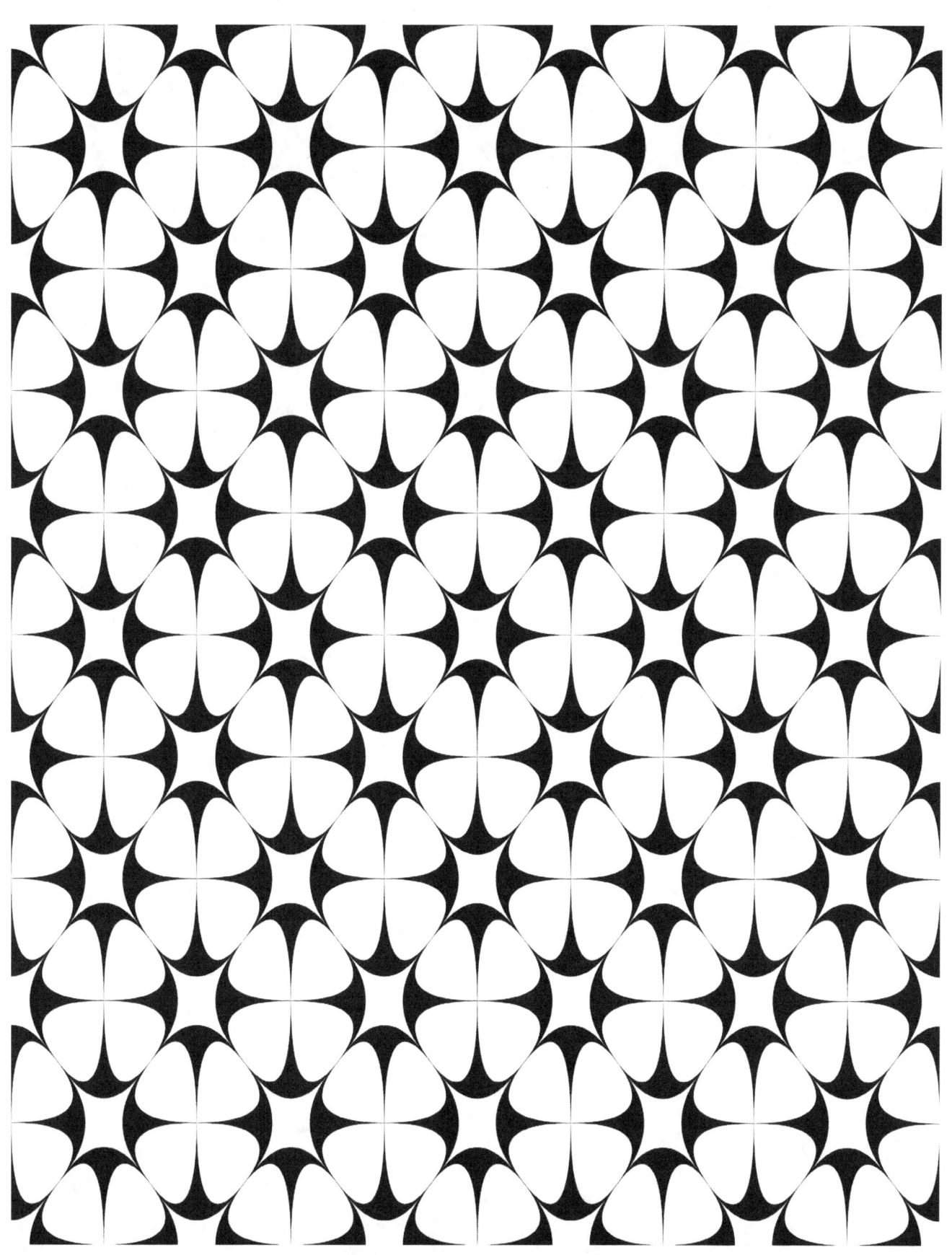

Copyright © 2018 Michael Weiner

Copyright © 2018 Michael Weiner

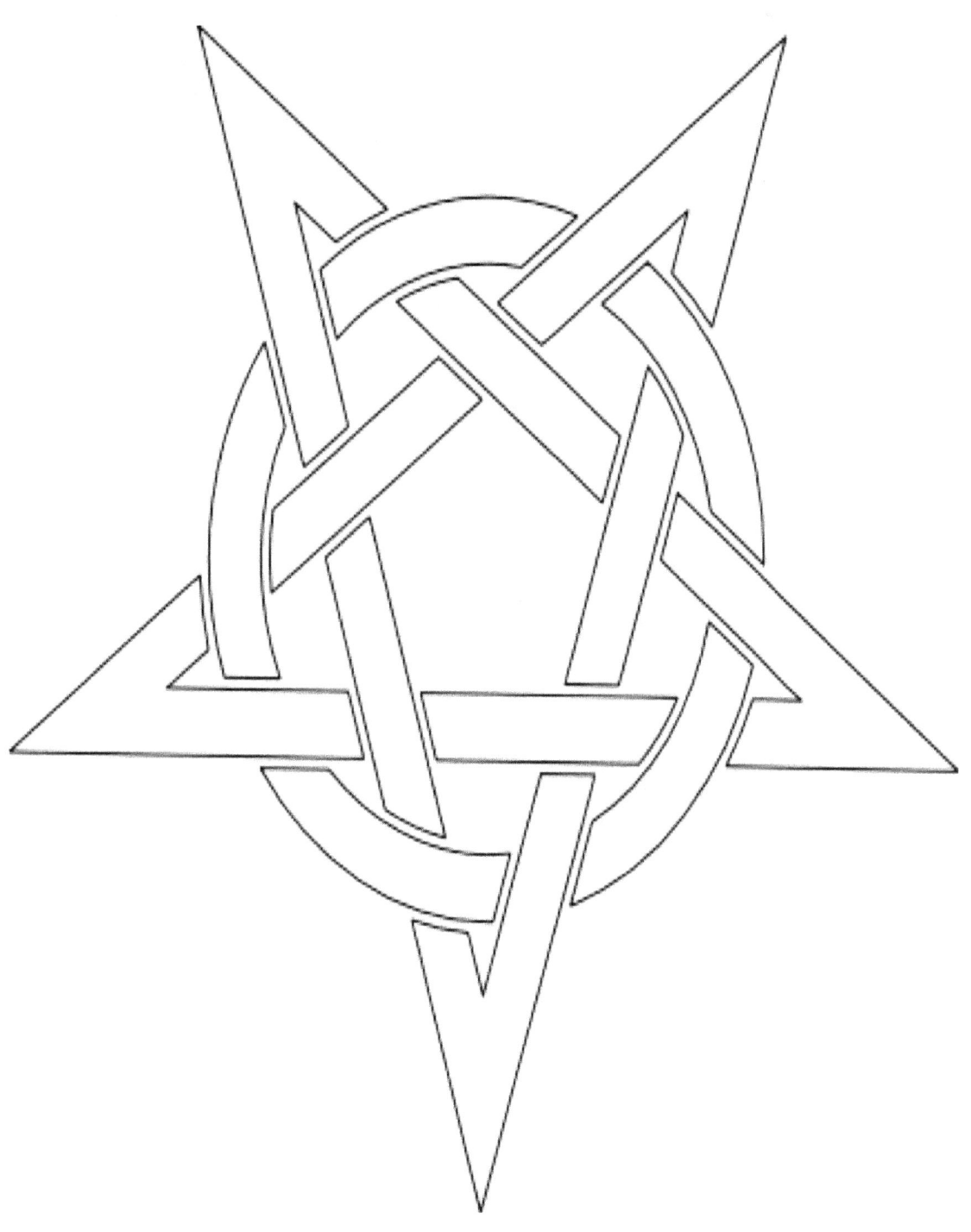

Copyright © 2018 Michael Weiner

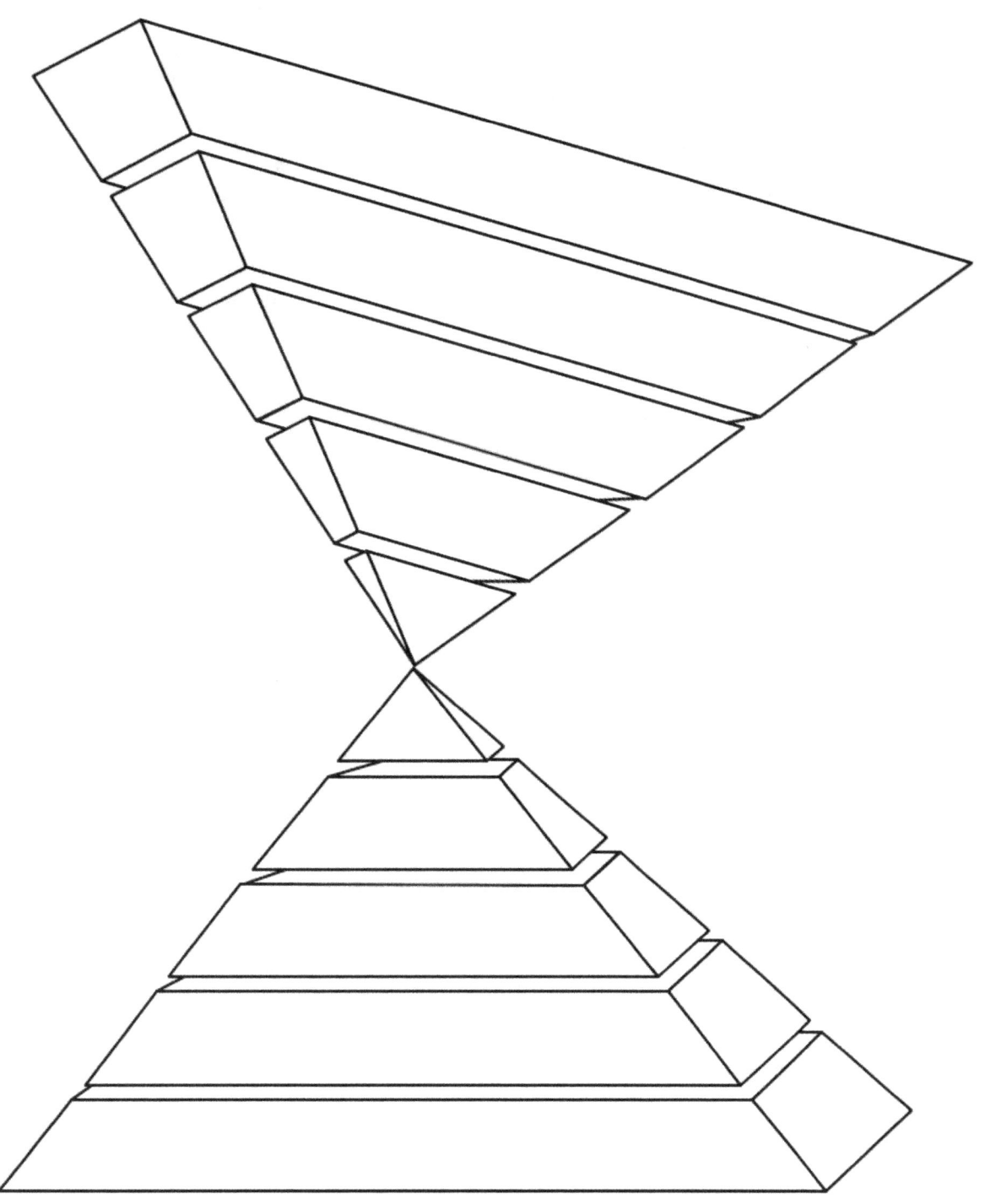

Copyright © 2018 Michael Weiner

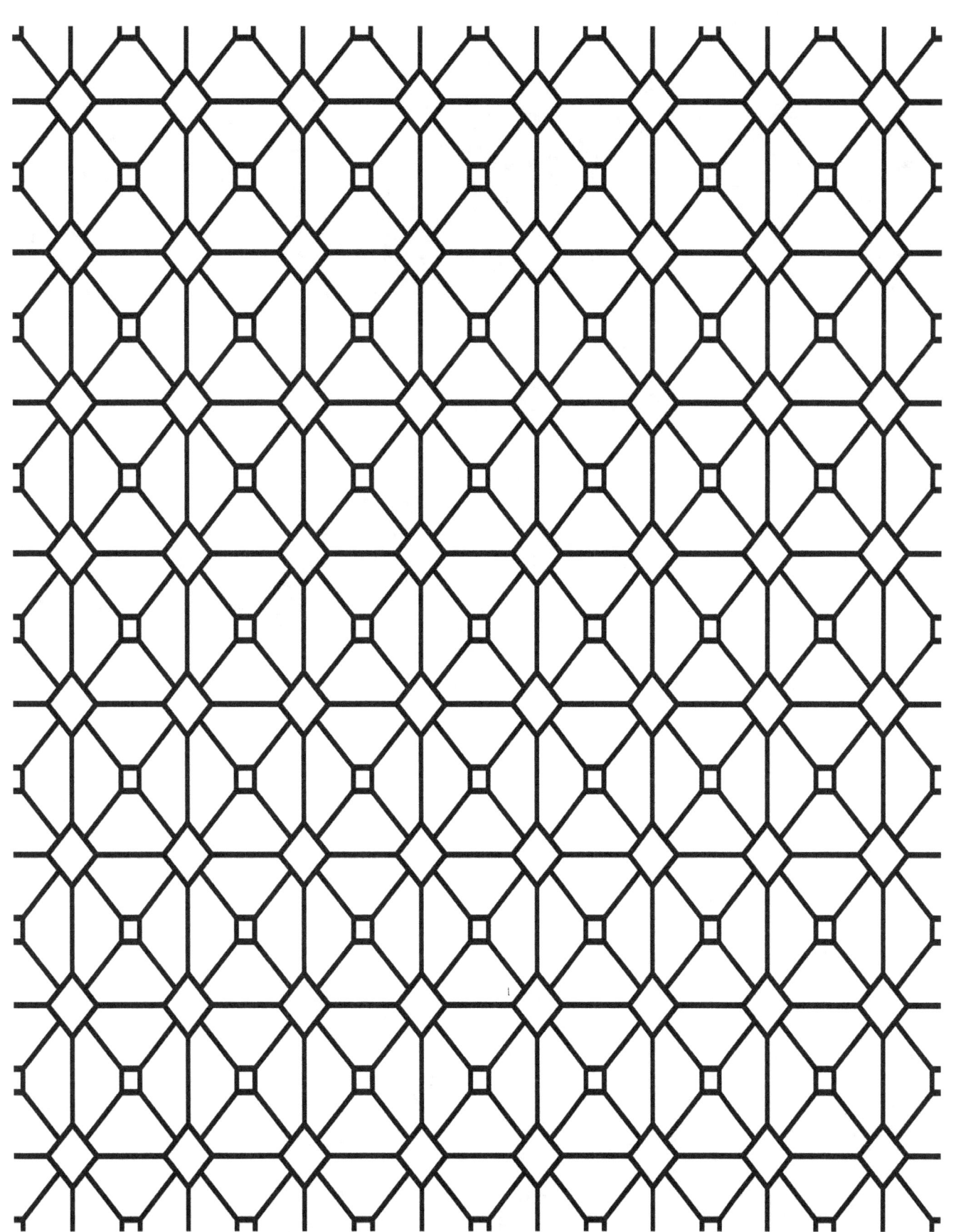

Copyright © 2018 Michael Weiner

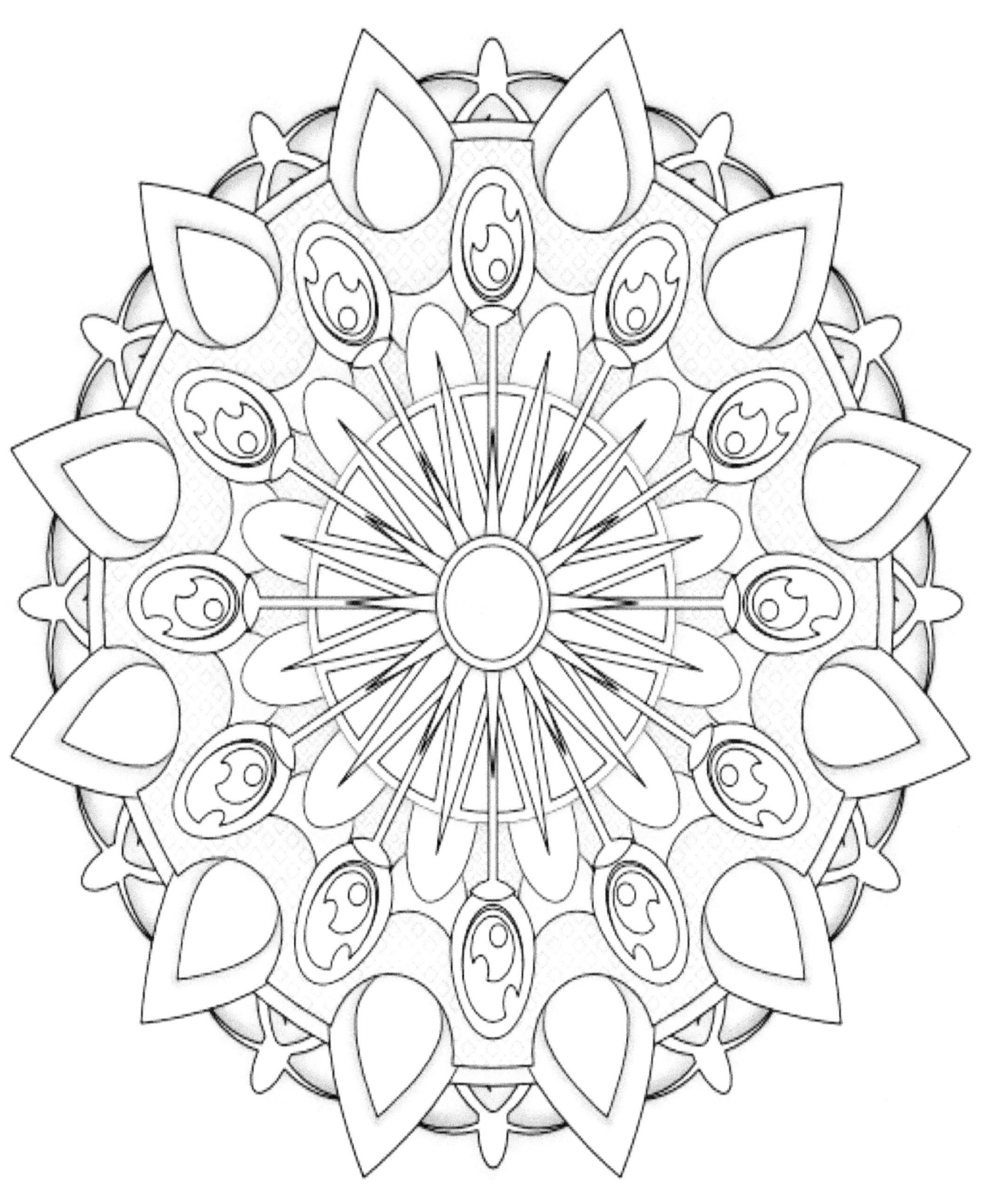

Copyright © 2018 Michael Weiner

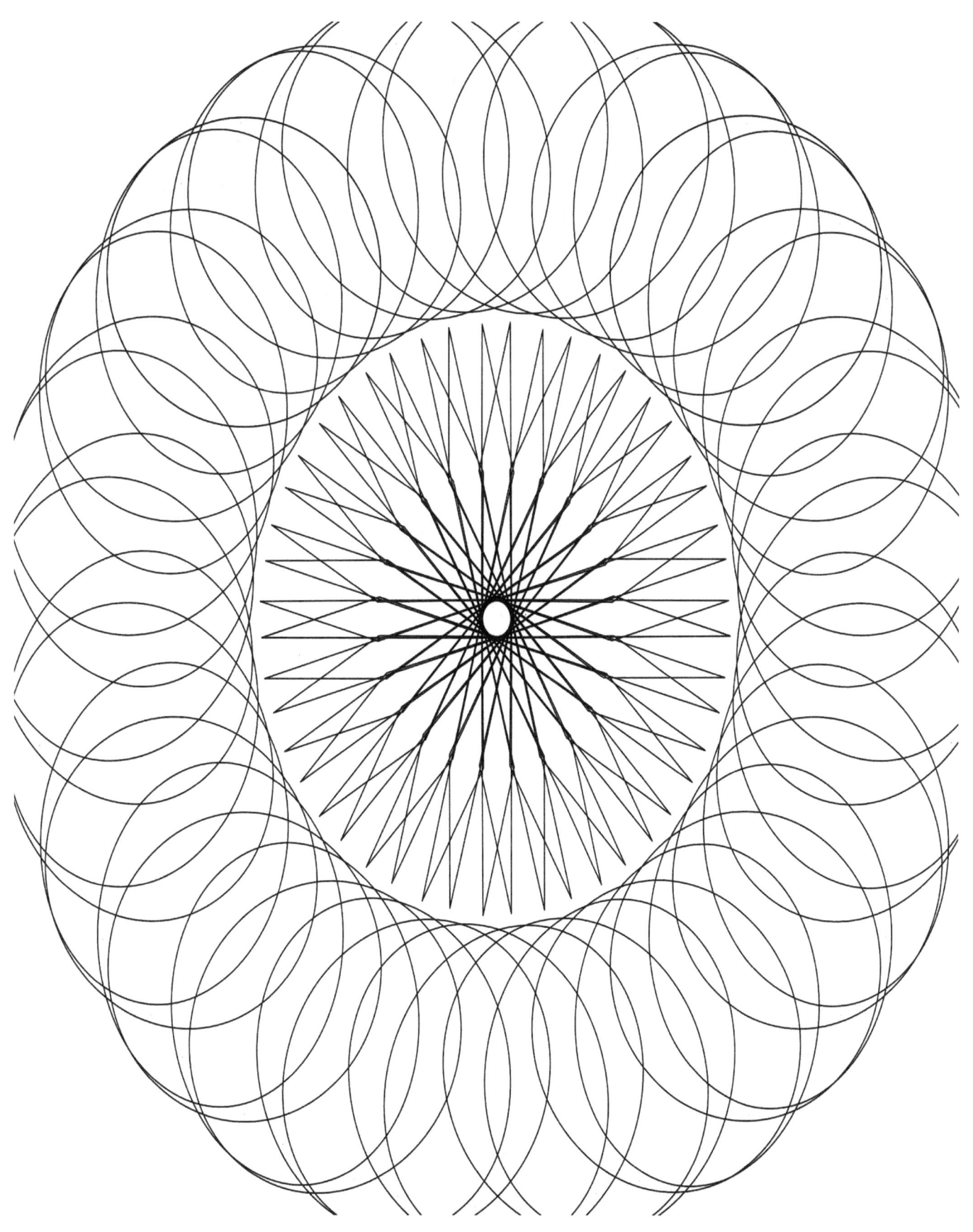

Copyright © 2018 Michael Weiner

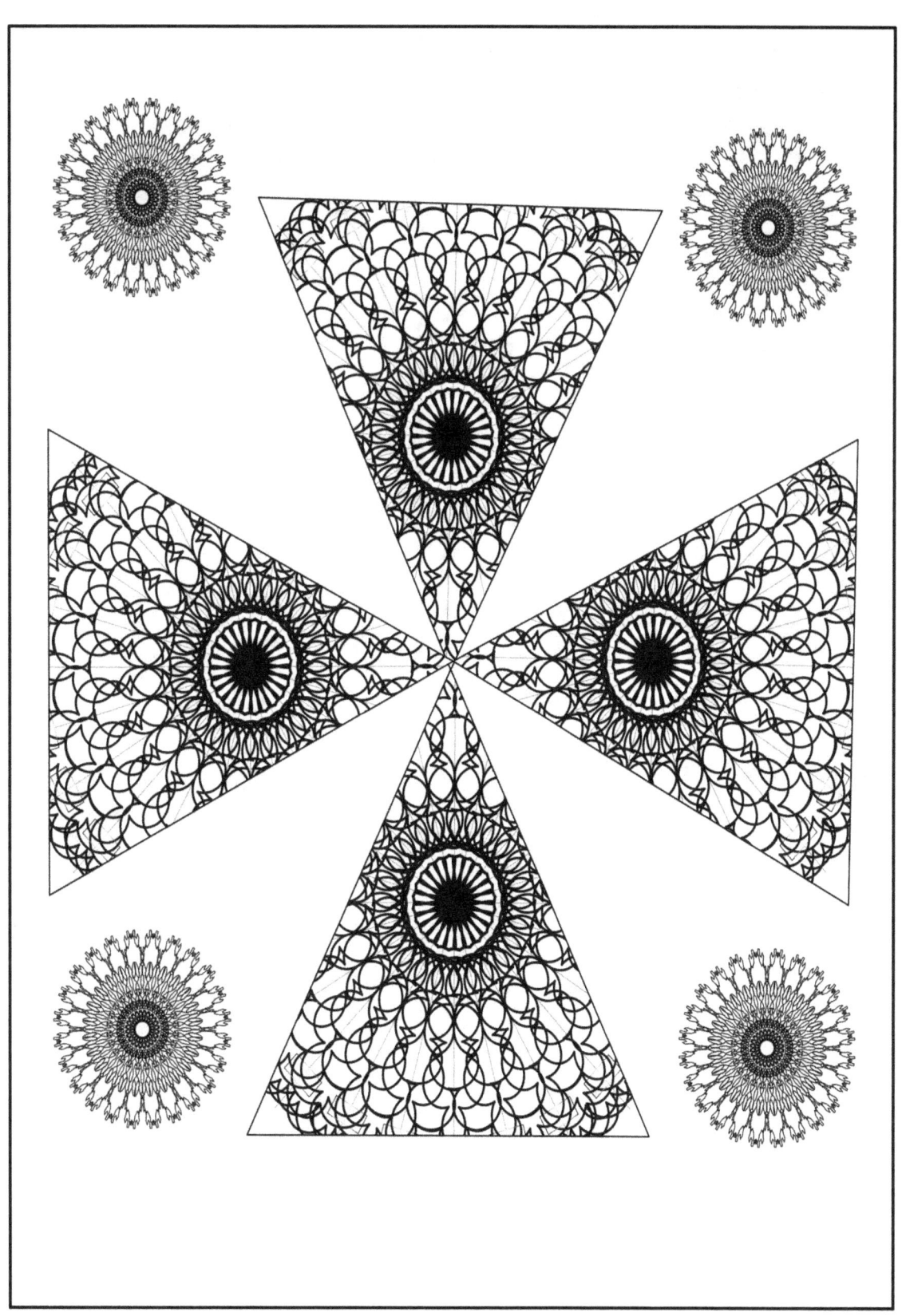

Copyright © 2018 Michael Weiner

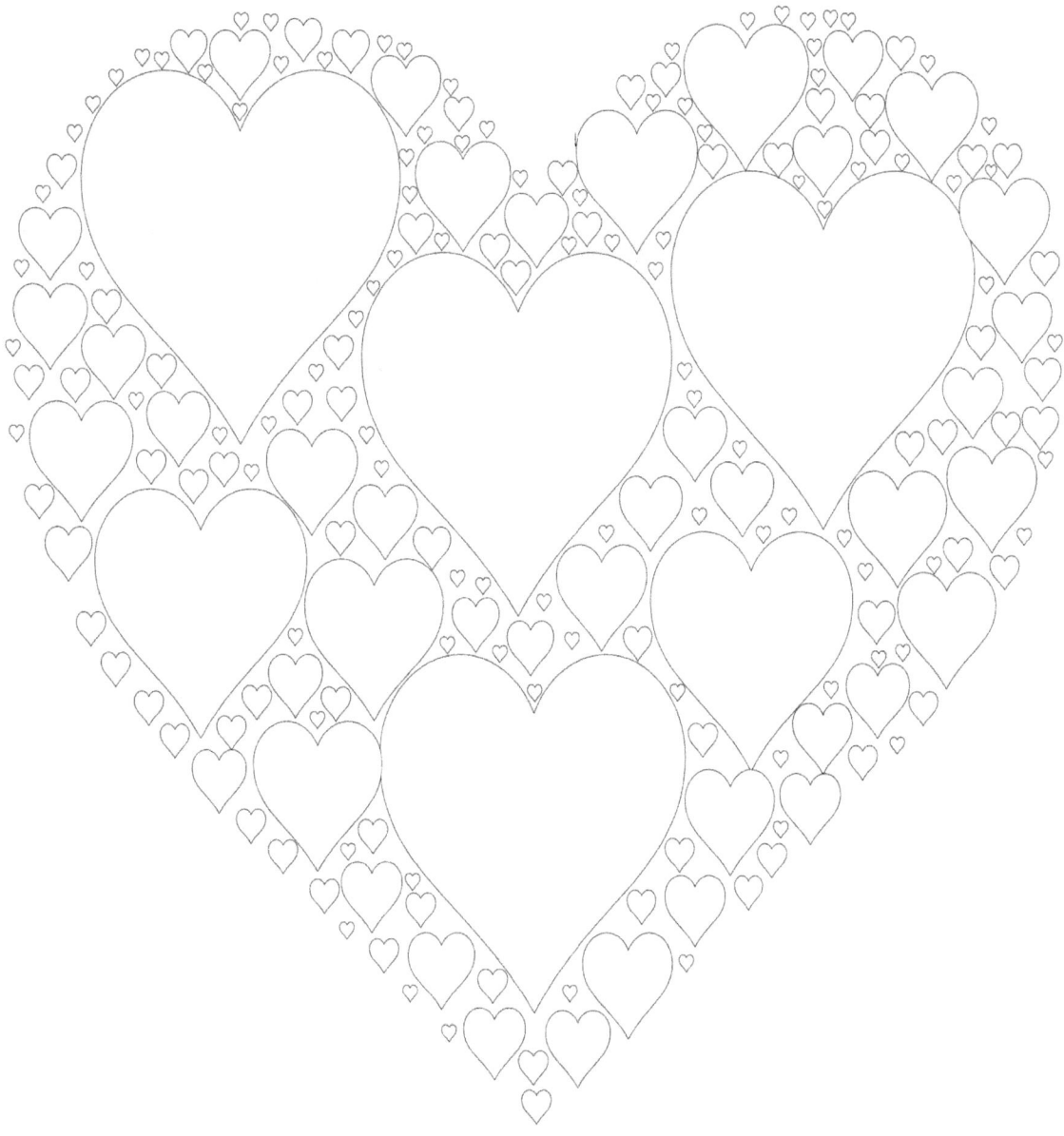

Copyright © 2018 Michael Weiner

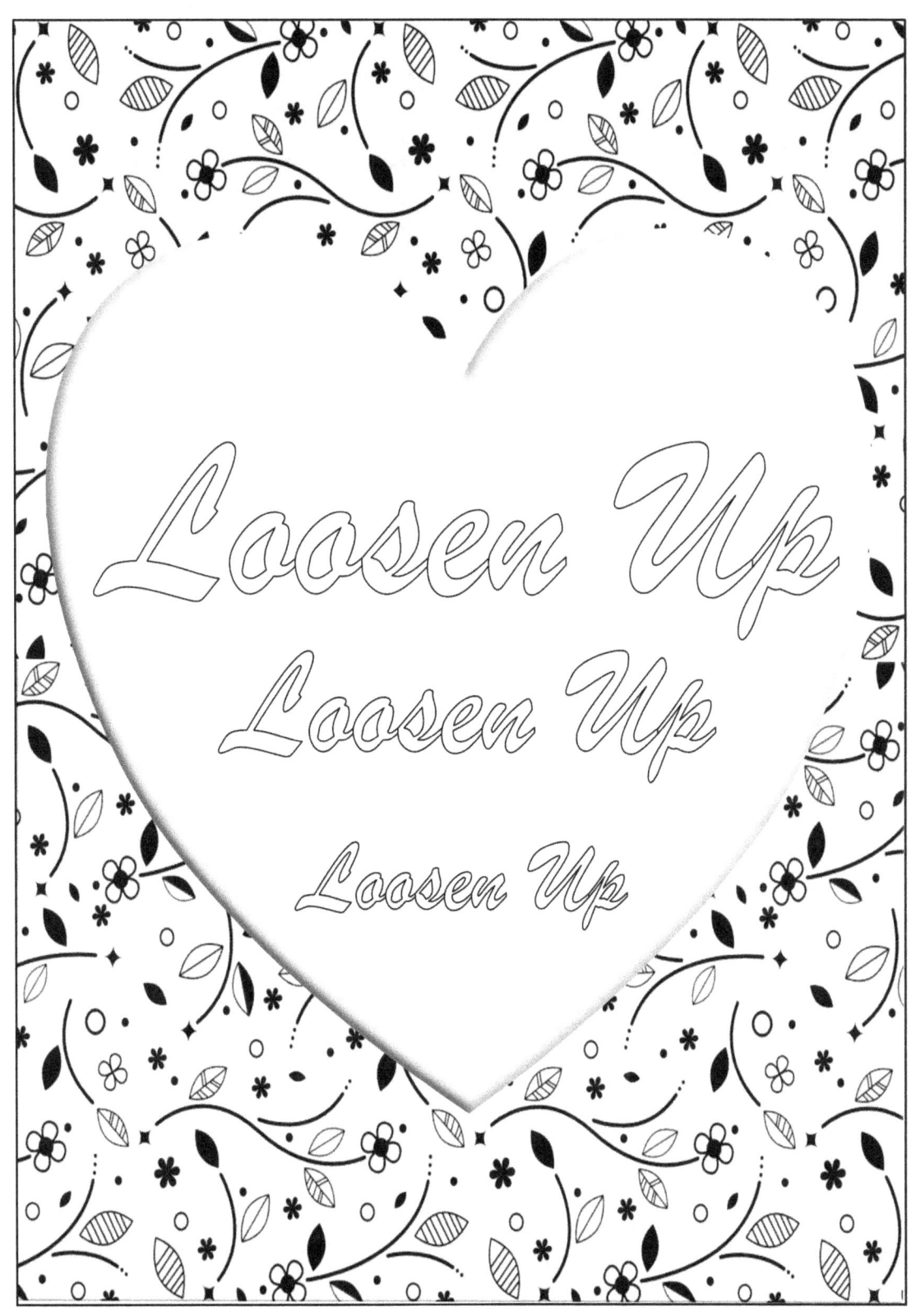

Copyright © 2018 Michael Weiner

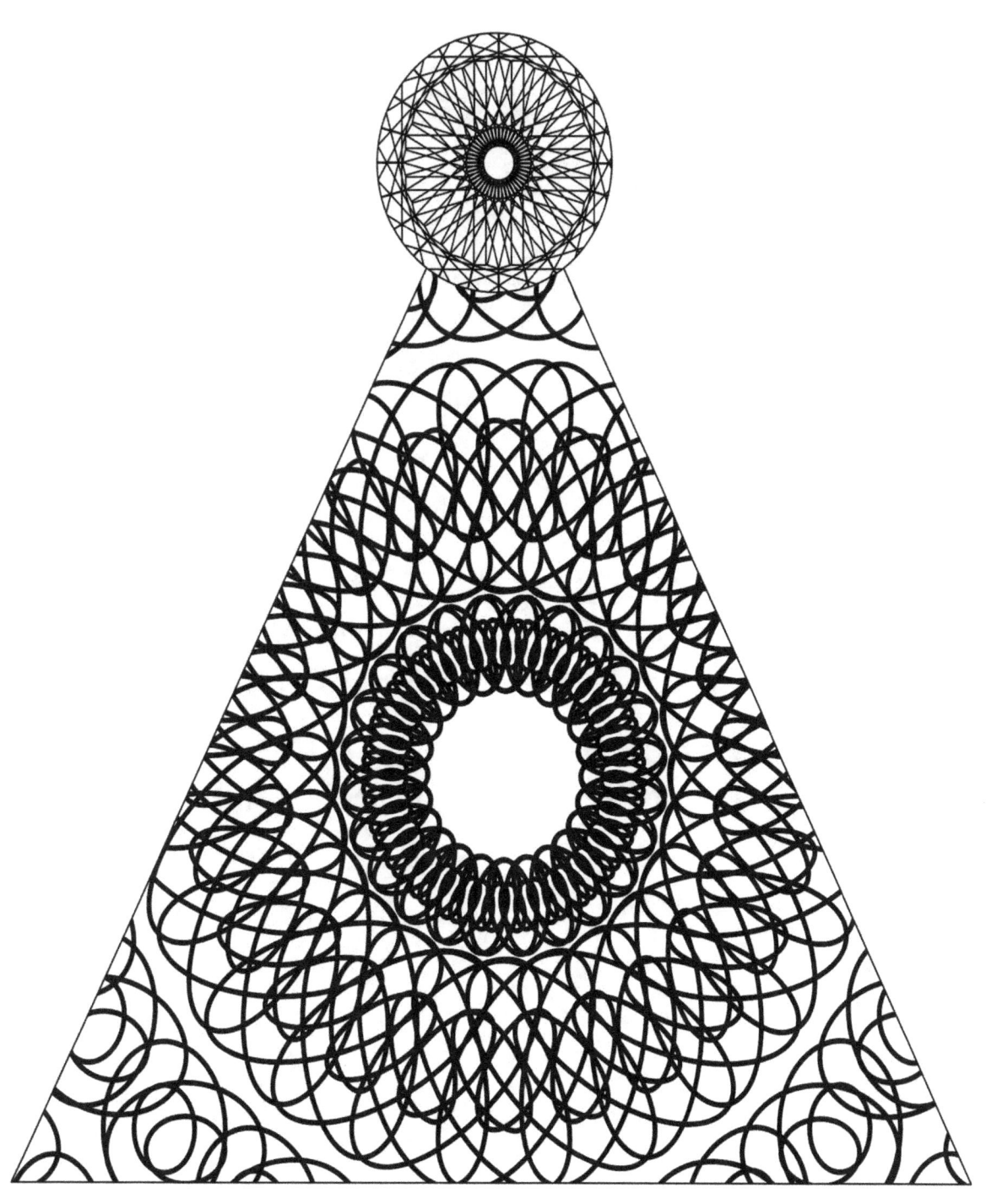

Copyright © 2018 Michael Weiner

Notes

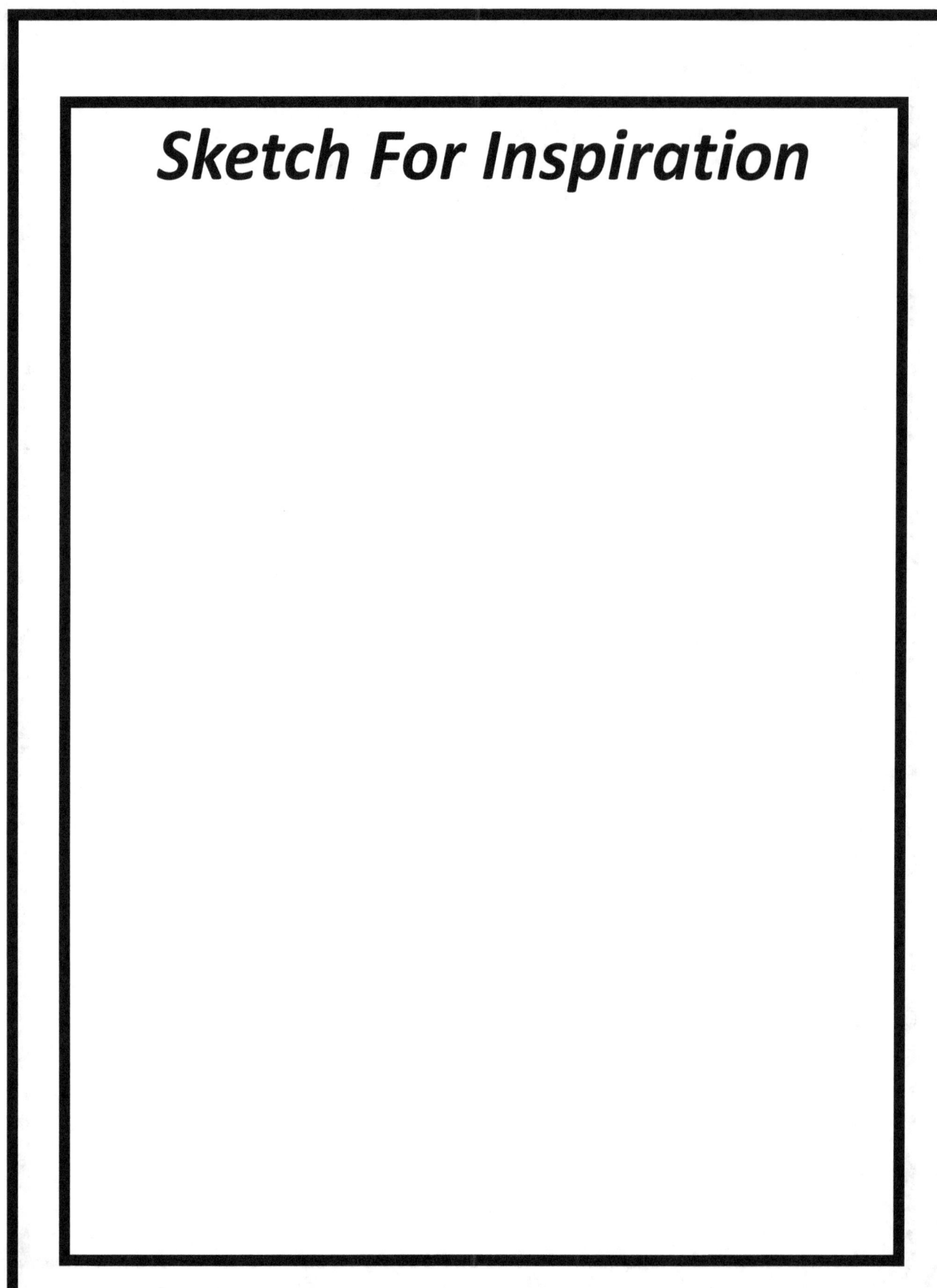

Beautiful Flowers
Coloring Book For Adults

Inspiring Flowers
Adult Coloring Book For Women Men Teens & Seniors
(50 stress-relieving and Relaxation designs)

Copyright © 2018 Michael Weiner

Copyright © 2018 by Michael Weiner

All rights reserved. No part of this publication may be reproduced, distributed, or transmitted in any form or by any means, including photocopying, recording, or other electronic or mechanical methods, without the prior written permission of the publisher, except in the case of brief quotations embodied in critical reviews and certain other noncommercial uses permitted by copyright law. For permission requests, write to the publisher, addressed "Attention: Permissions Coordinator," at the address below.

Glass By Michael, LLC
michael@liveasuperchargedlife.com
liveasuperchargedlife.com

Ordering Information:
Quantity sales. Special discounts are available on quantity purchases by corporations, associations, and others. For details, contact the publisher at the address above.

Orders by U.S. trade bookstores and wholesalers. Please contact Live A Supercharged Life
michael@liveasuperchargedlife.com
liveasuperchargedlife.com
First Edition

Copyright © 2018 Michael Weiner

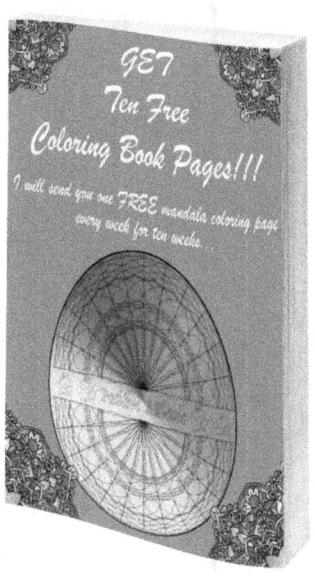

Sign Up For Your 10
FREE
Printable Mandala Coloring Book Pages Now!
http://www.liveasuperchargedlife.com/free-mandala-coloring-pages/

Check Us Out on Social Media

Email: michael@liveasuperchargedlife.com
https://www.facebook.com/liveasuperchargedlife/
https://www.instagram.com/liveasuperchargedlife/
https://www.youtube.com/channel/UCwfgl-GmDbQf5C0m7bLEiUQ
https://www.pinterest.com/liveasupercharg/
https://twitter.com/Superchargedway

Check Out Our Other Books

http://www.liveasuperchargedlife.com/books-by-michael/

Copyright © 2018 Michael Weiner

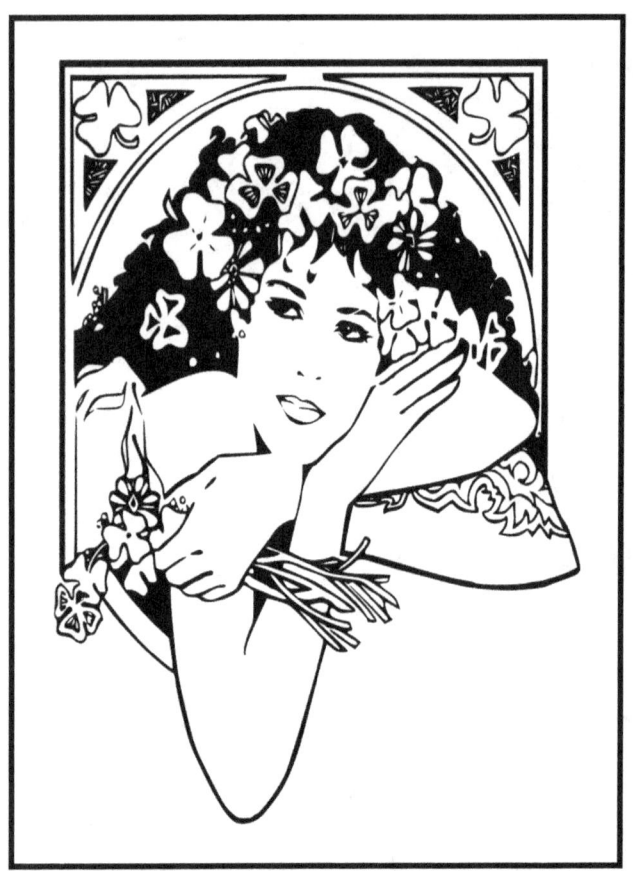
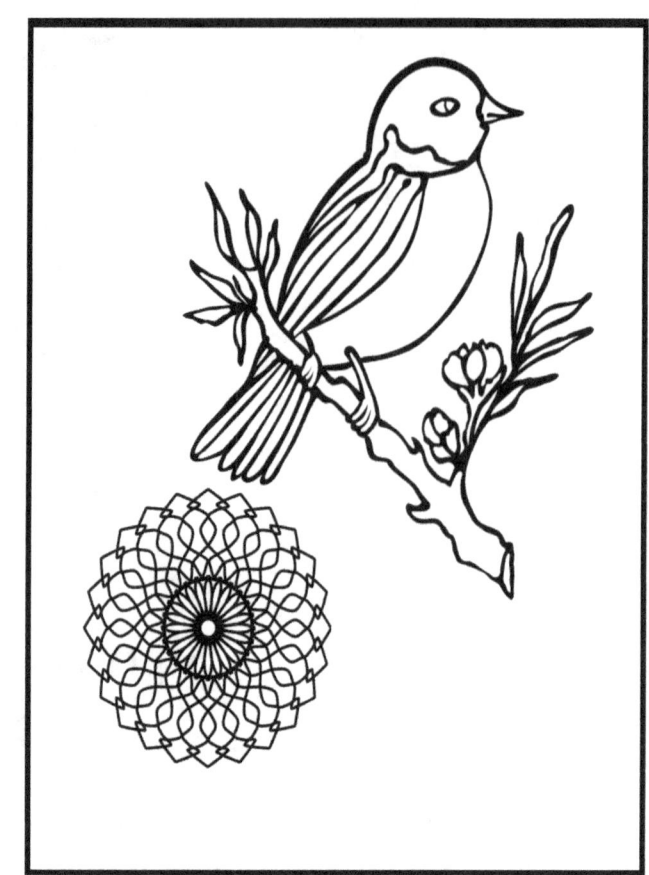

Sample Pages

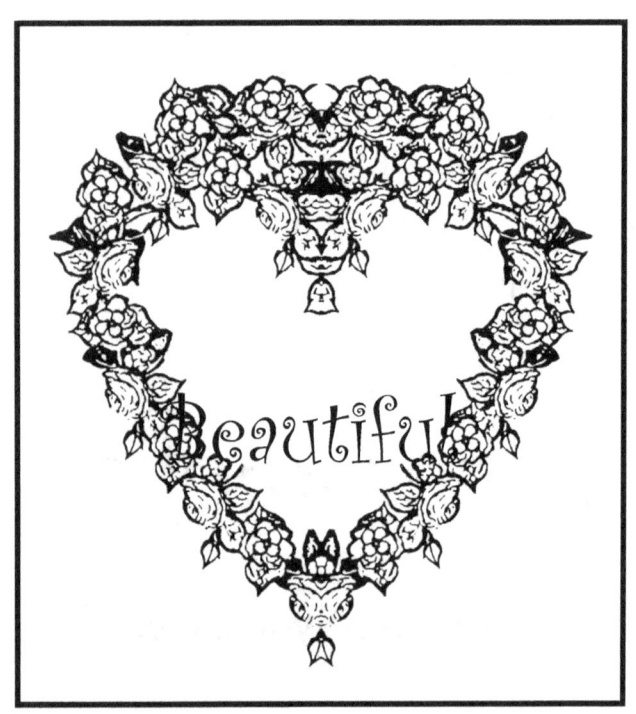
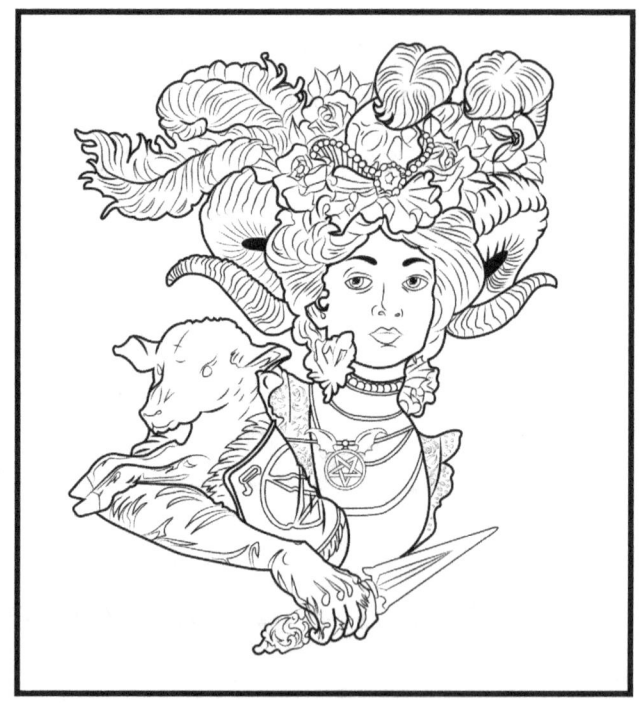

Copyright © 2018 Michael Weiner

This Book Belongs To

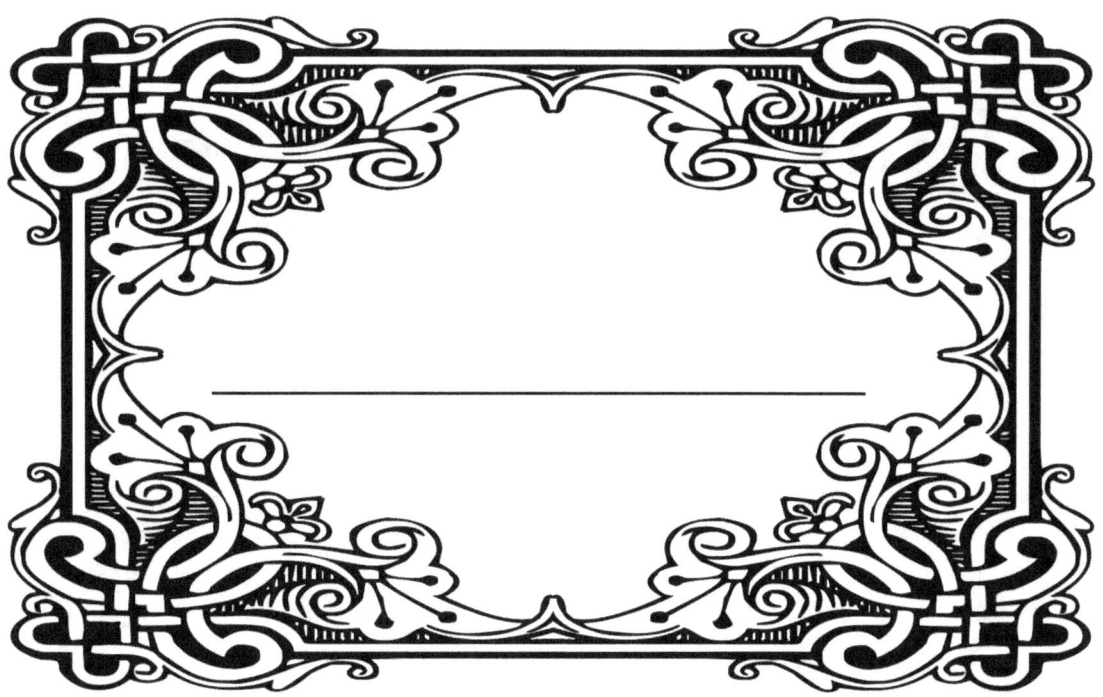

Copyright © 2018 Michael Weiner

Test your color palette

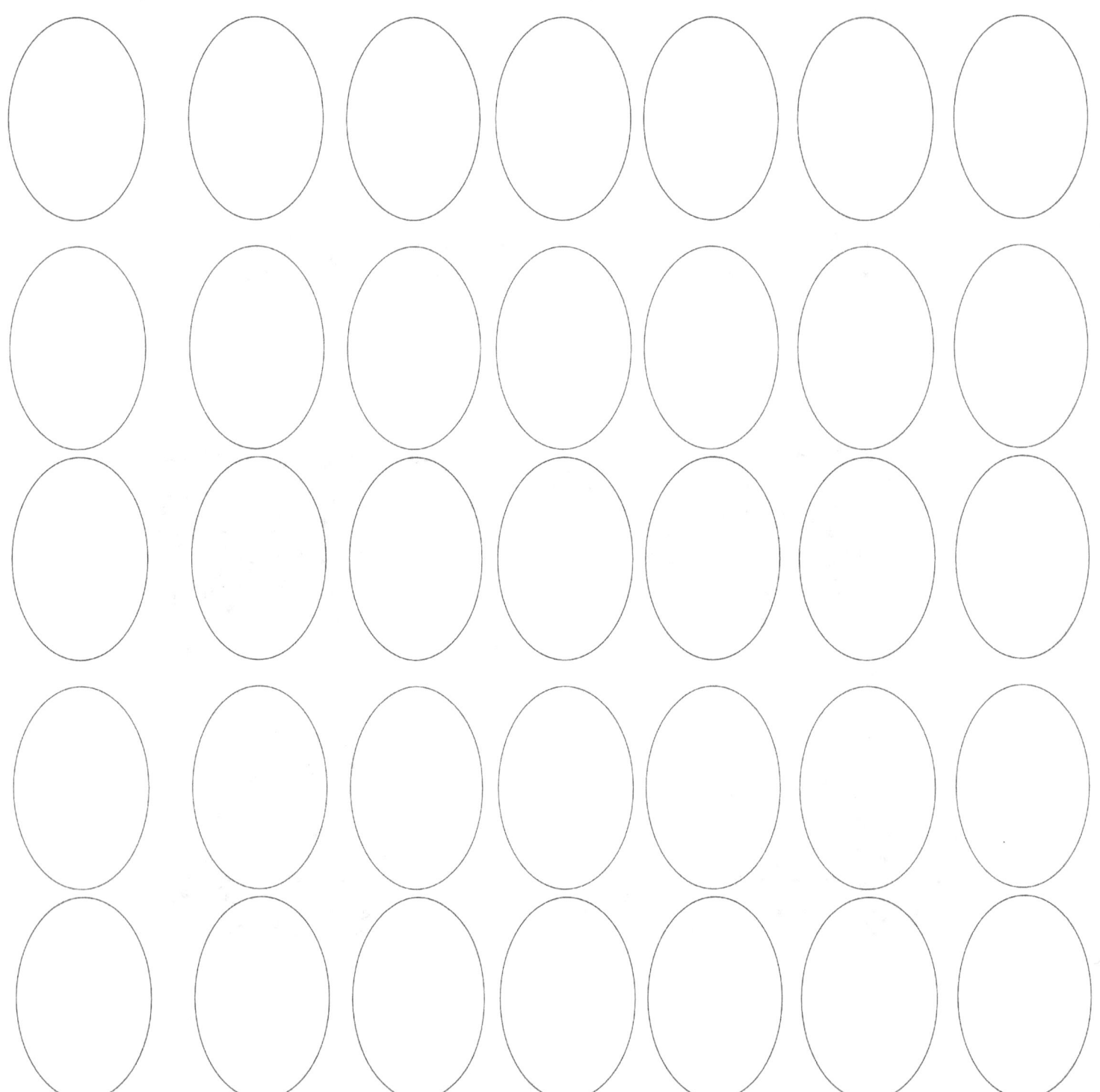

Copyright © 2018 Michael Weiner

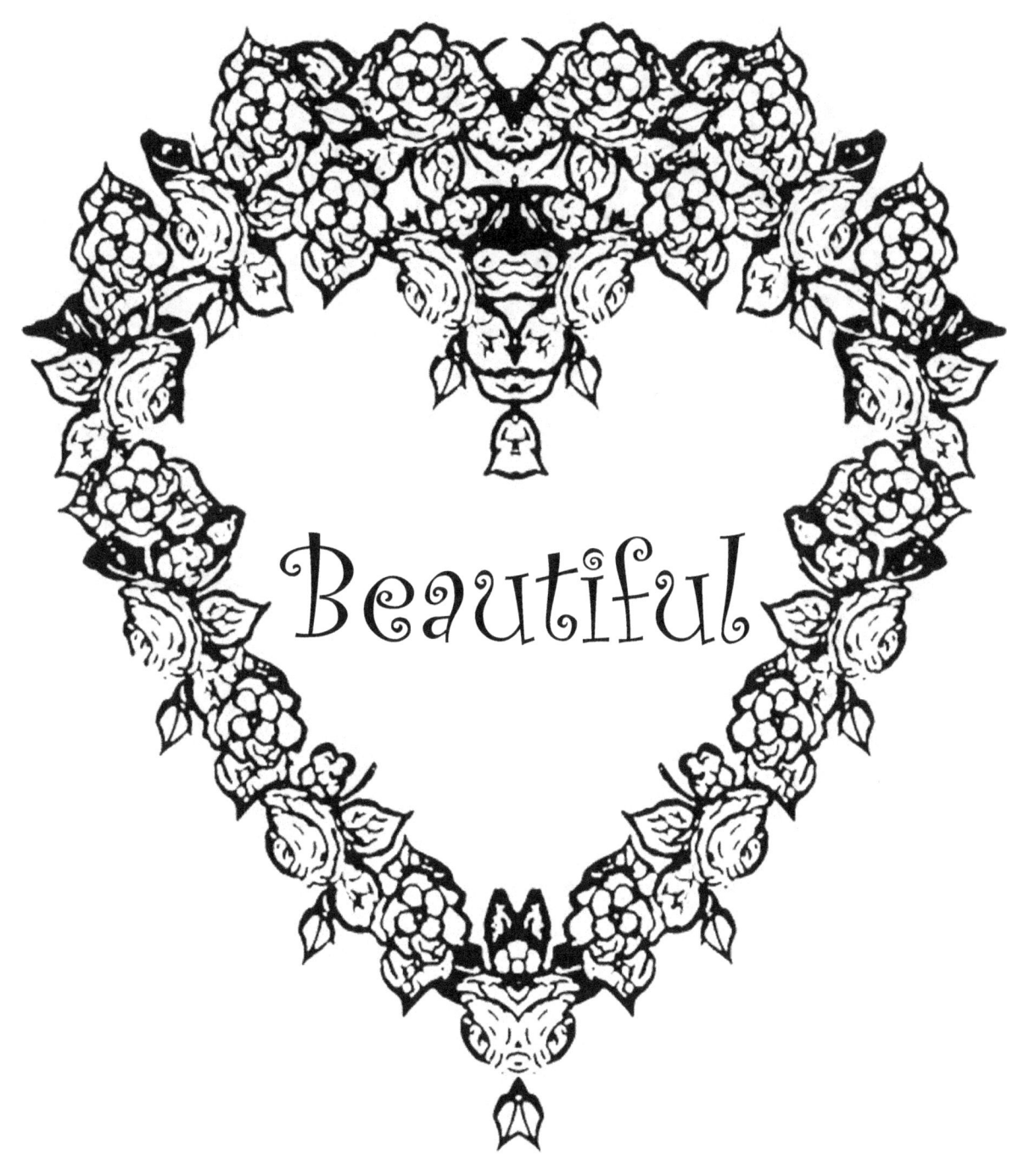

Copyright © 2018 Michael Weiner

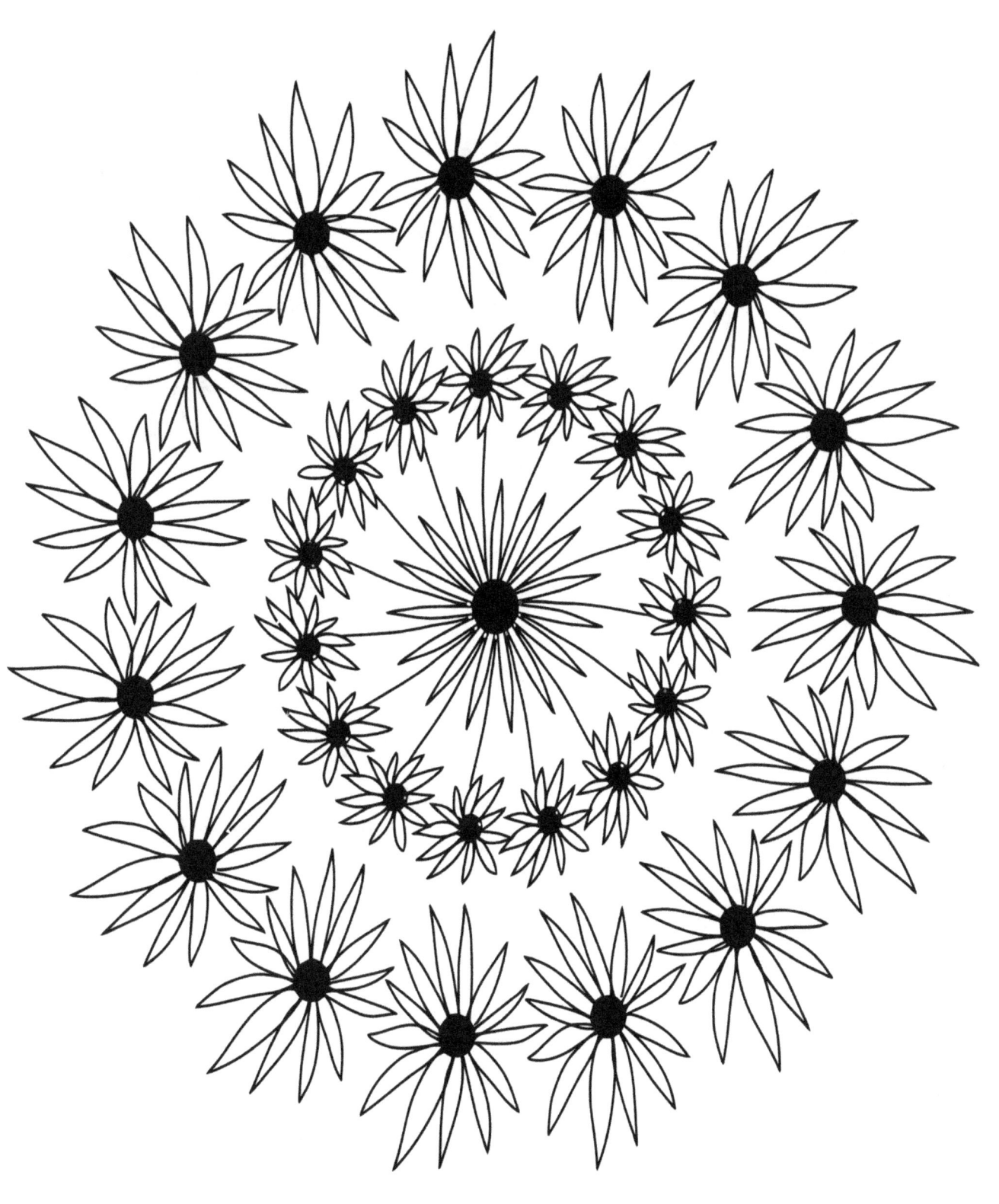

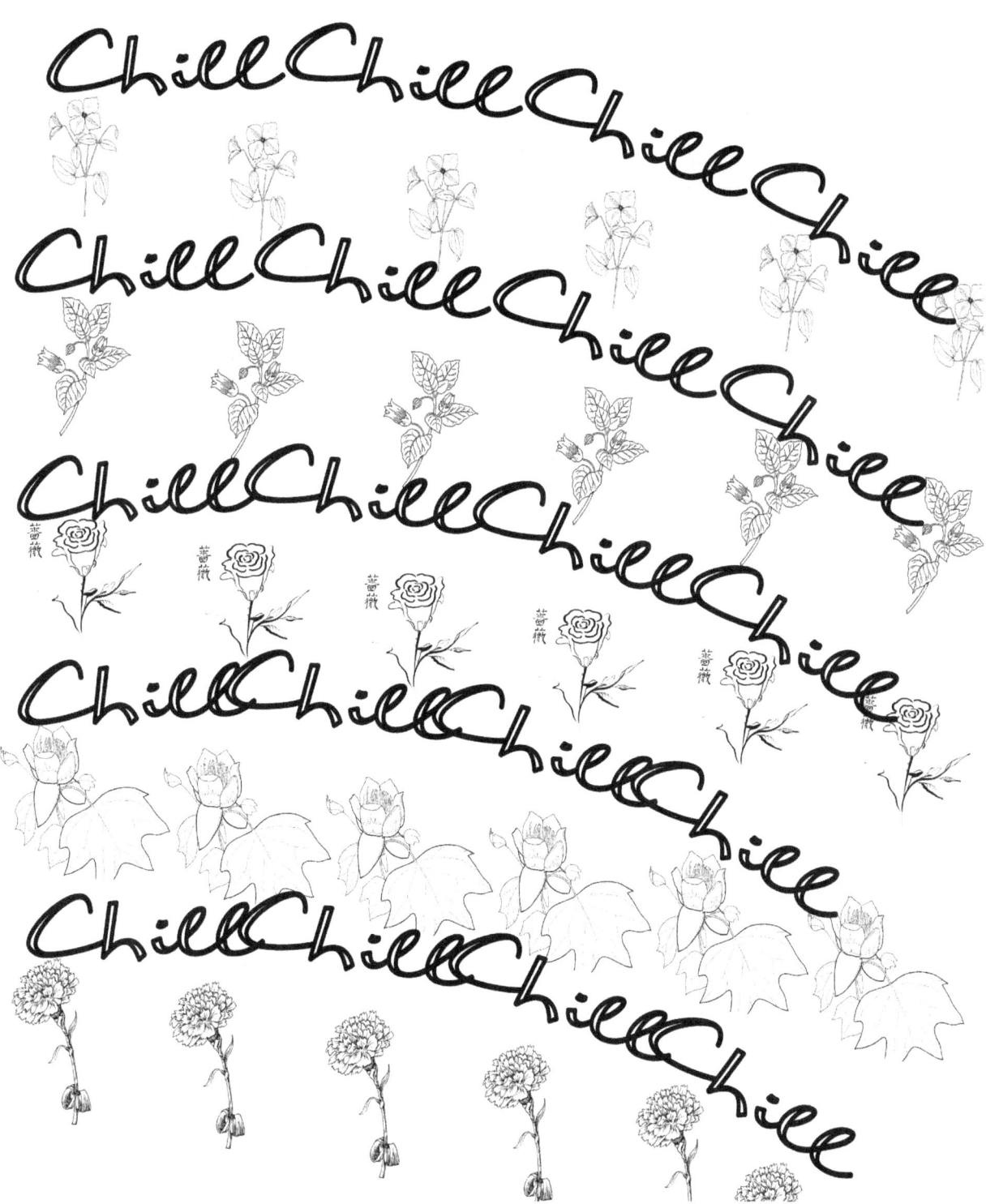

Copyright © 2018 Michael Weiner

Copyright © 2018 Michael Weiner

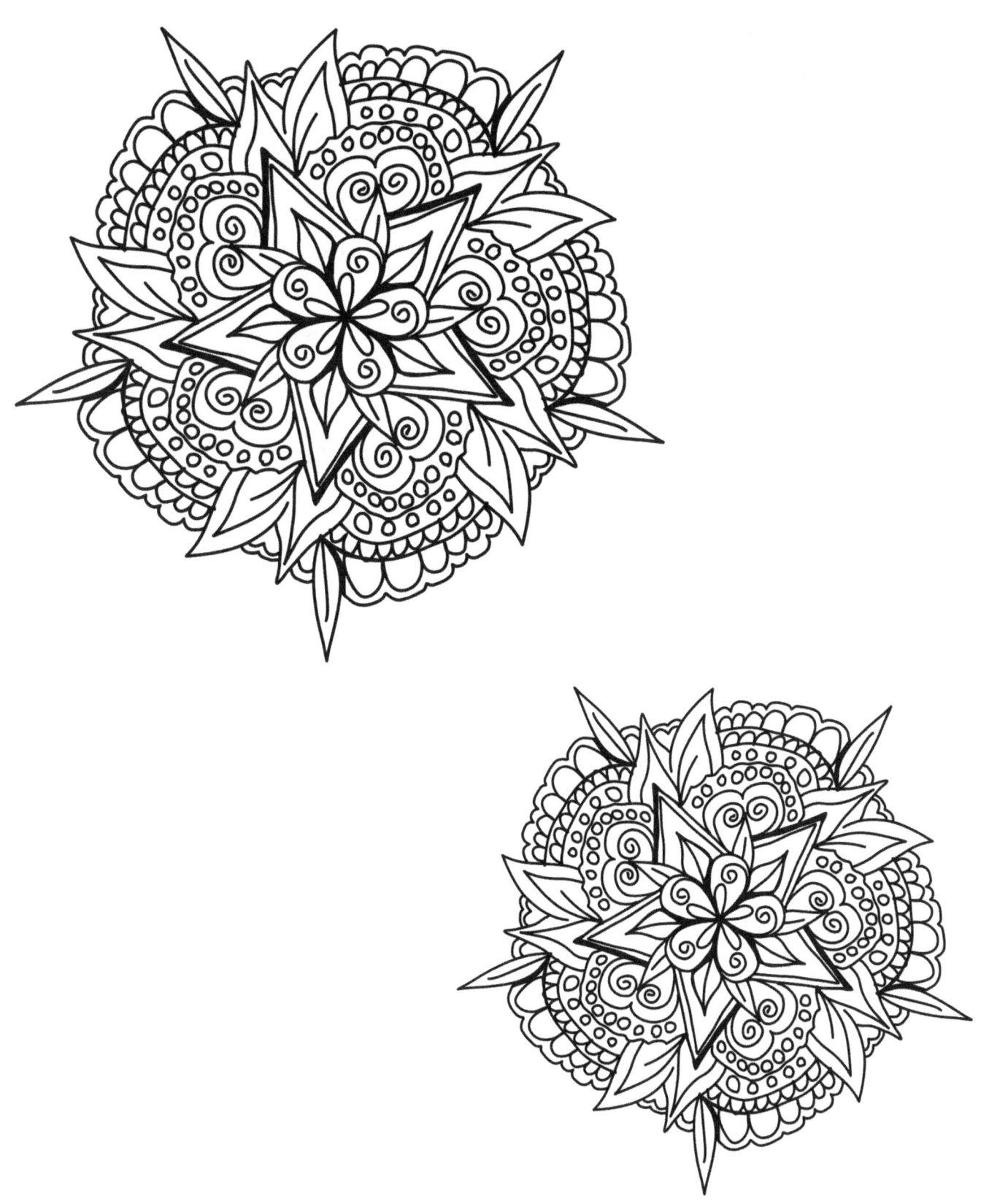

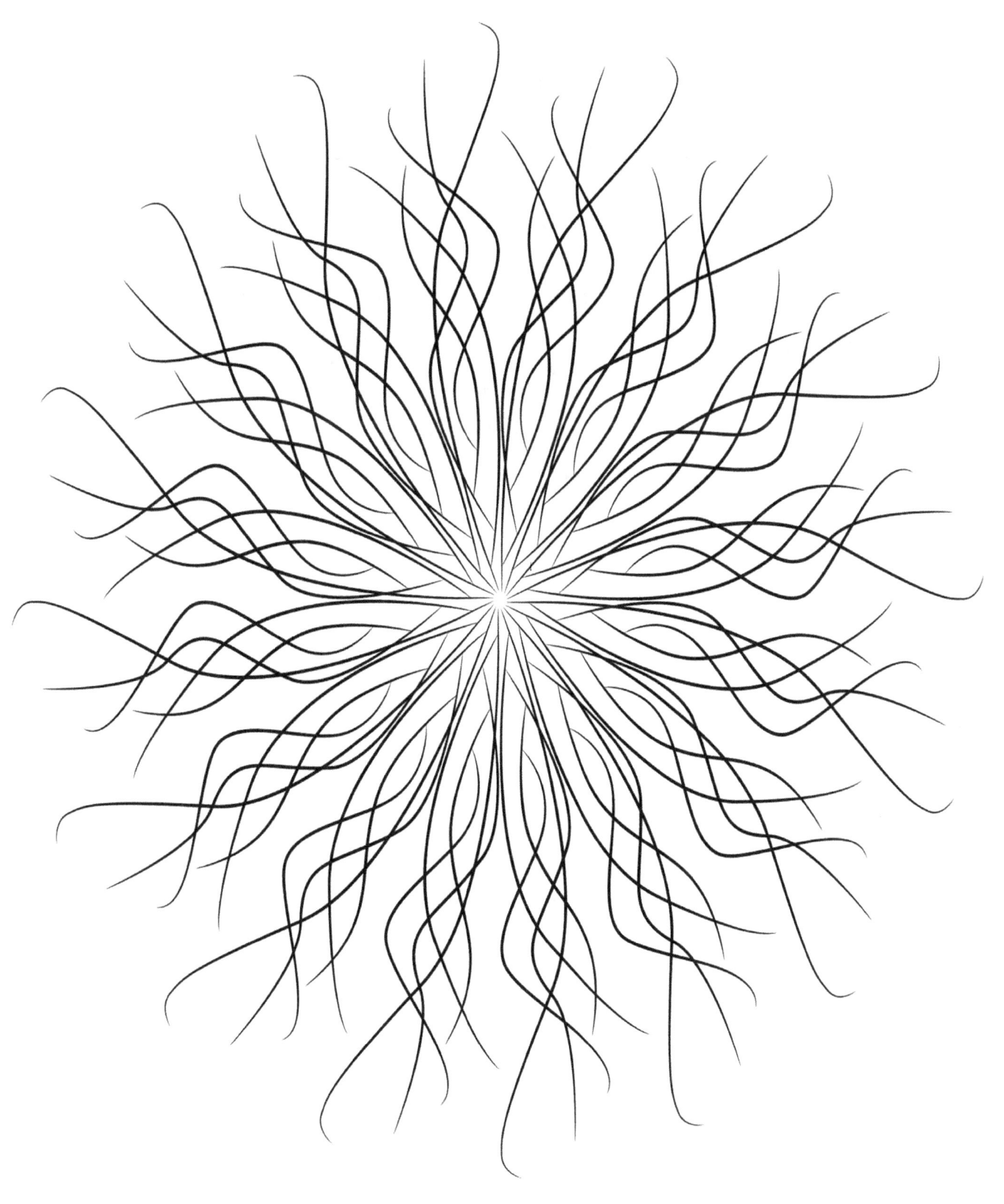

Copyright © 2018 Michael Weiner

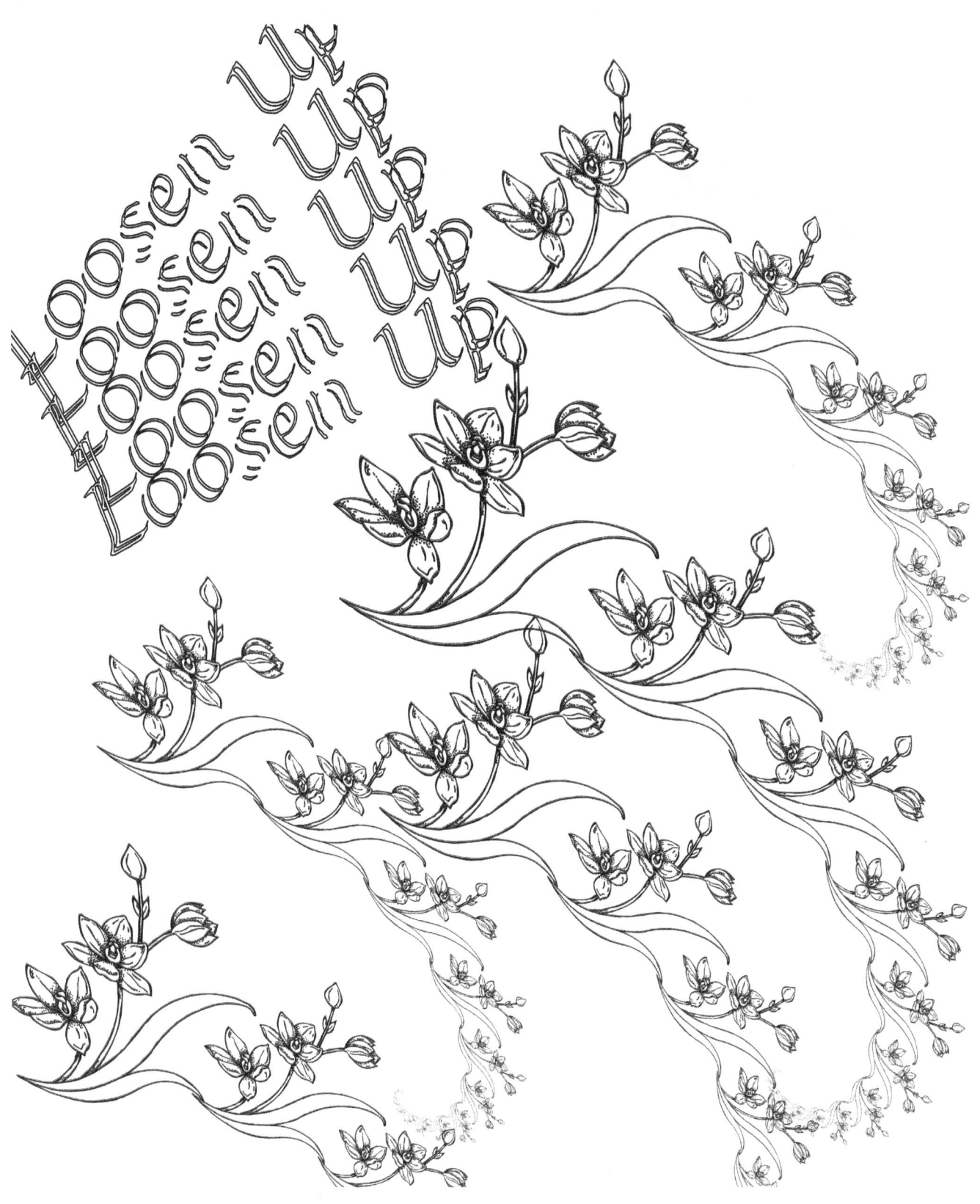

Copyright © 2018 Michael Weiner

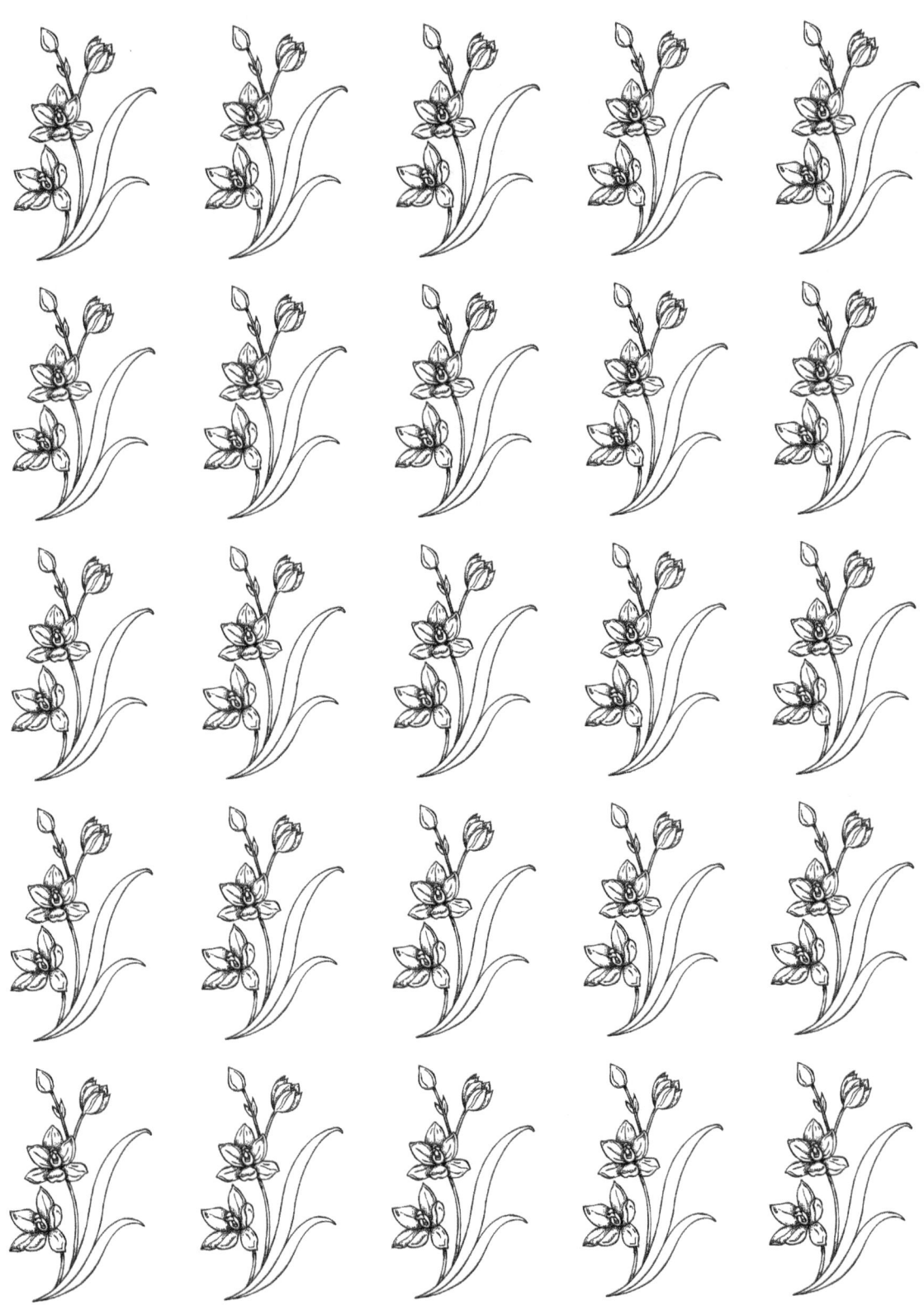

Copyright © 2018 Michael Weiner

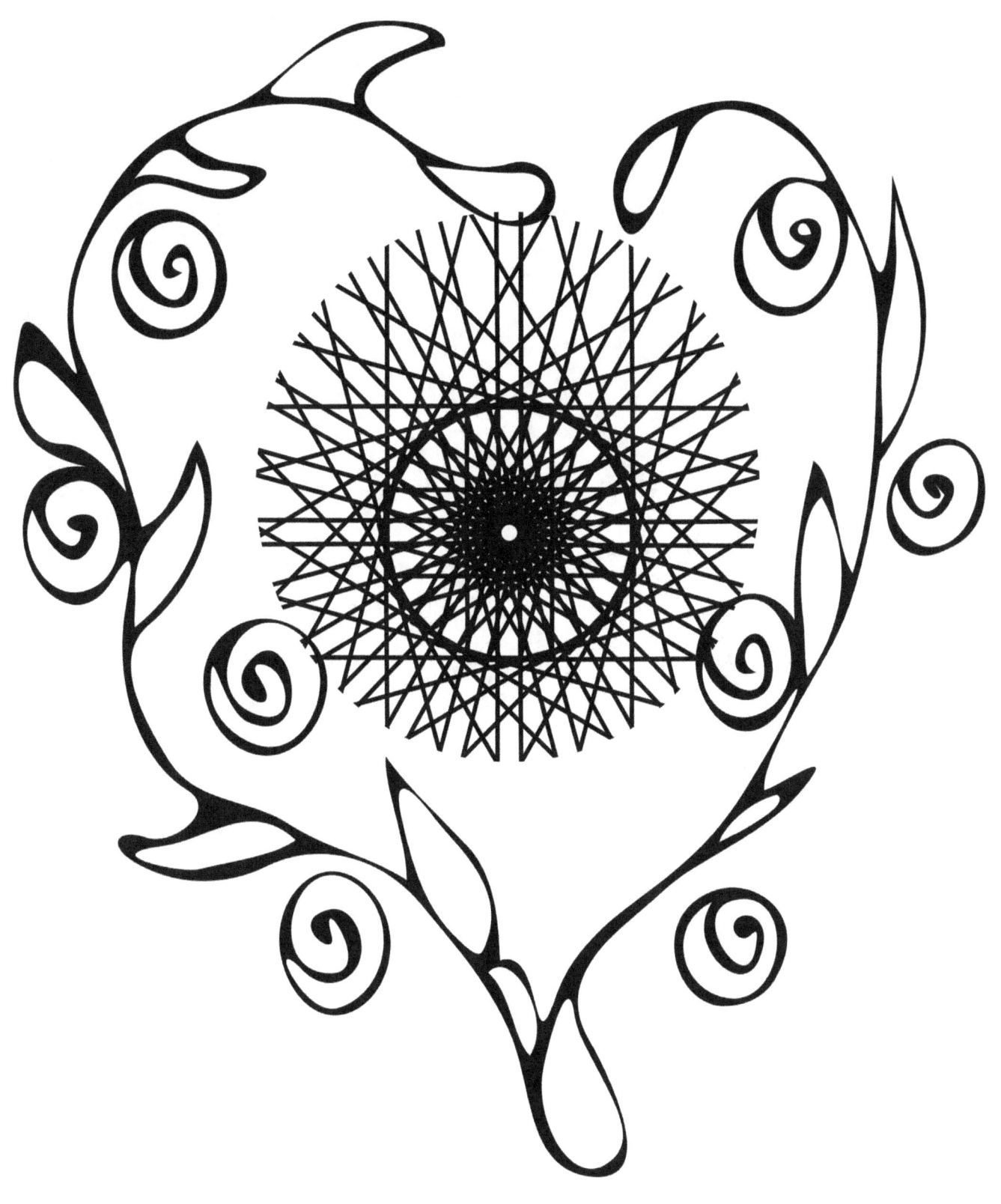

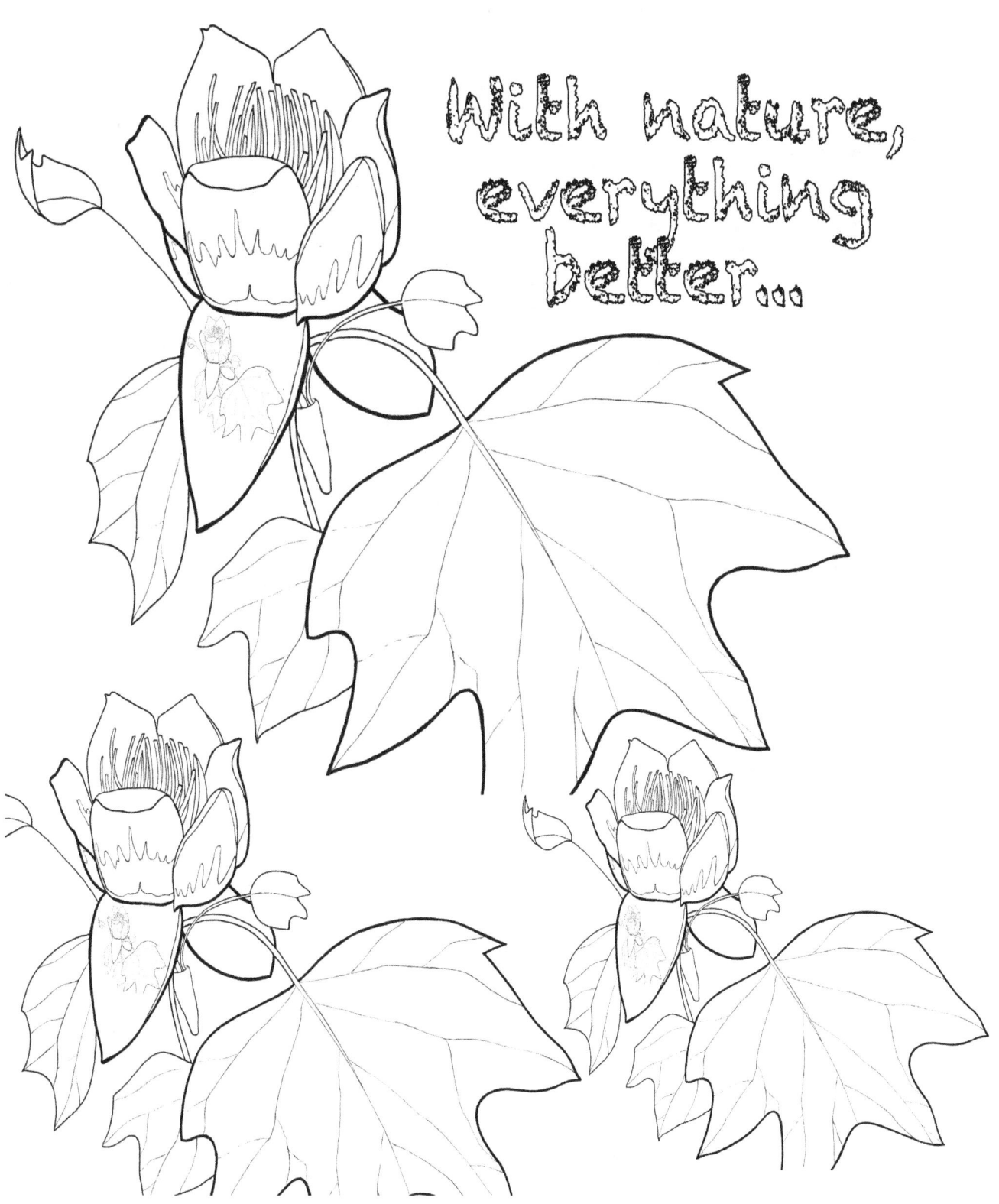

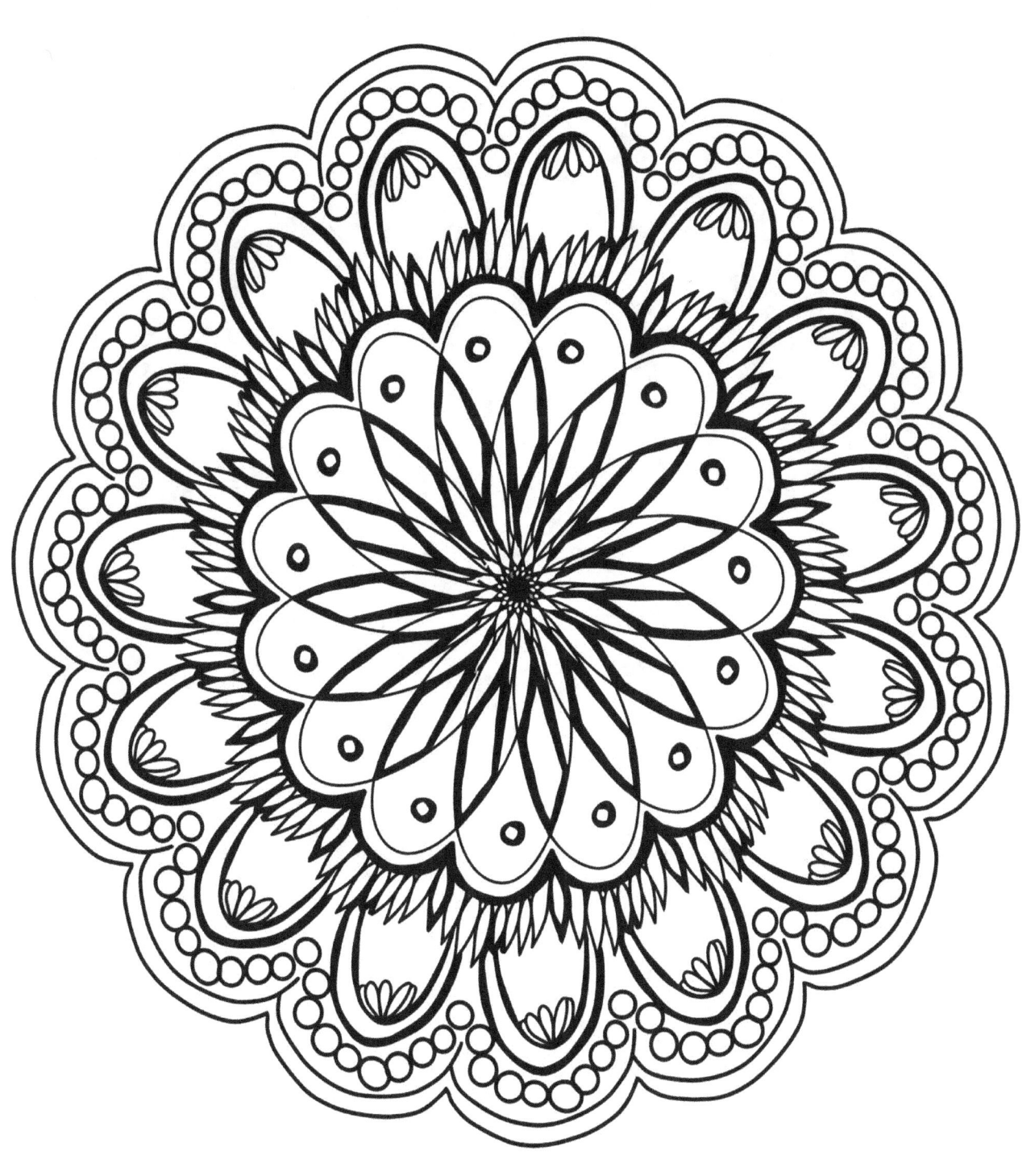

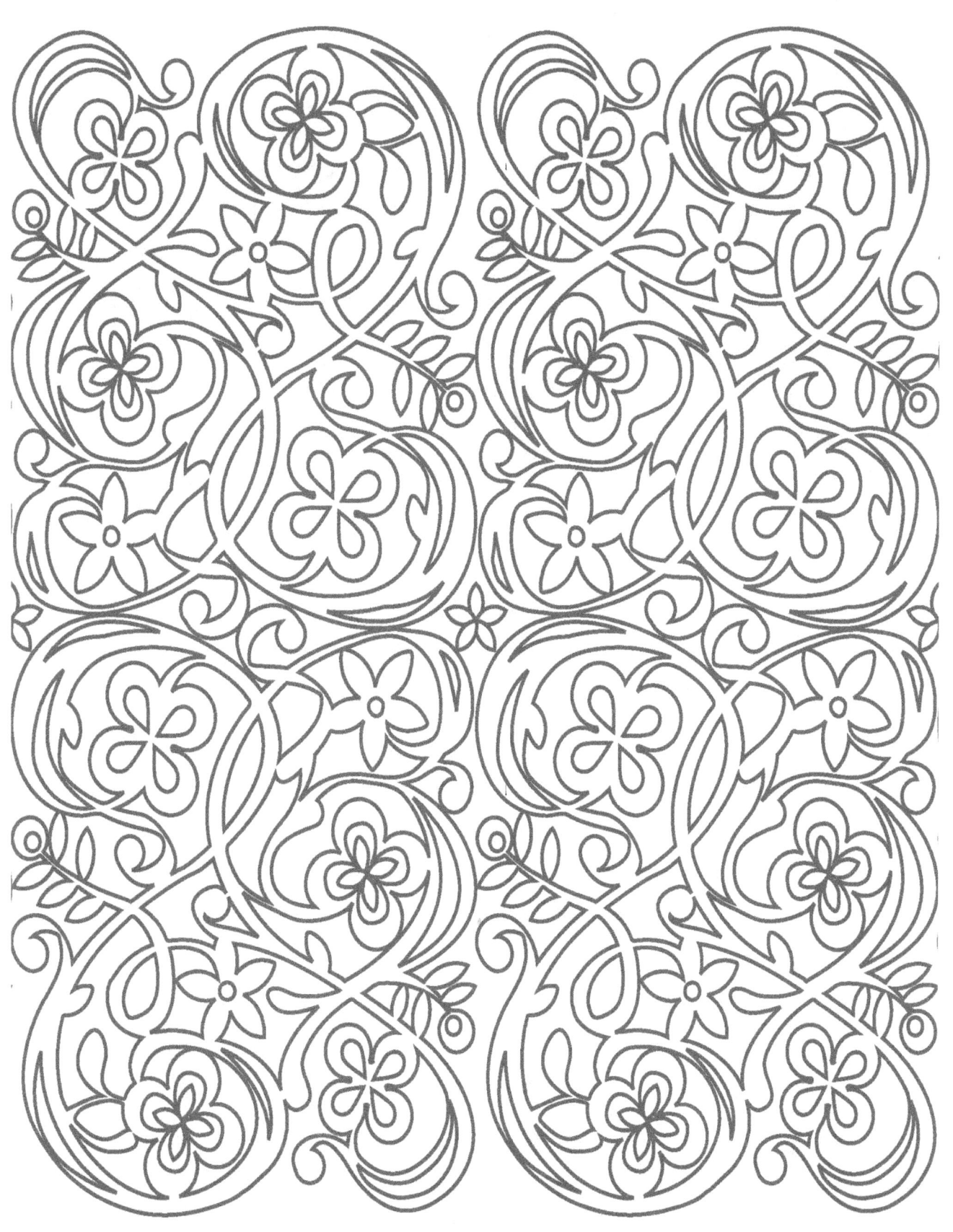

Copyright © 2018 Michael Weiner

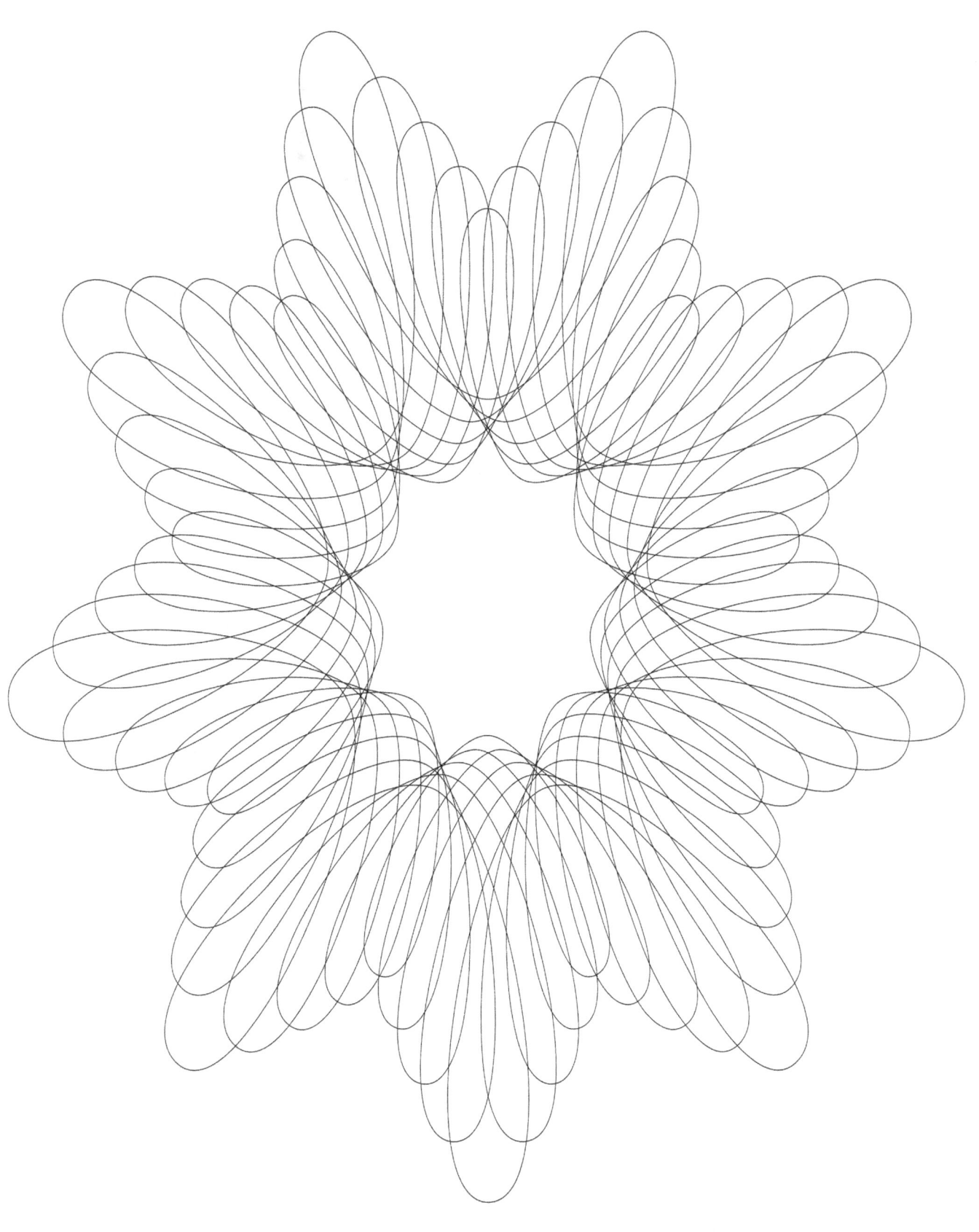
Copyright © 2018 Michael Weiner

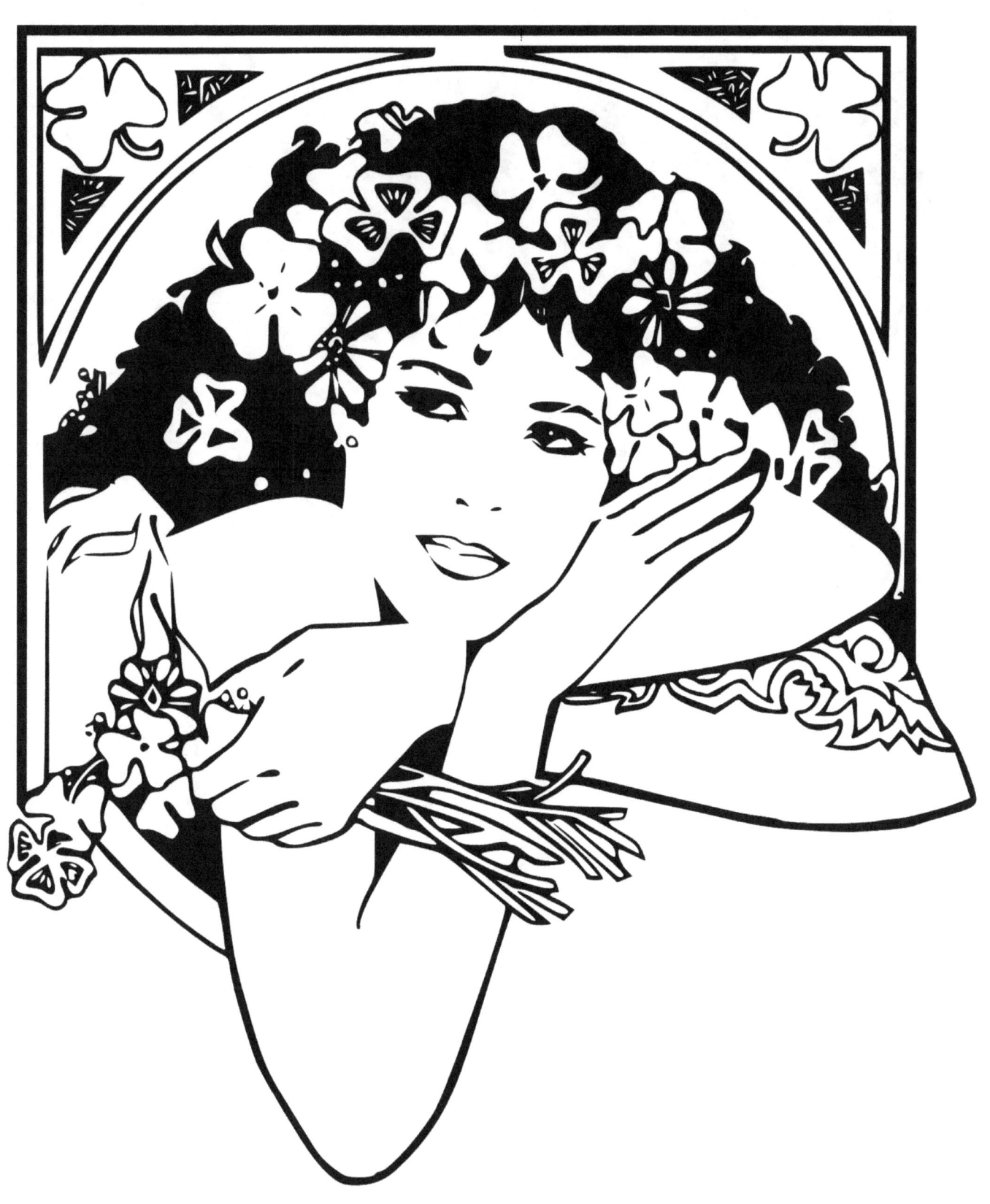

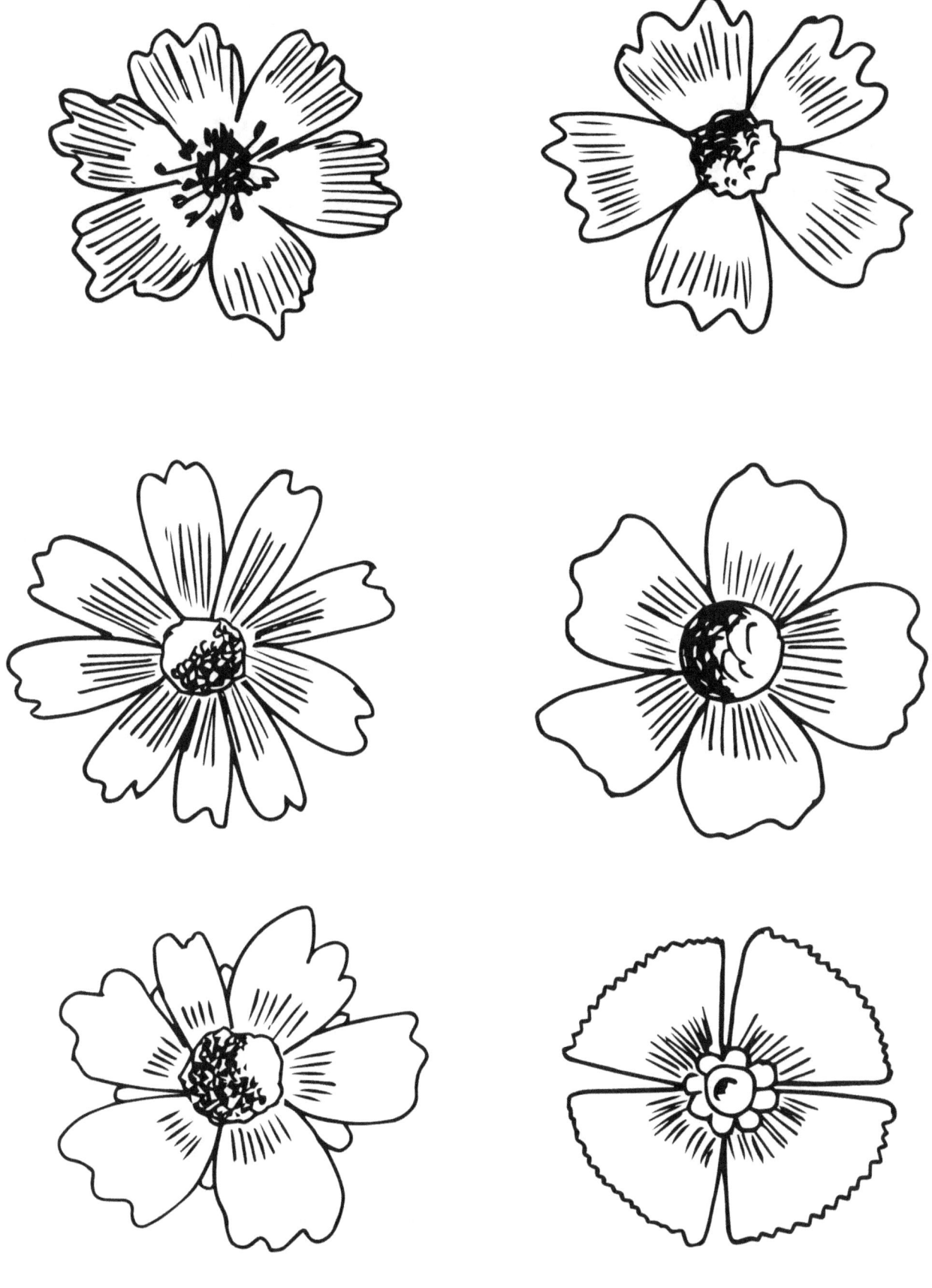

Copyright © 2018 Michael Weiner

Copyright © 2018 Michael Weiner

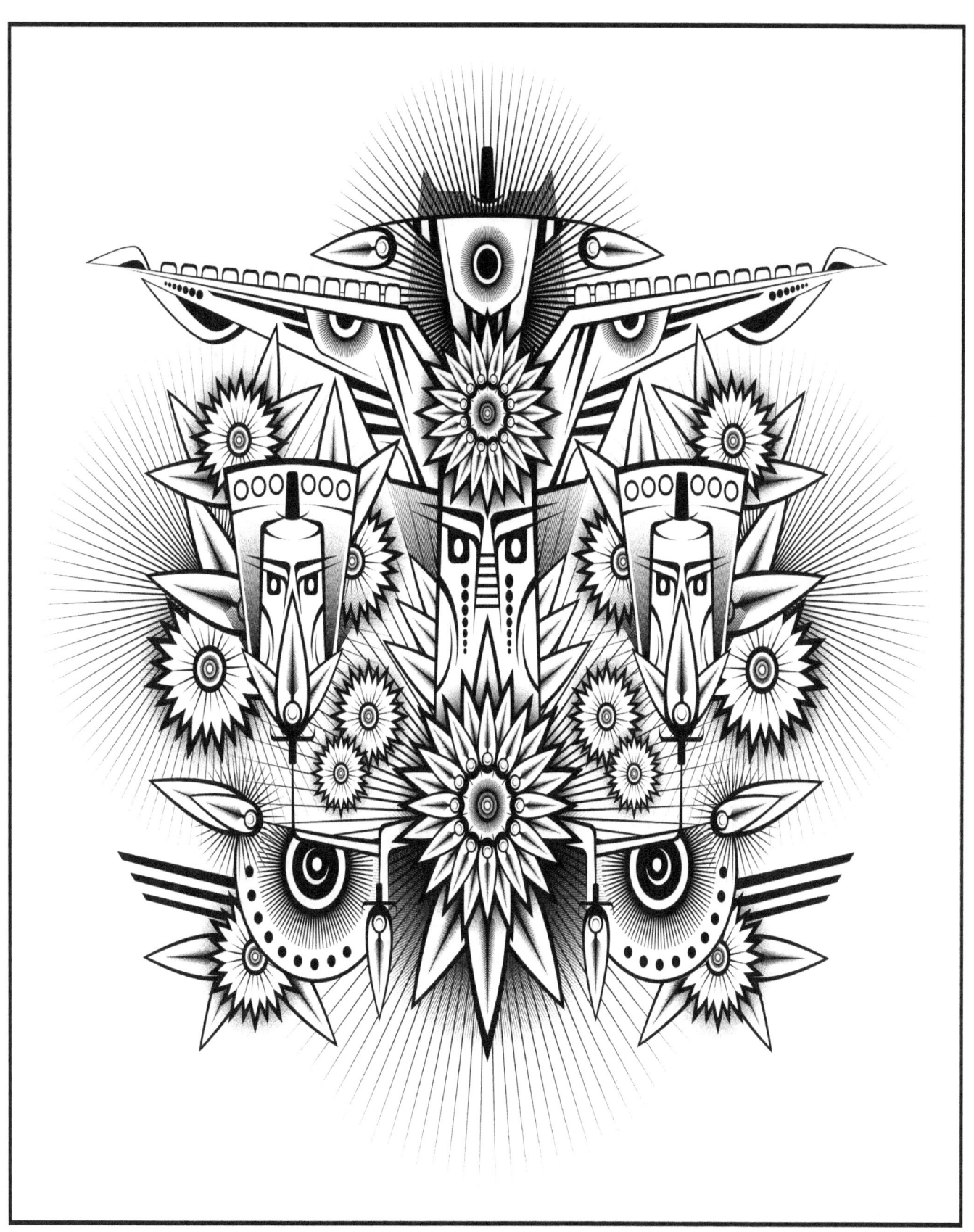

Copyright © 2018 Michael Weiner

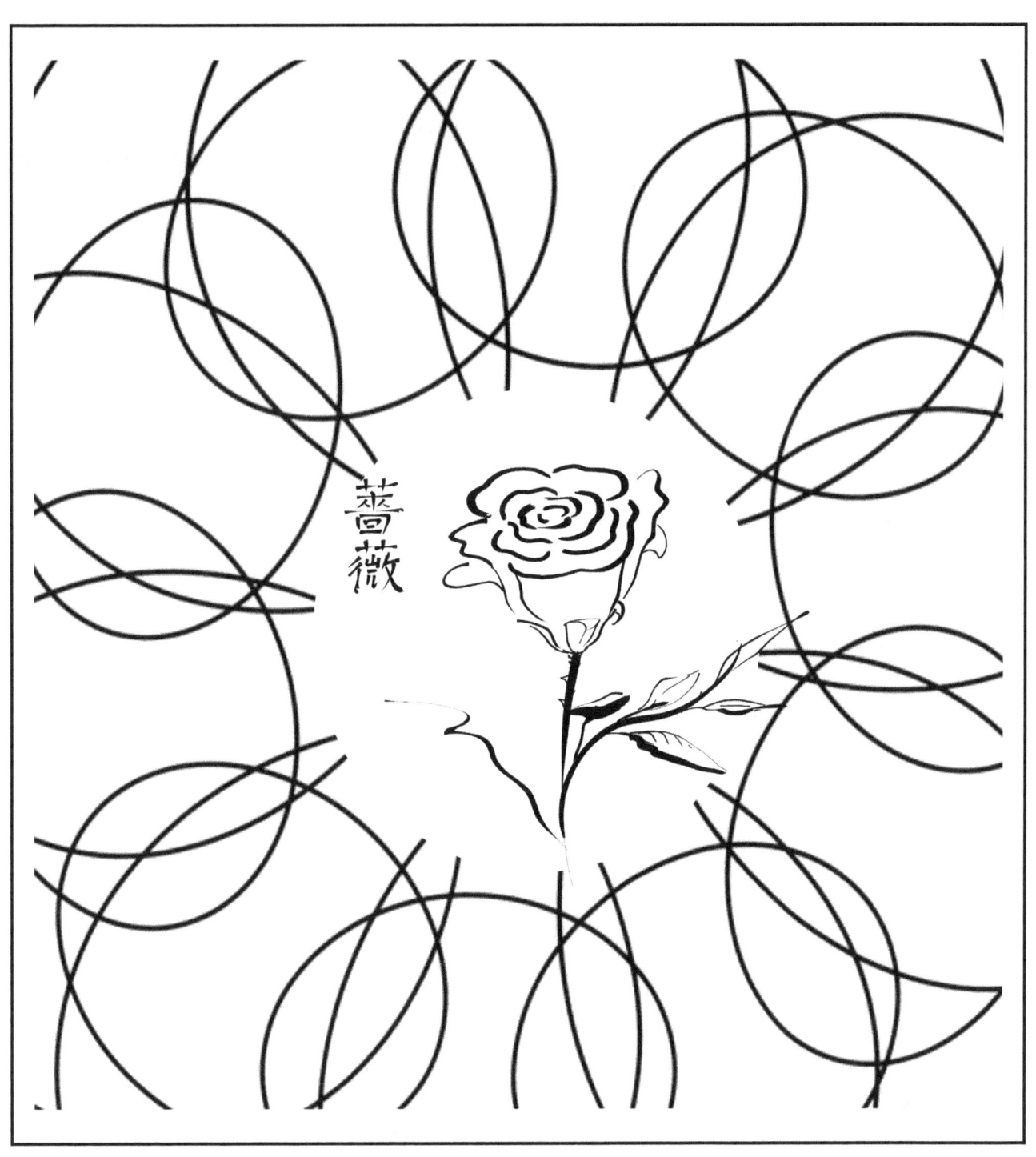

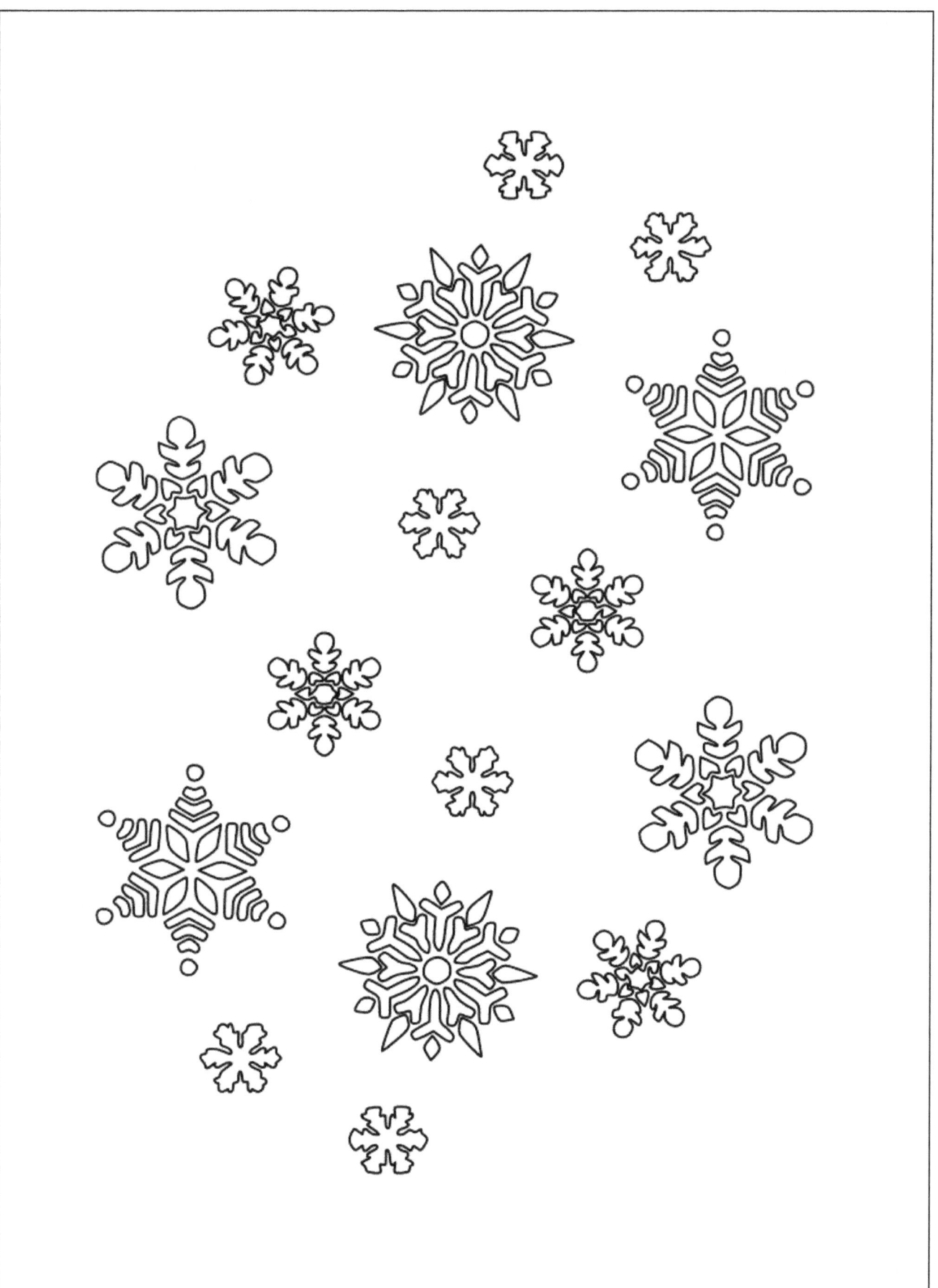

Copyright © 2018 Michael Weiner

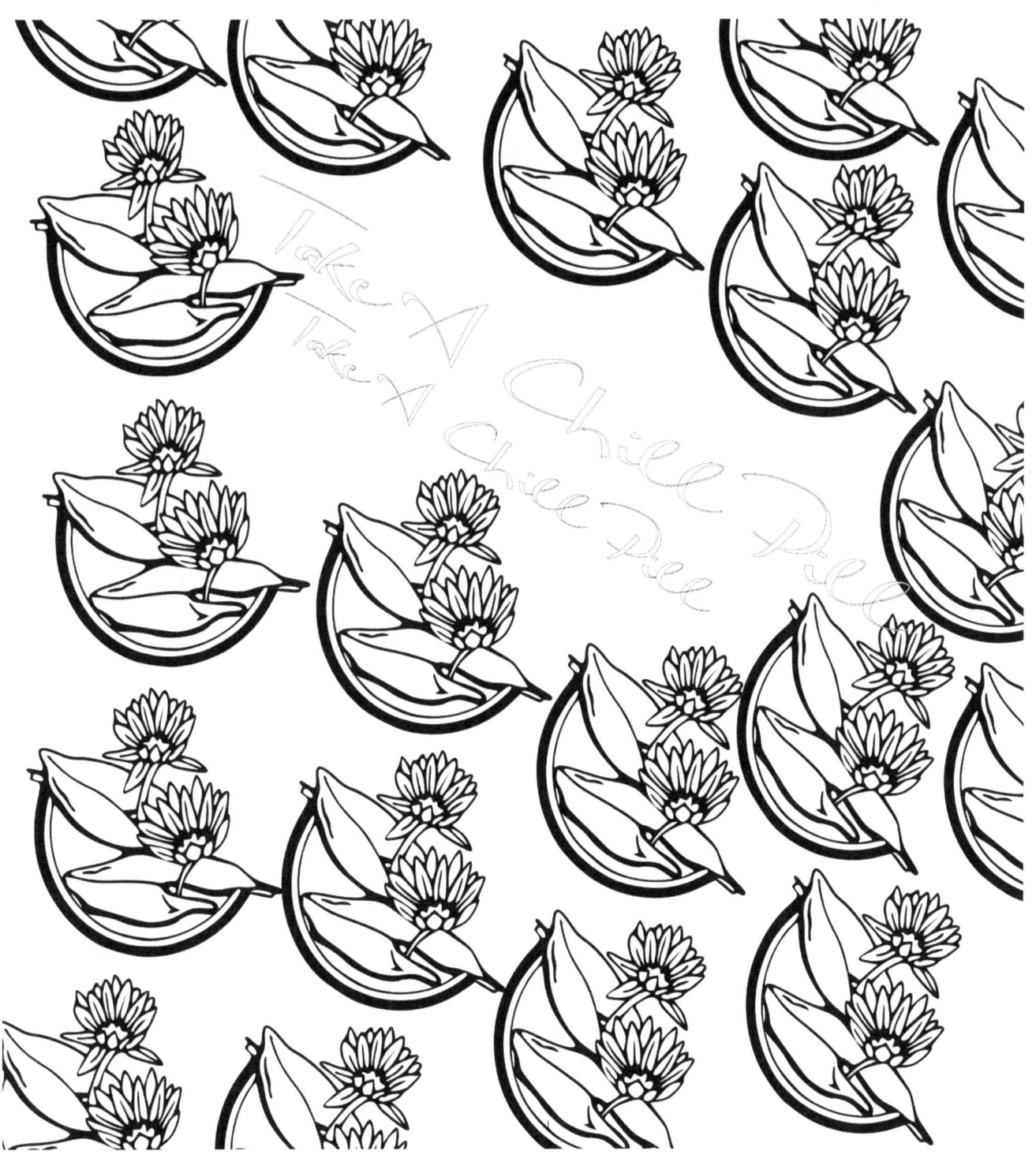

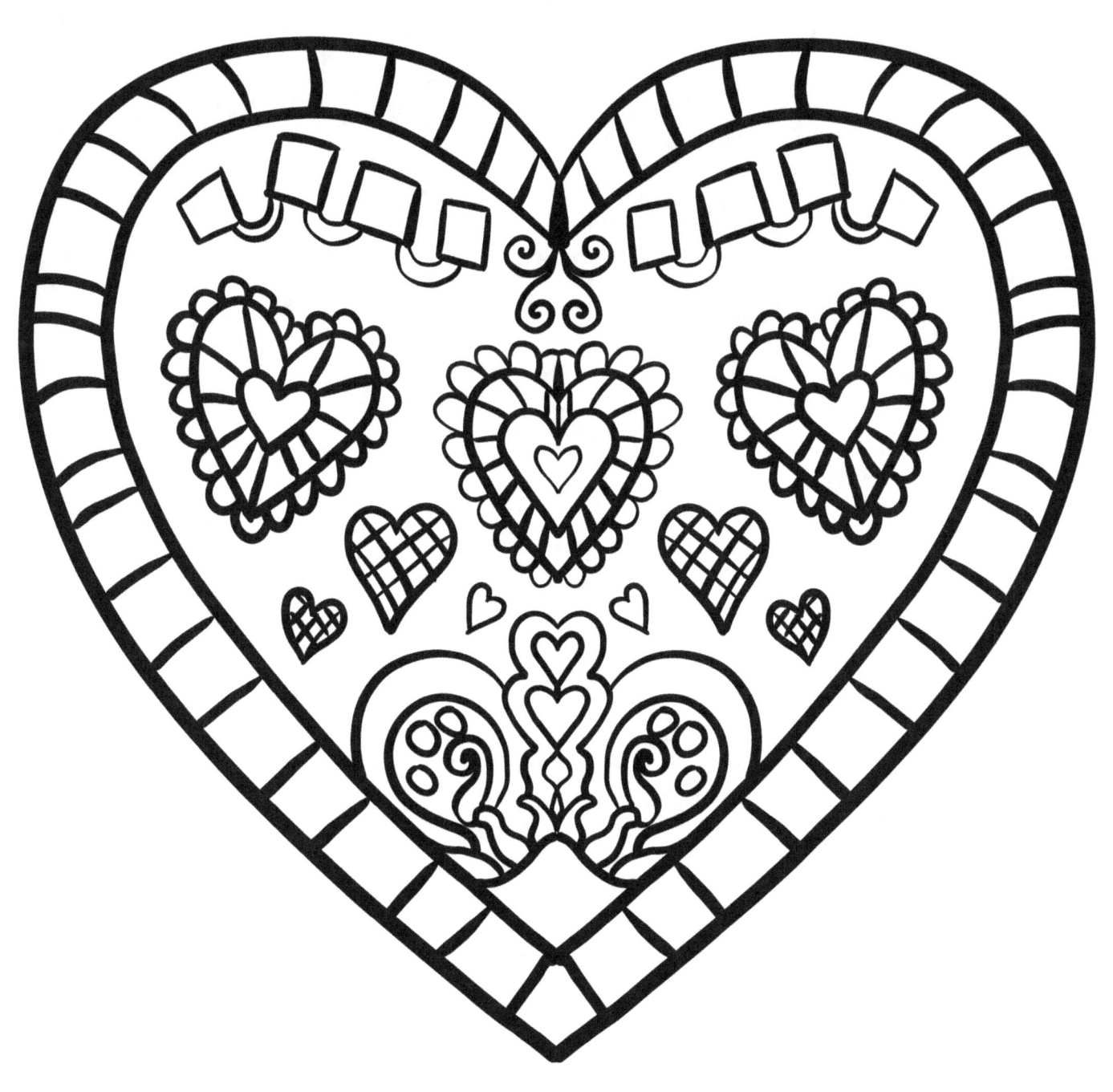

Copyright © 2018 Michael Weiner

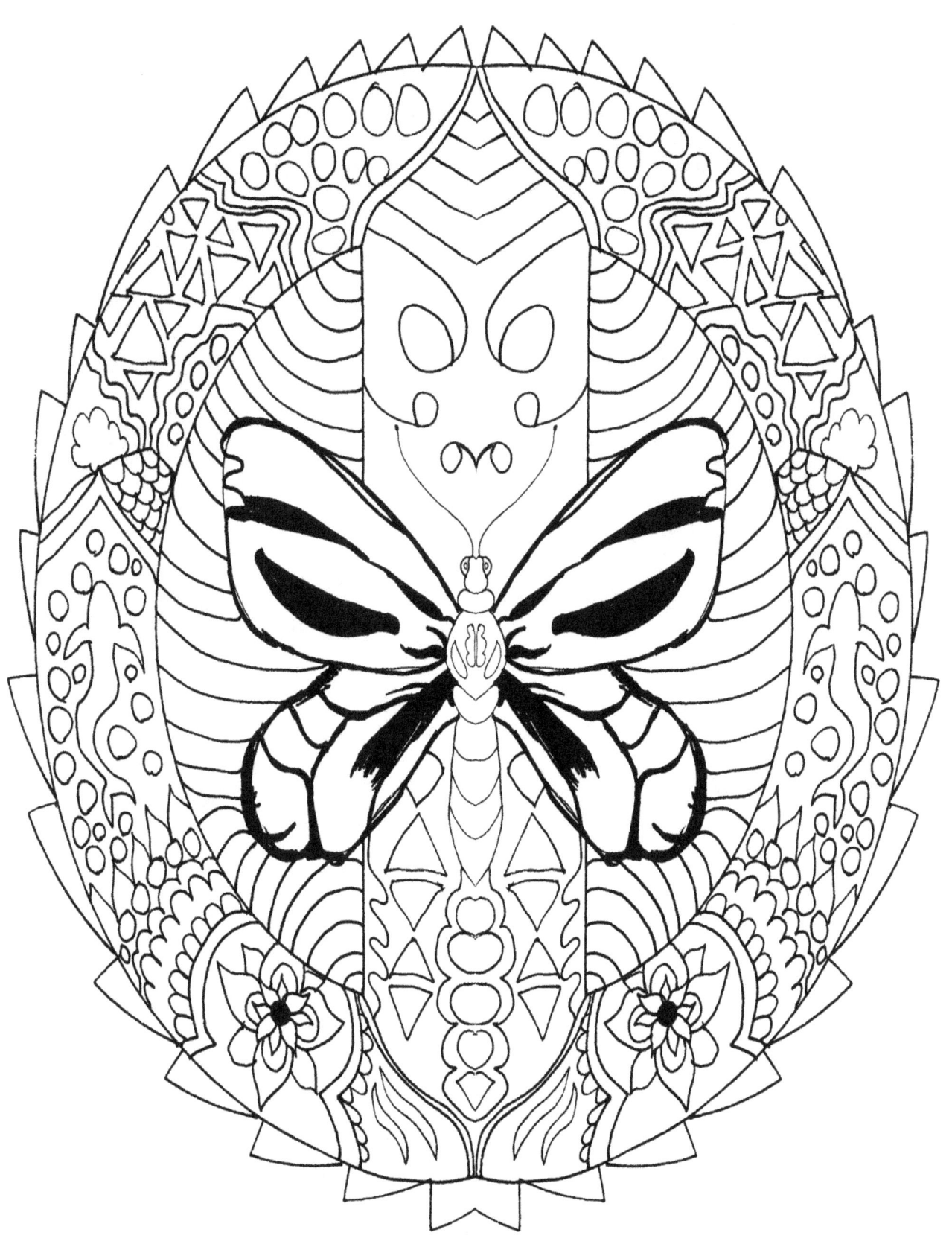

Copyright © 2018 Michael Weiner

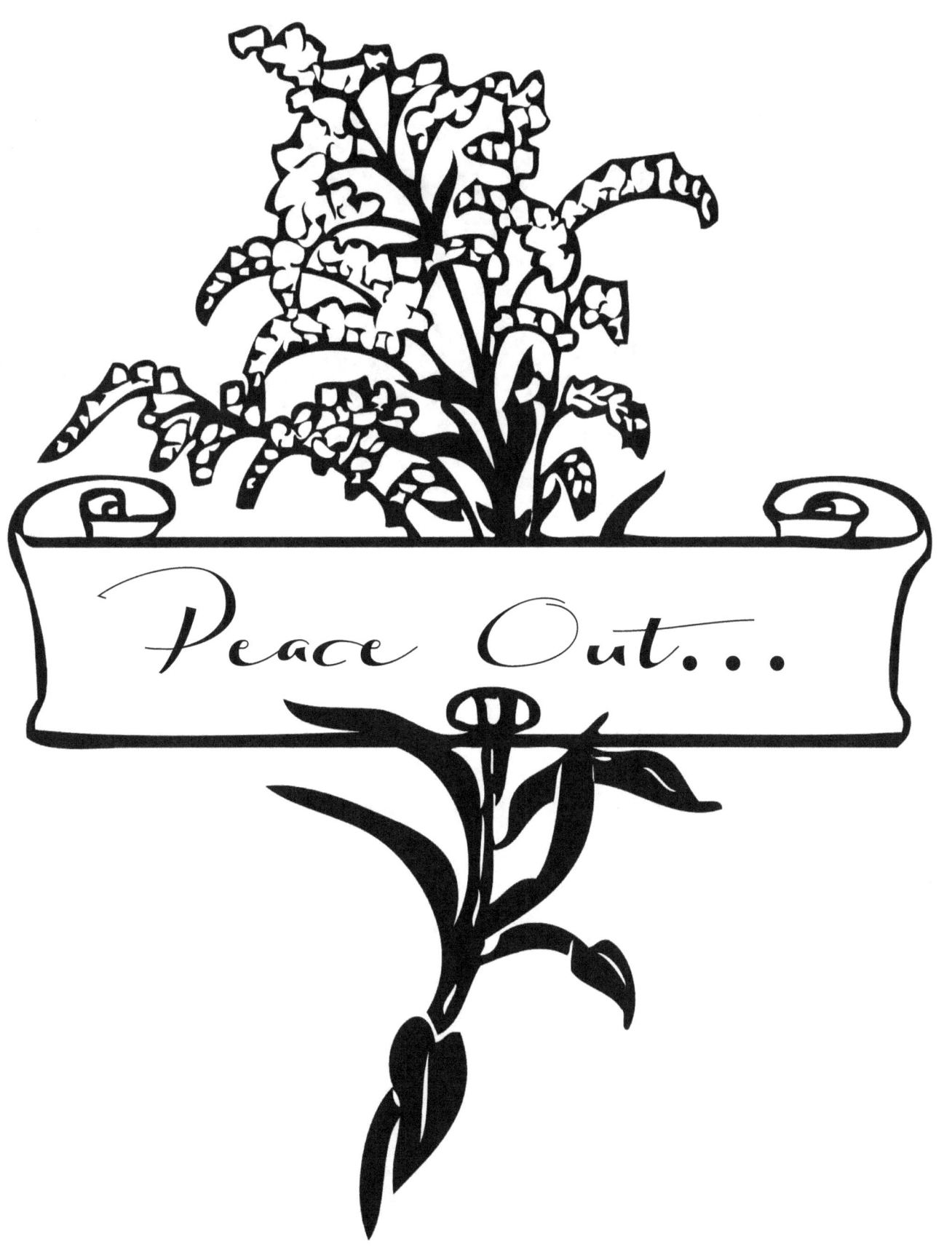

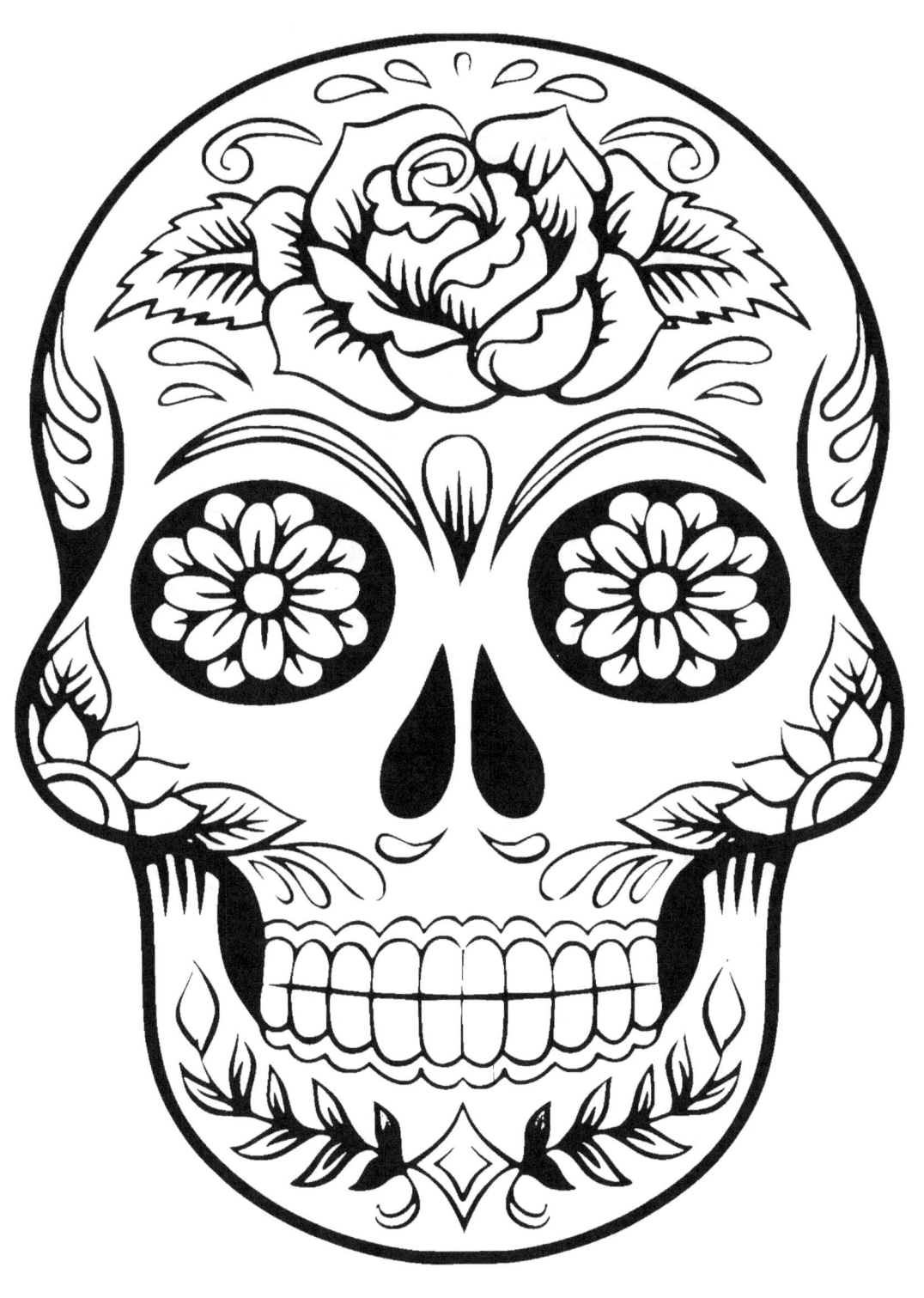

Copyright © 2018 Michael Weiner

Copyright © 2018 Michael Weiner

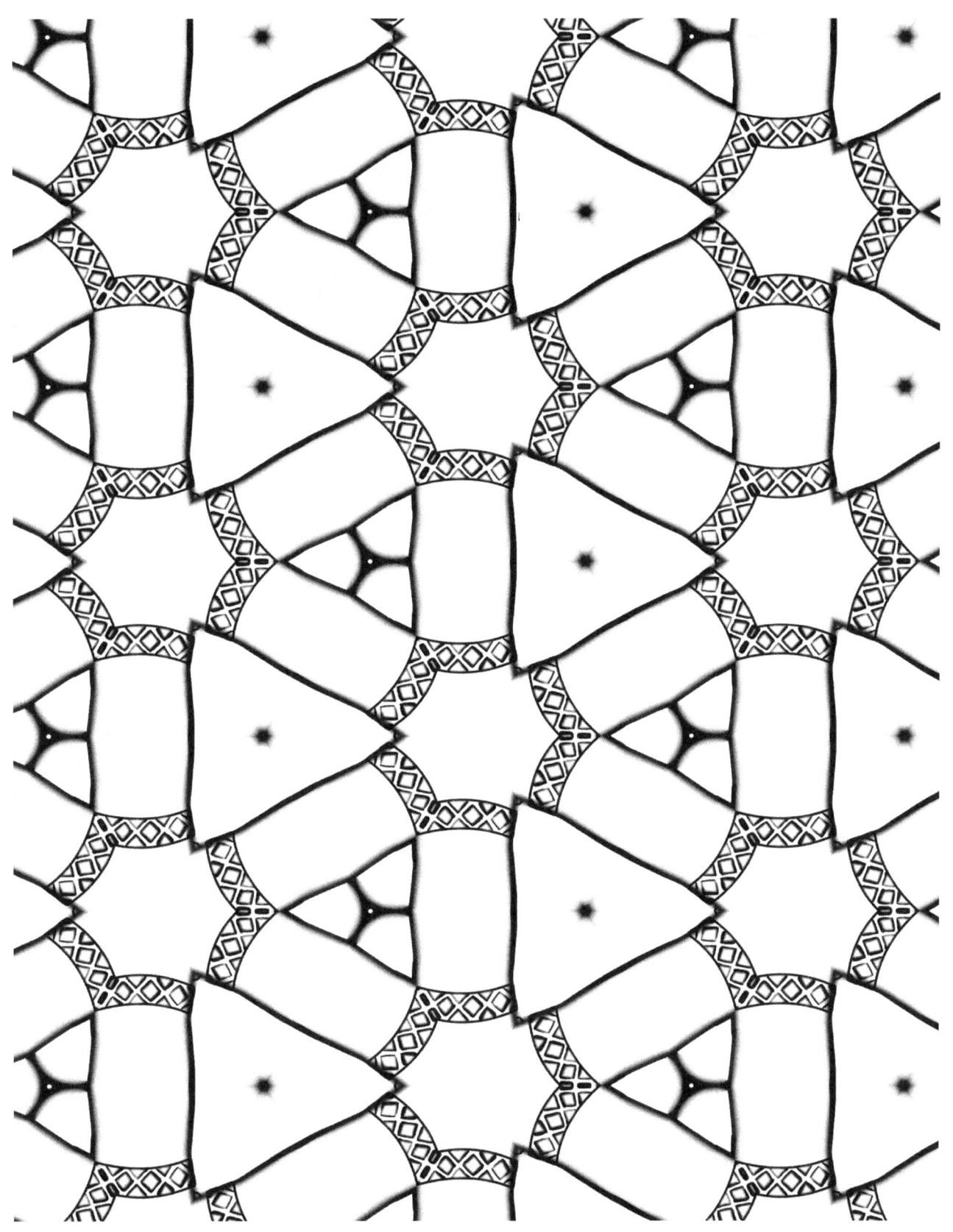

Copyright © 2018 Michael Weiner

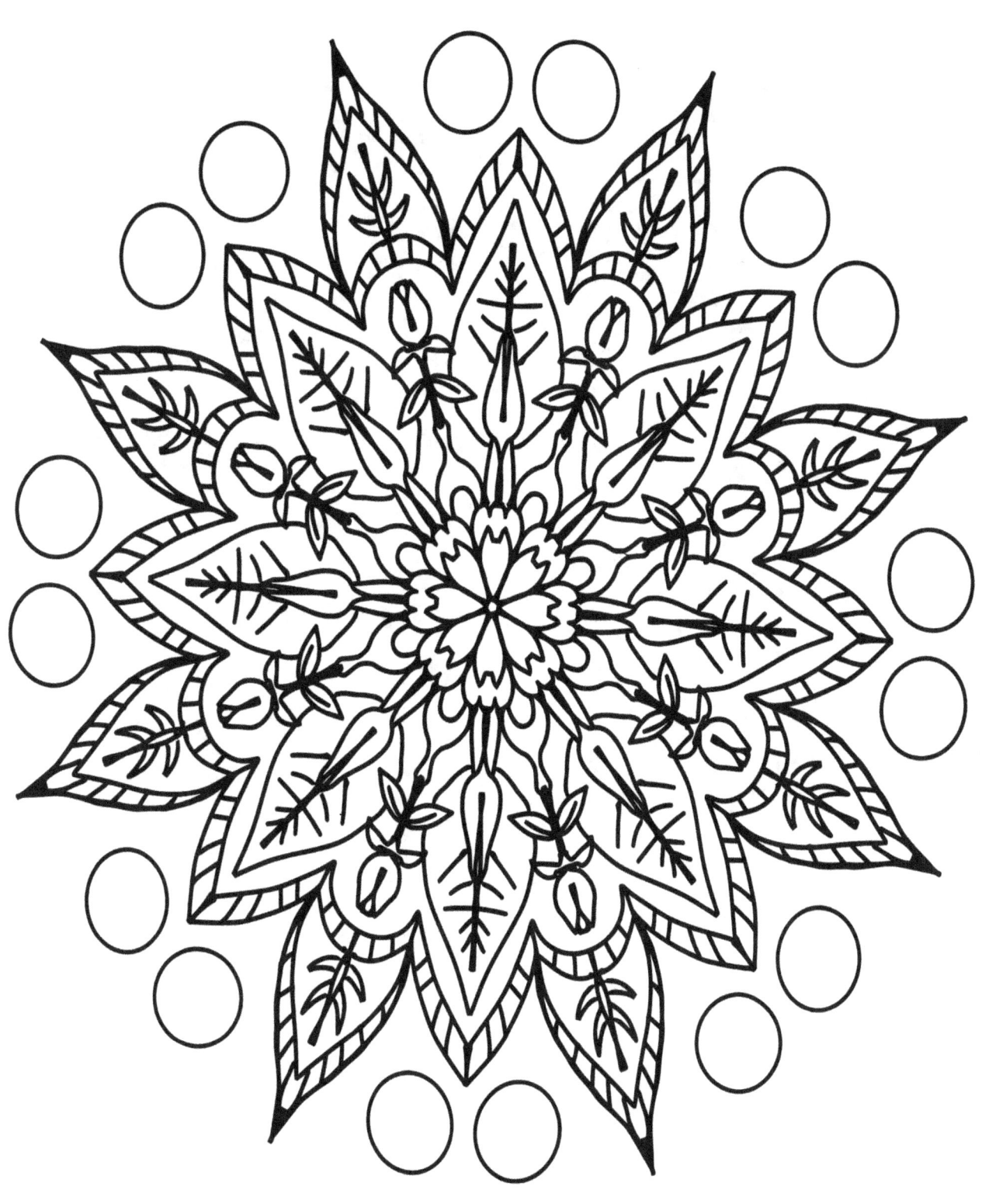

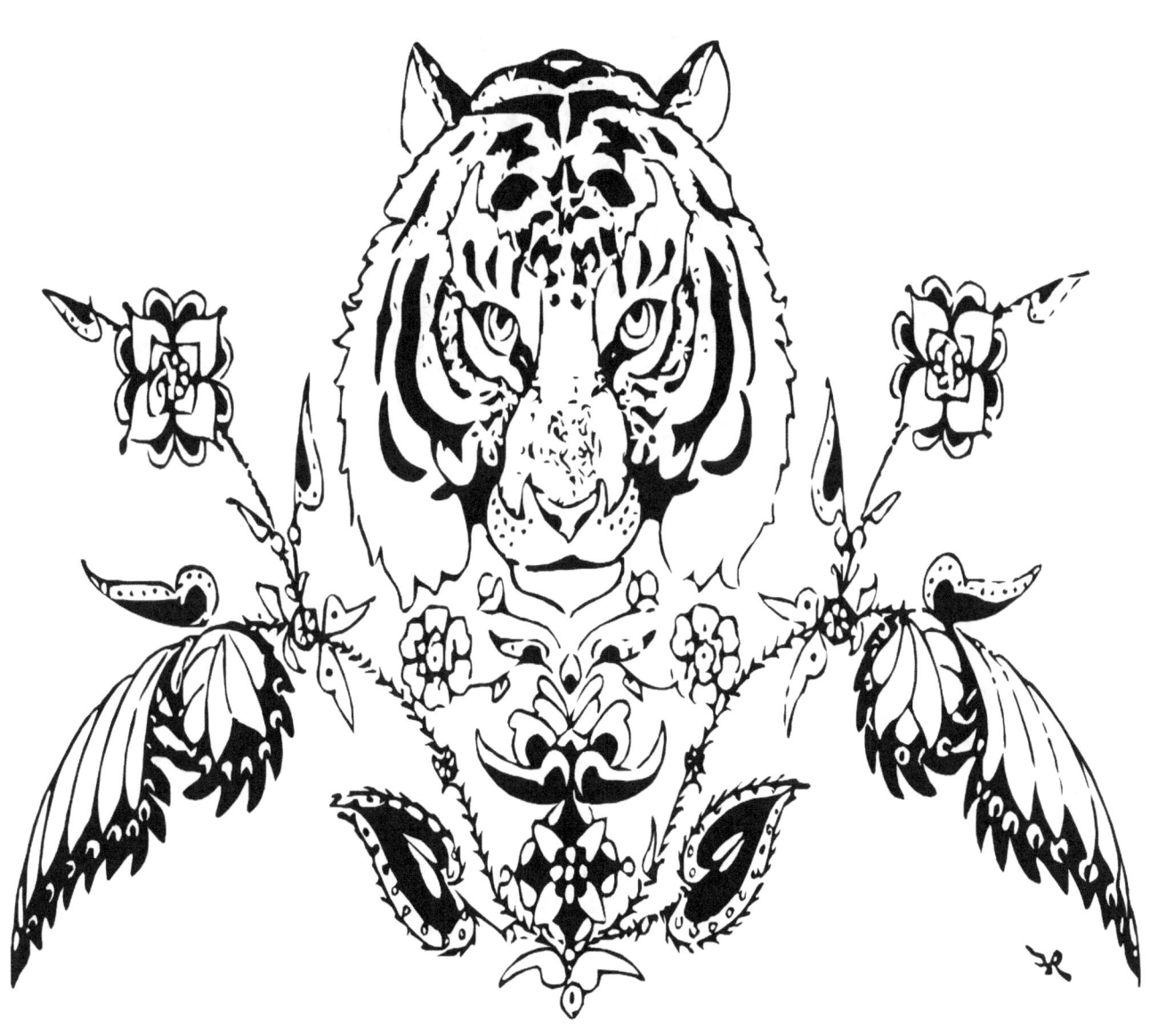

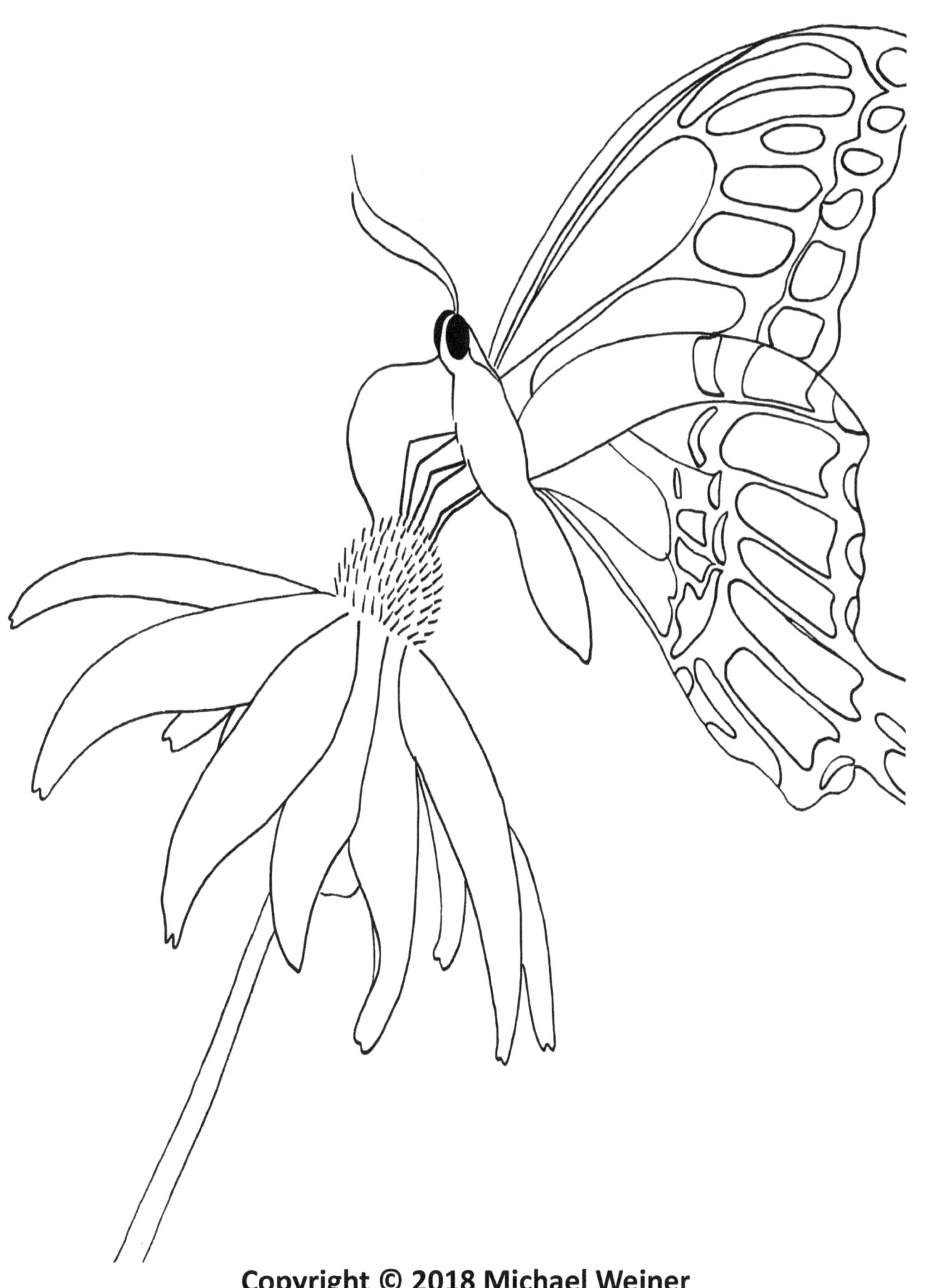

Copyright © 2018 Michael Weiner

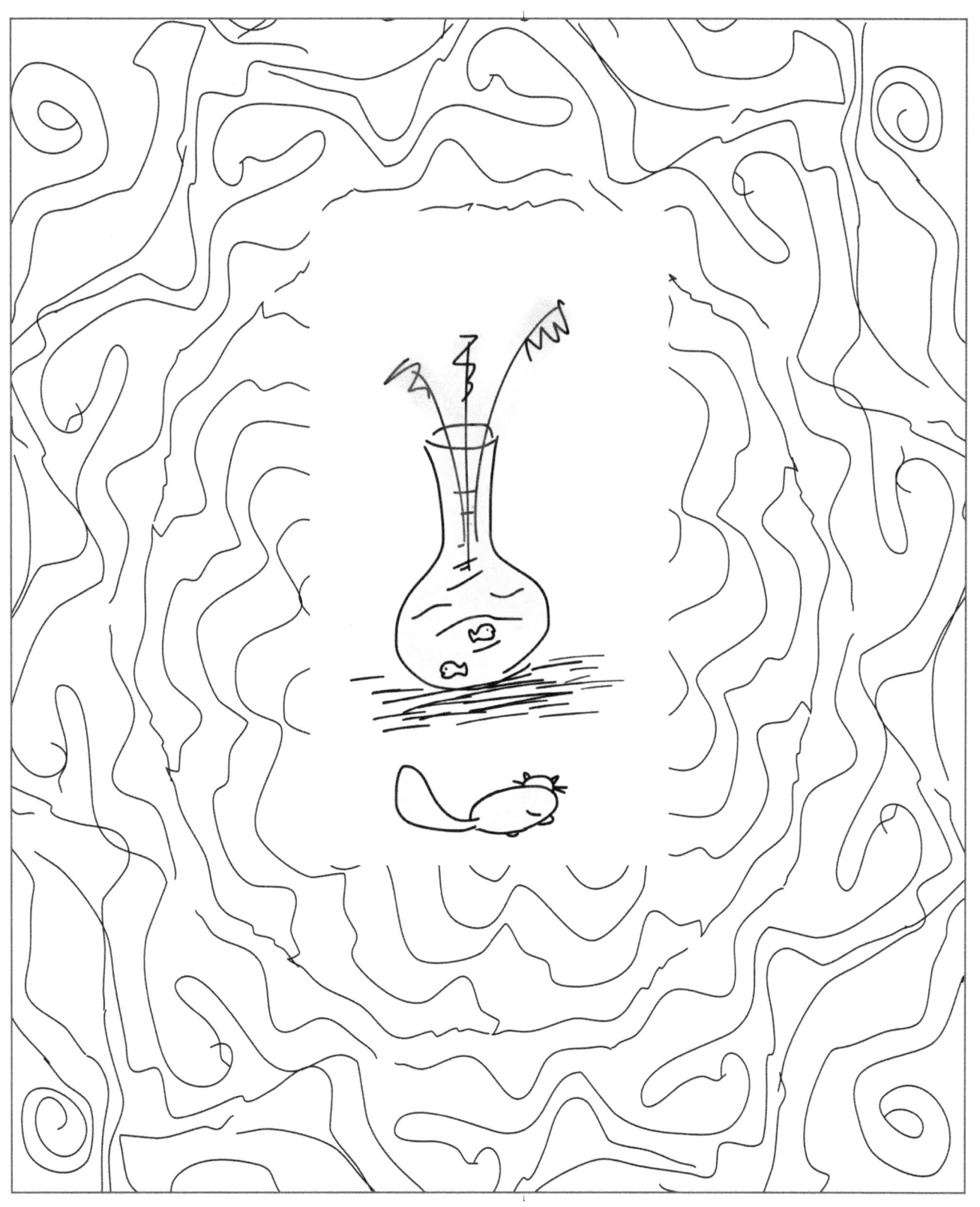

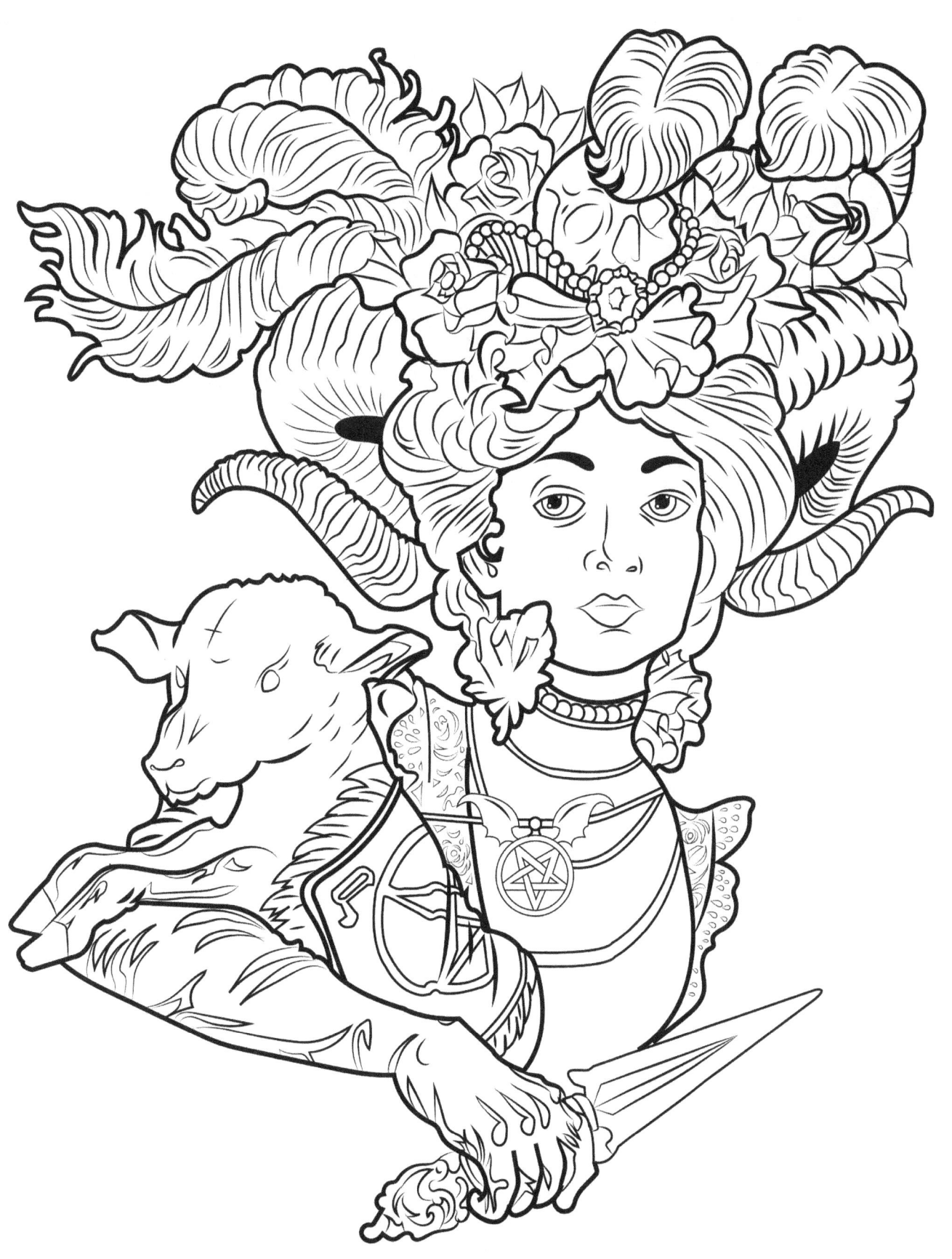

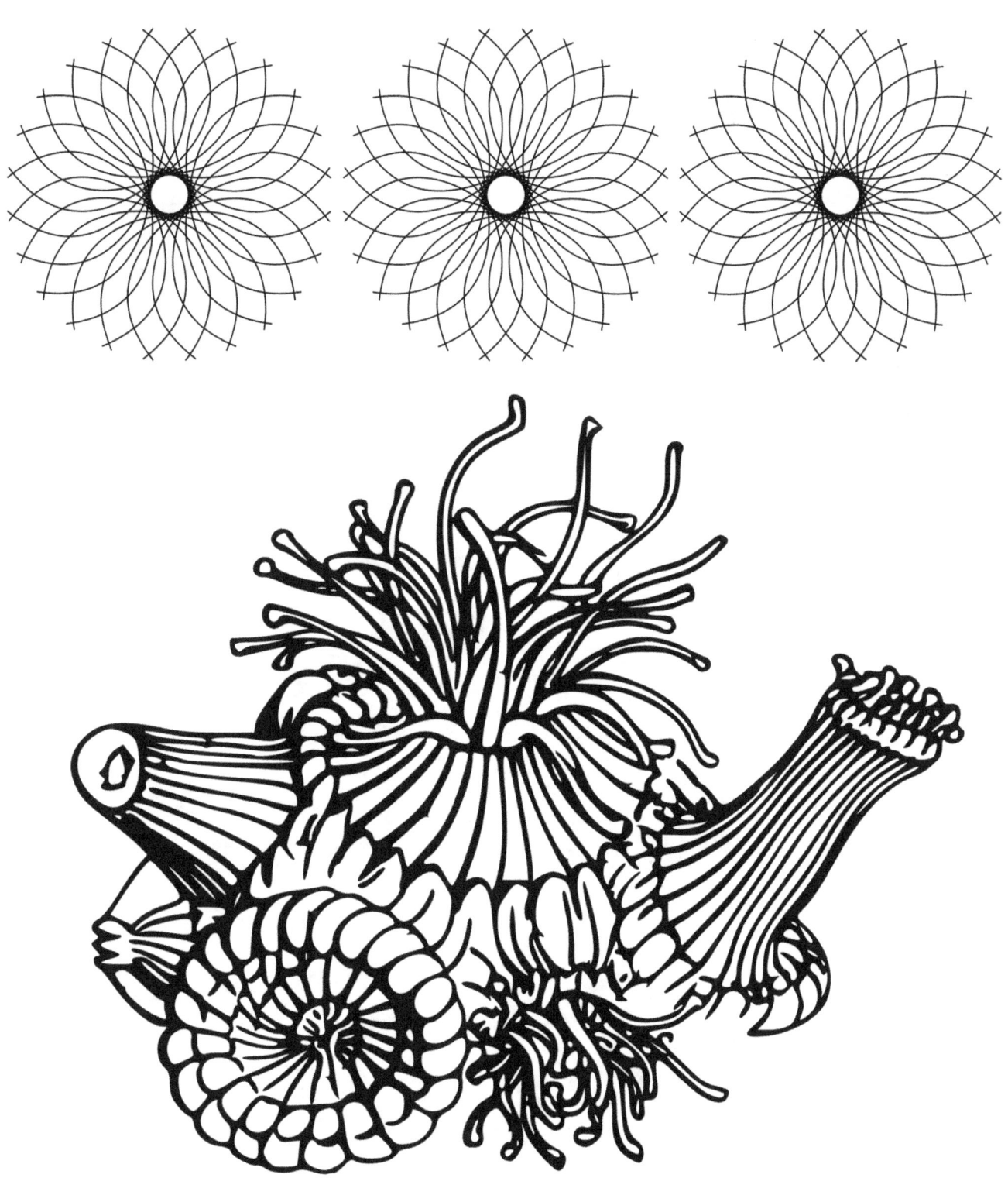

Copyright © 2018 Michael Weiner

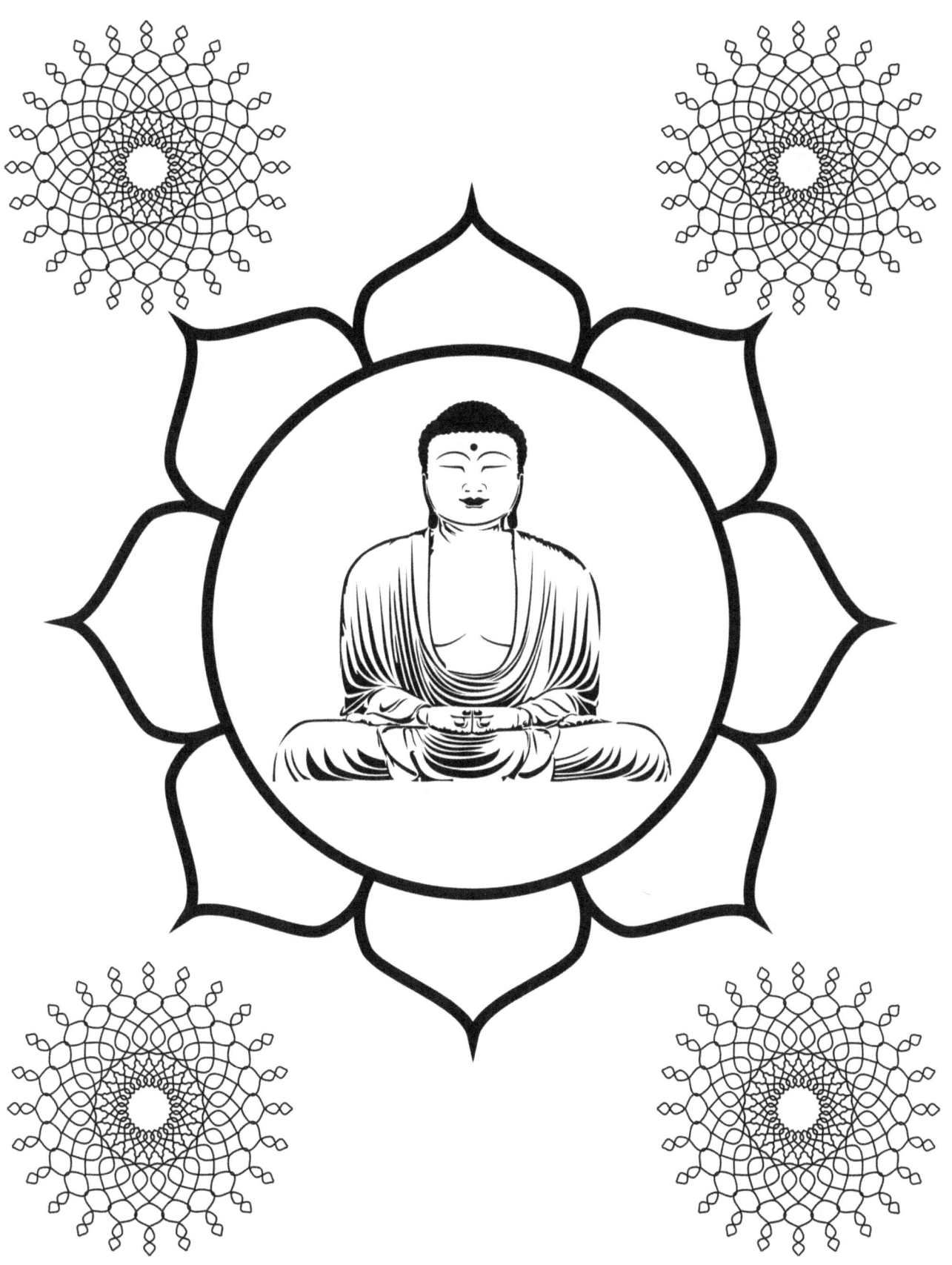

Copyright © 2018 Michael Weiner

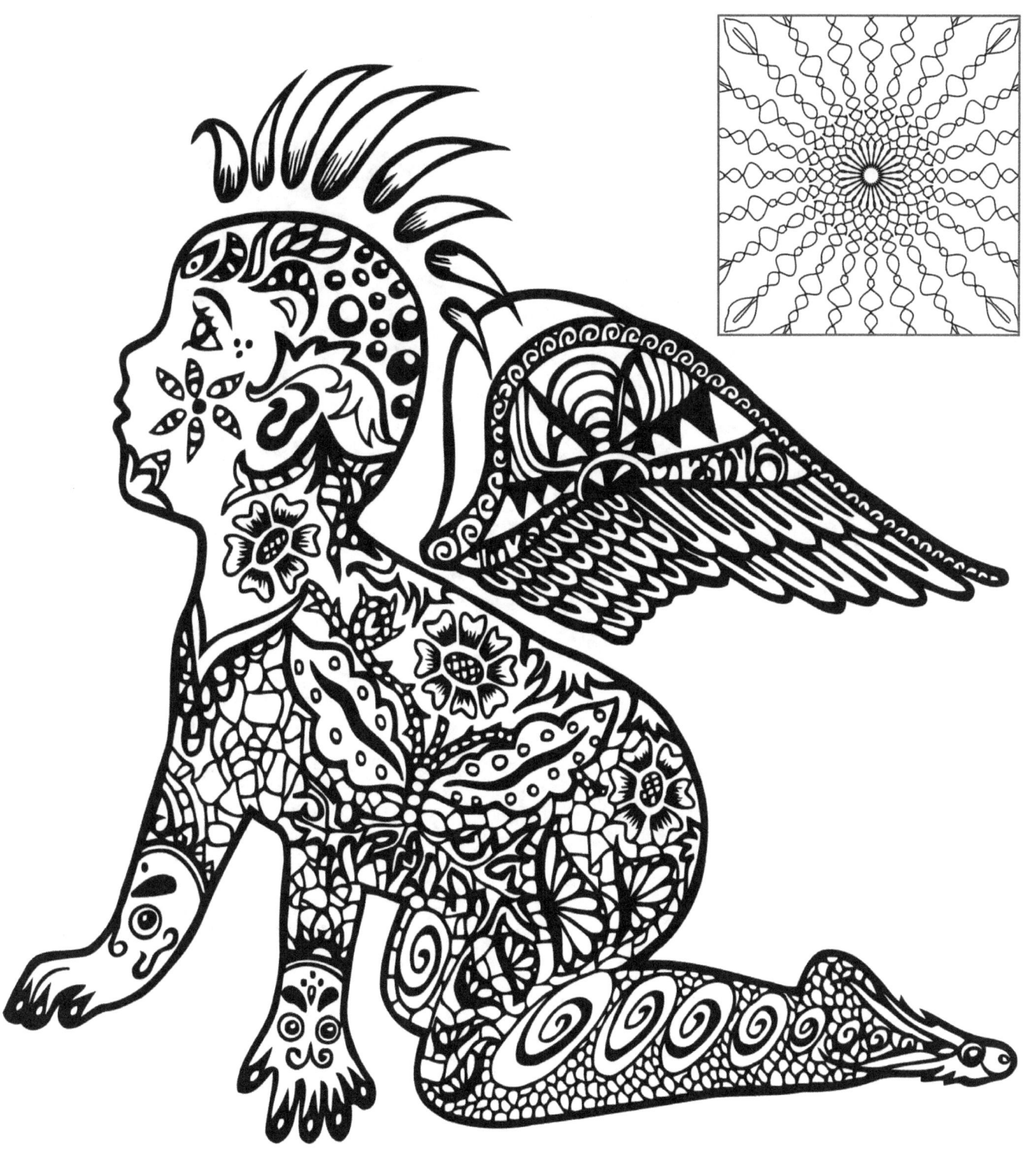

Copyright © 2018 Michael Weiner

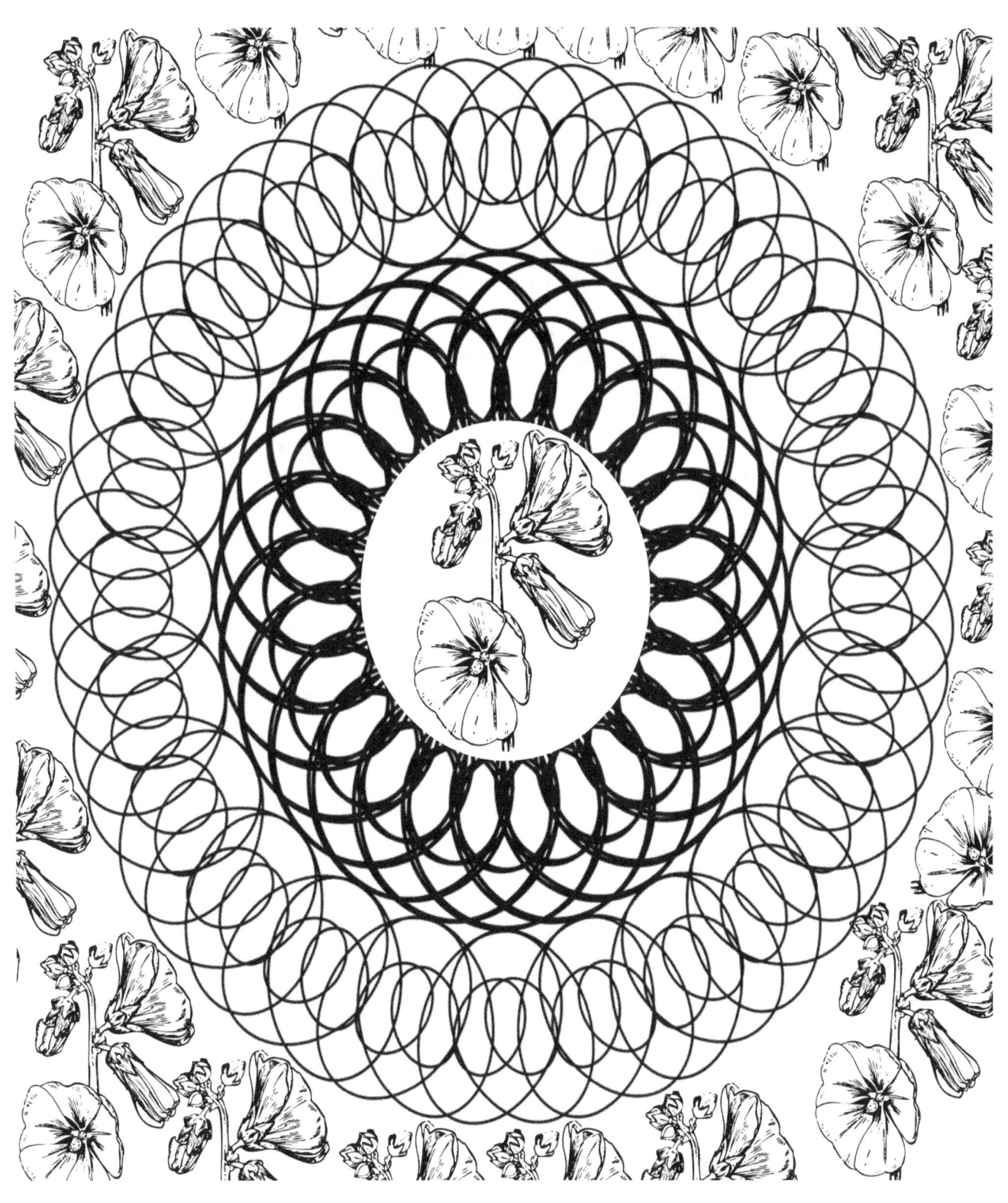

Copyright © 2018 Michael Weiner

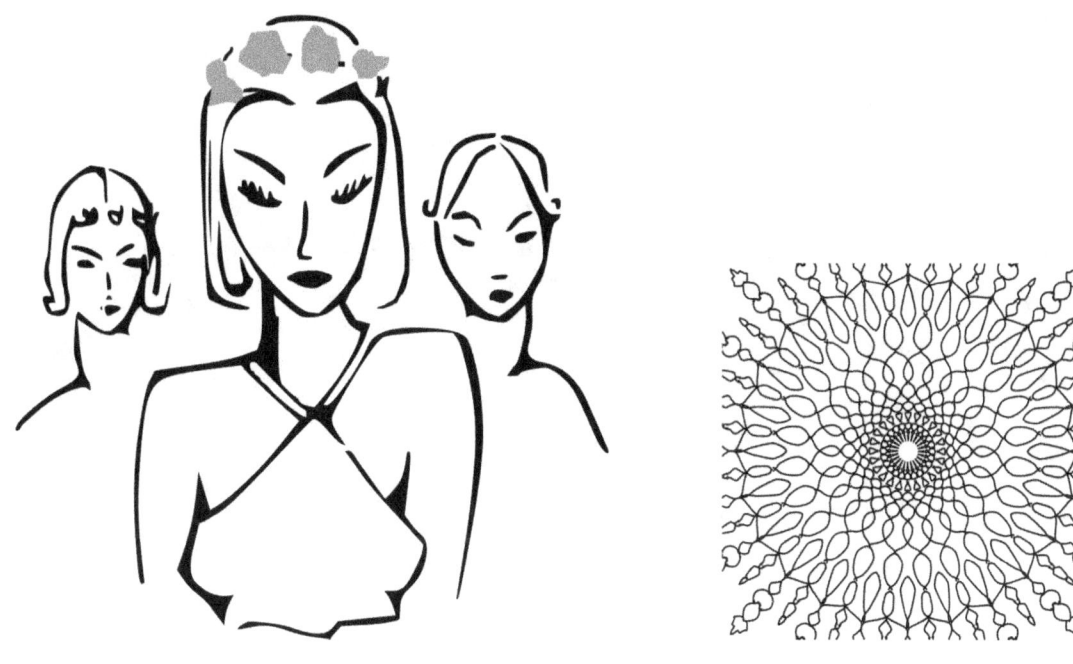

Friendship

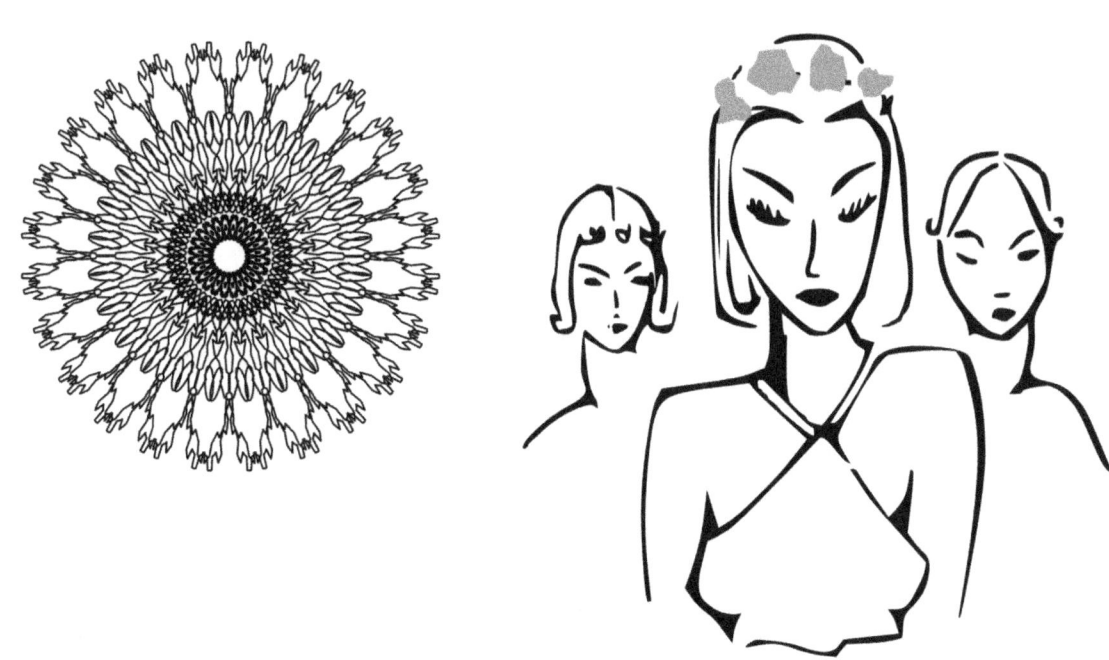

Copyright © 2018 Michael Weiner

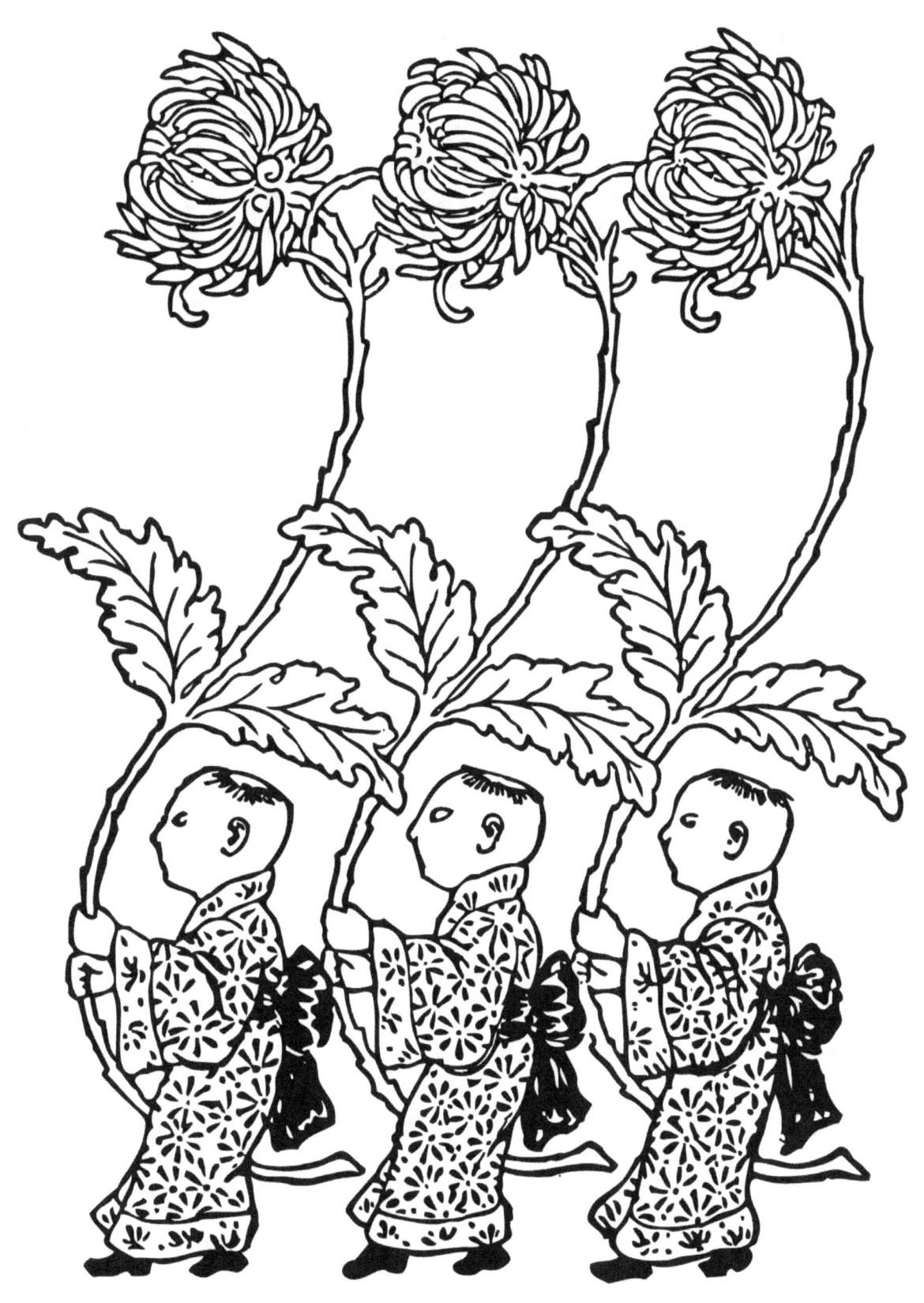

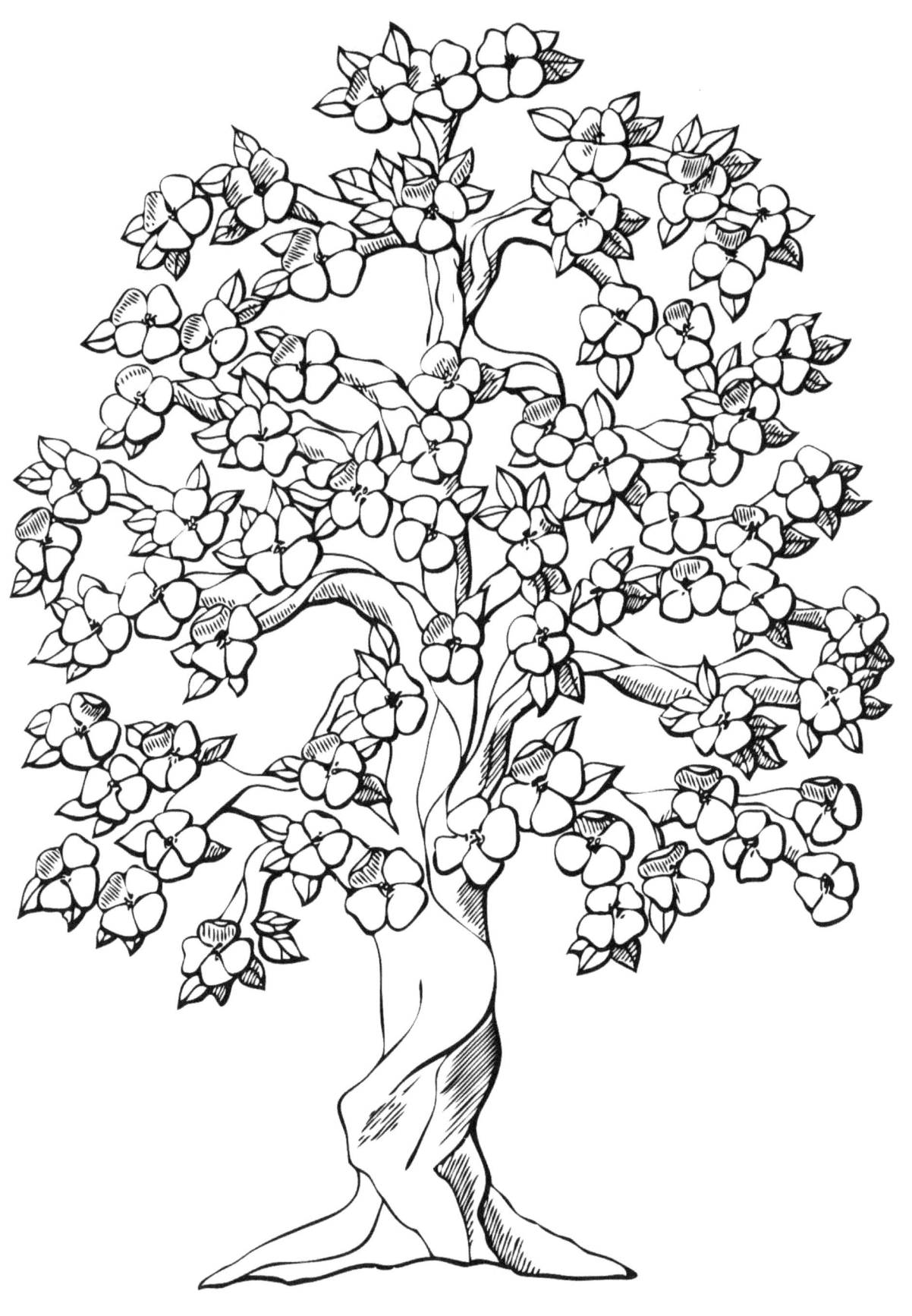

Copyright © 2018 Michael Weiner

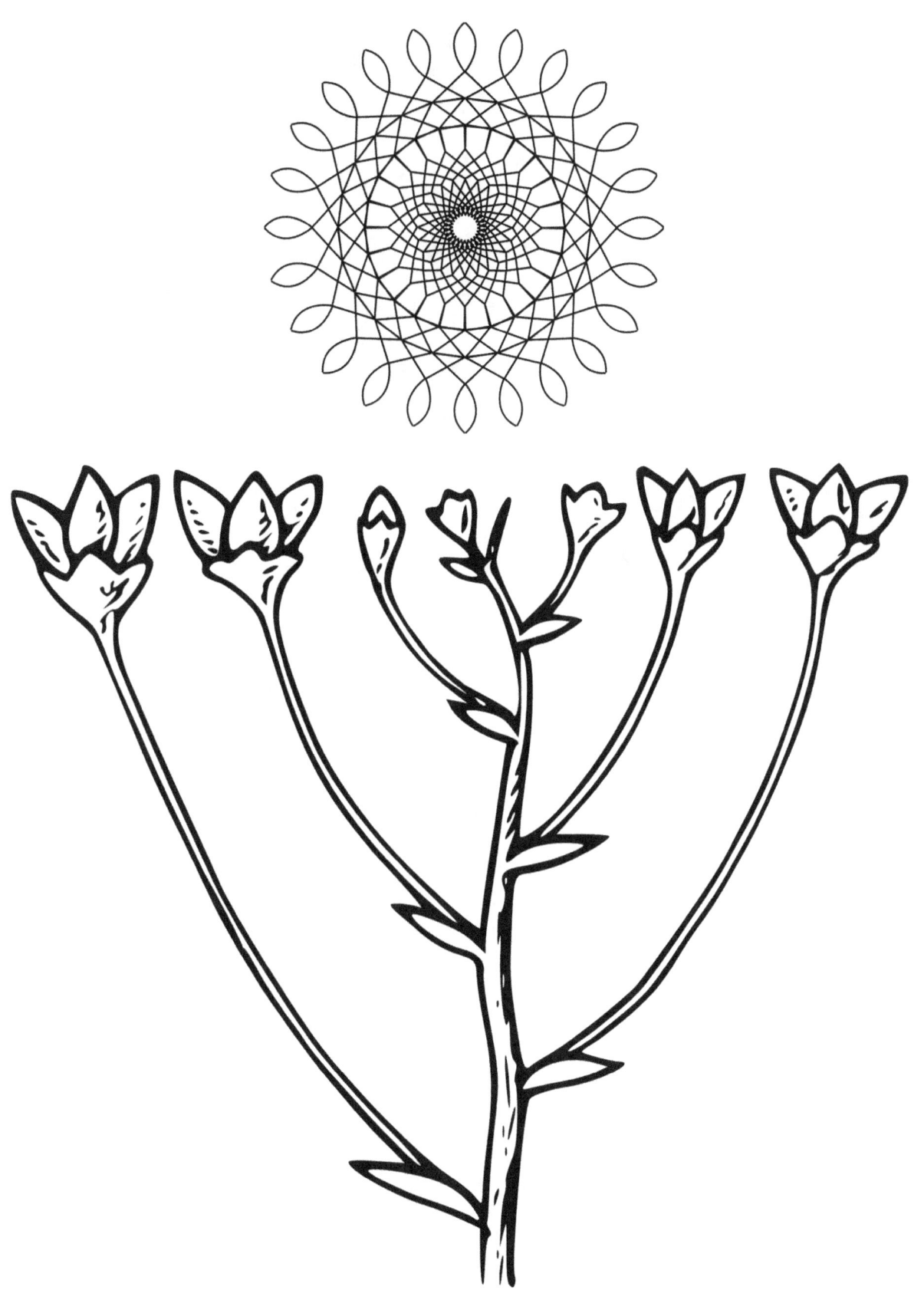

Copyright © 2018 Michael Weiner

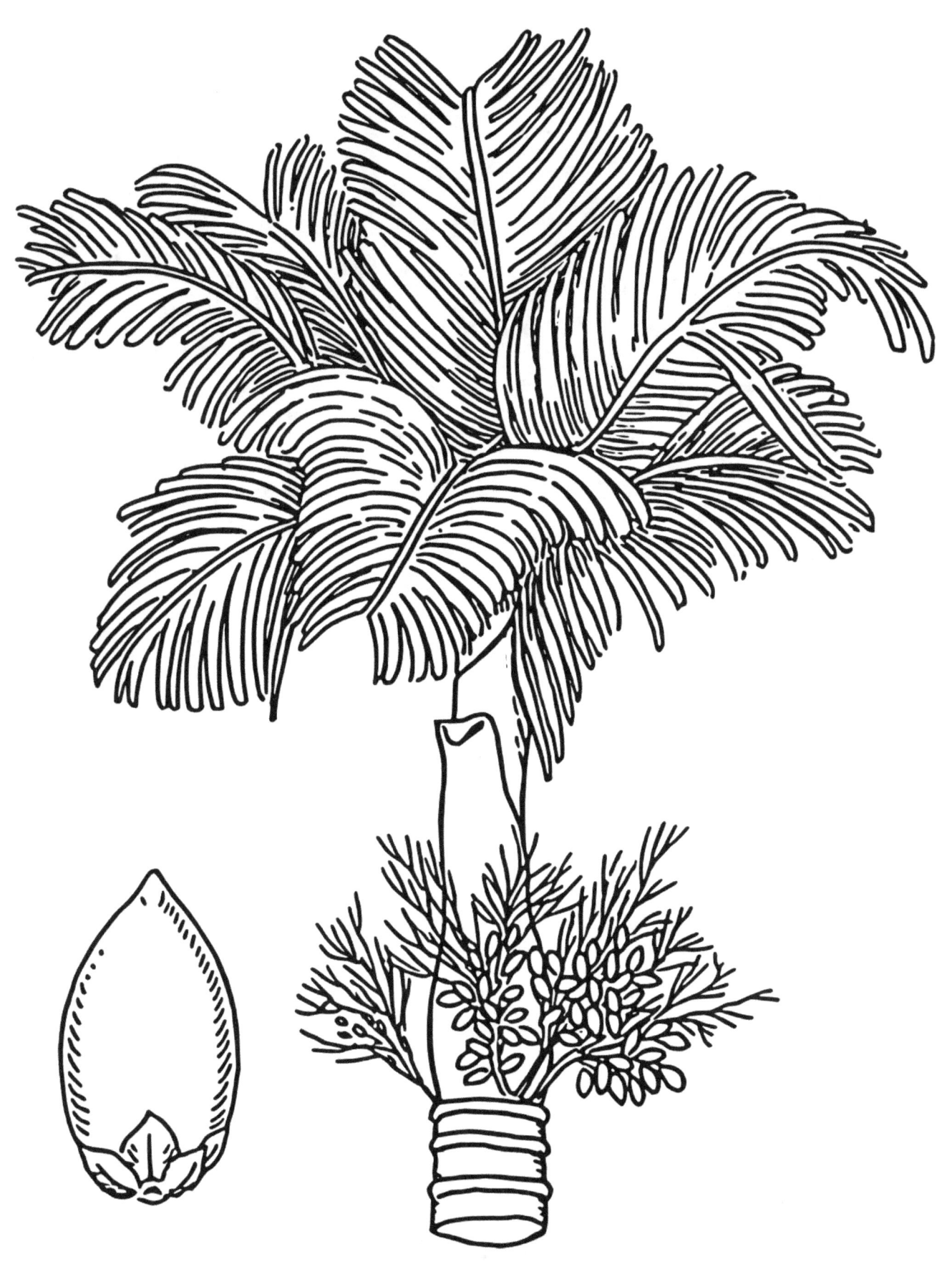

Copyright © 2018 Michael Weiner

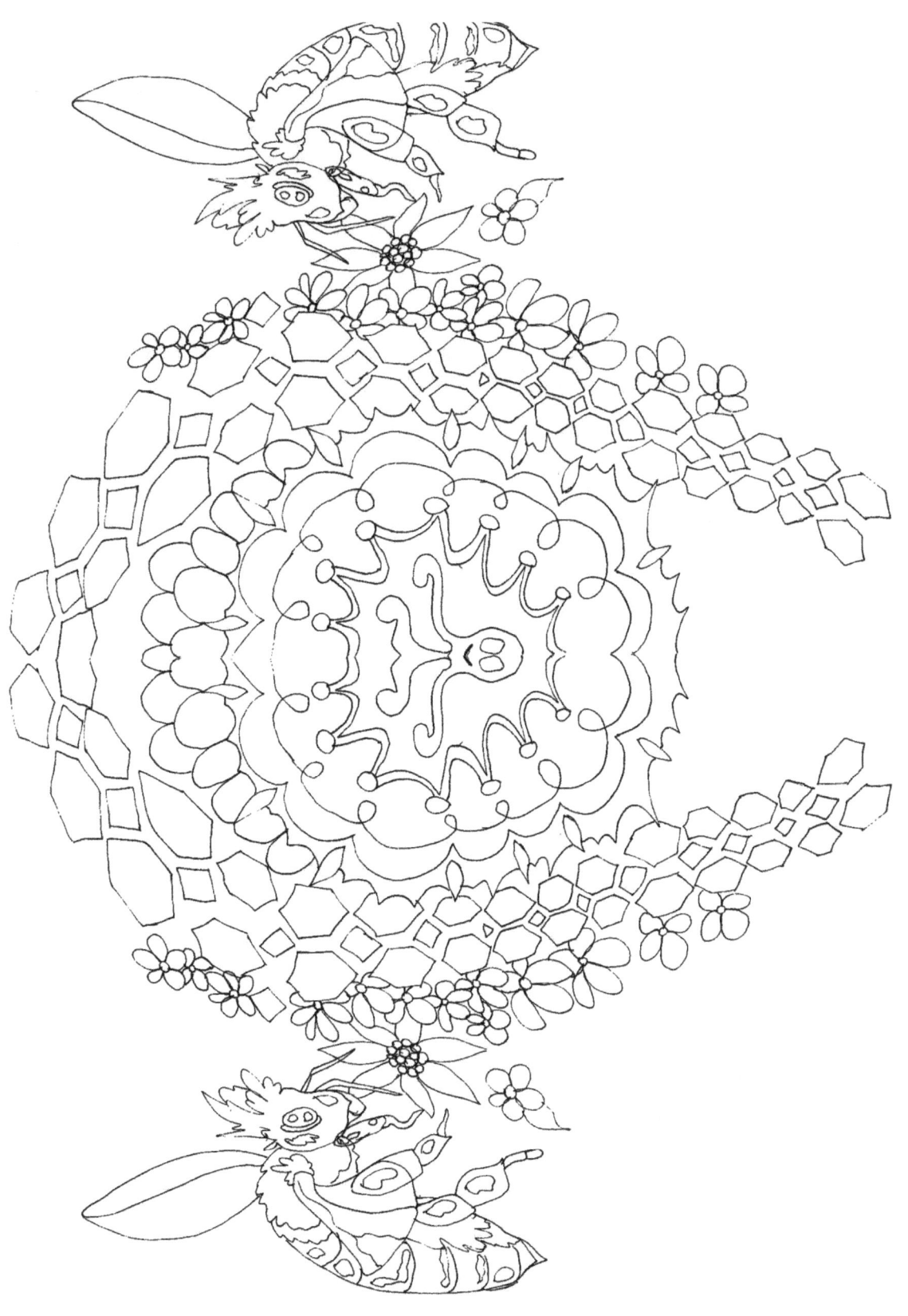

Copyright © 2018 Michael Weiner

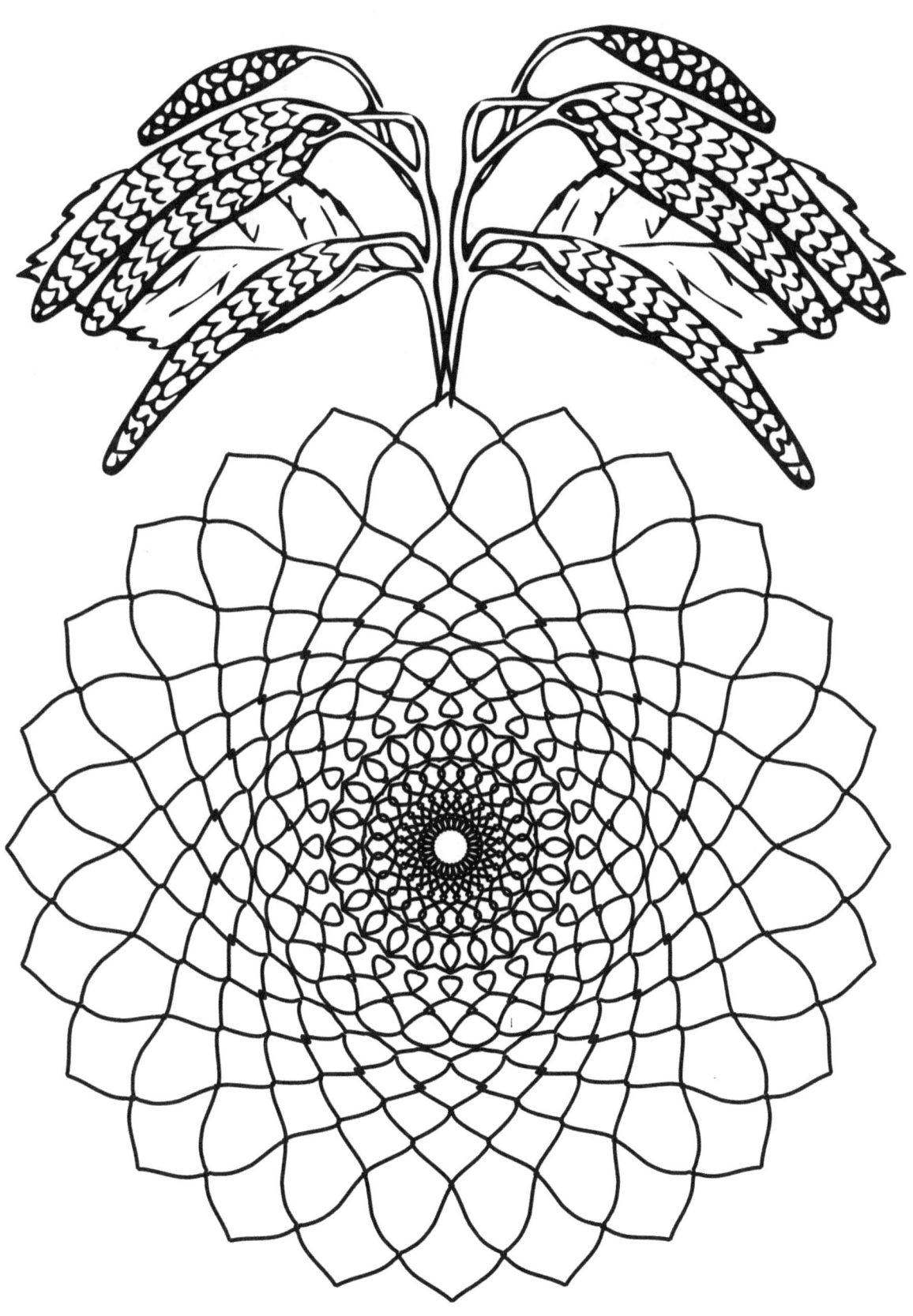

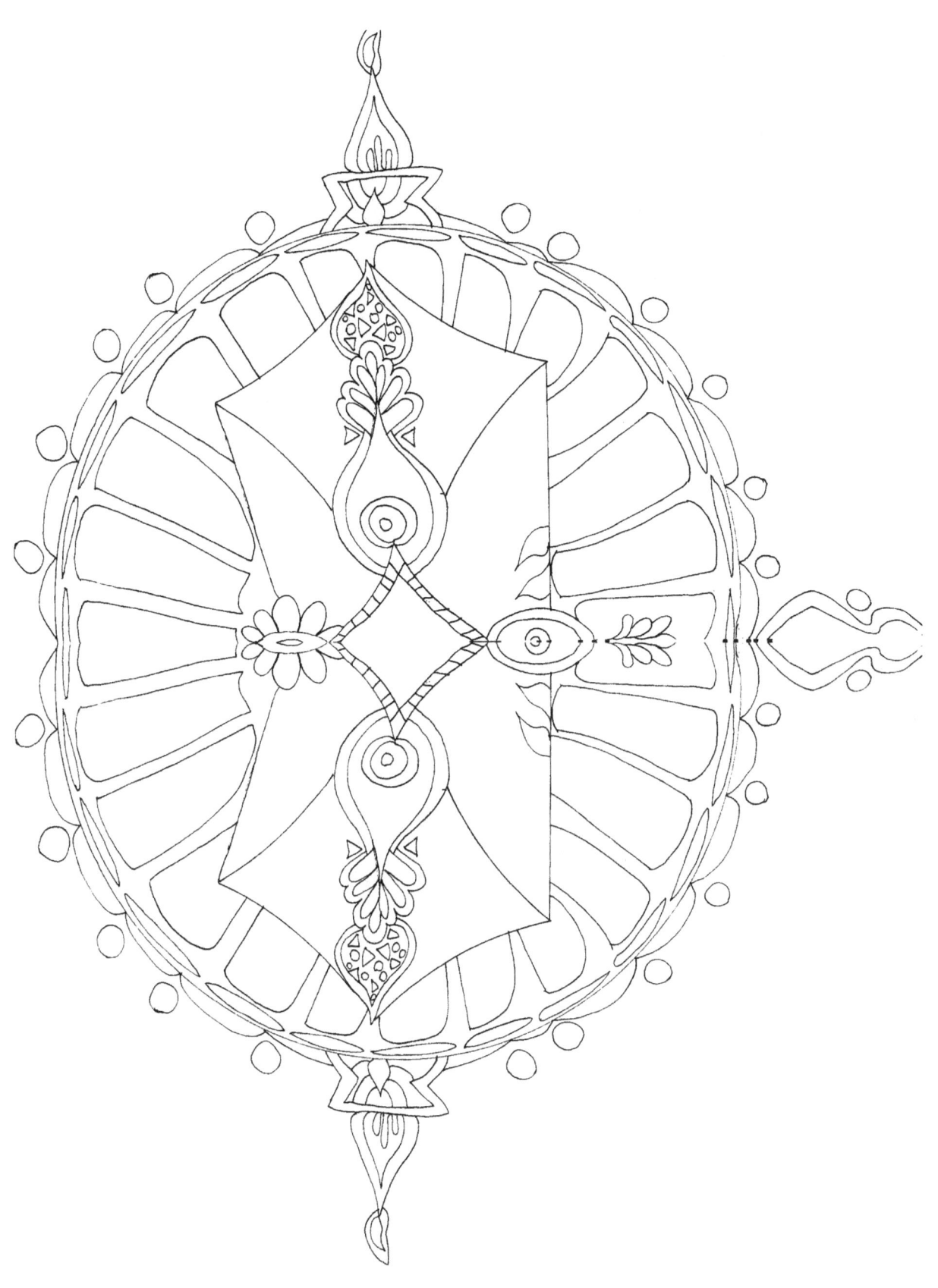

Copyright © 2018 Michael Weiner

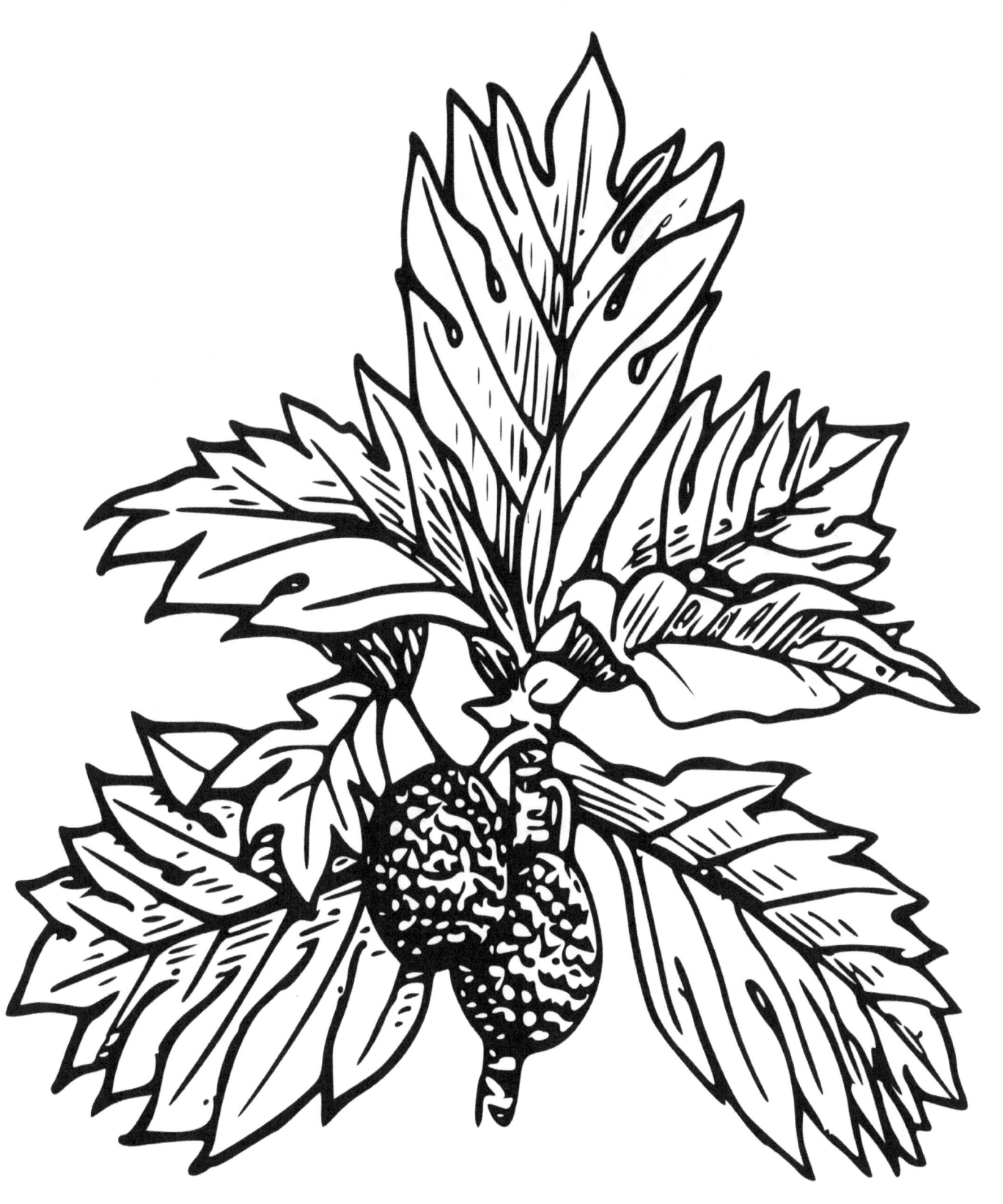

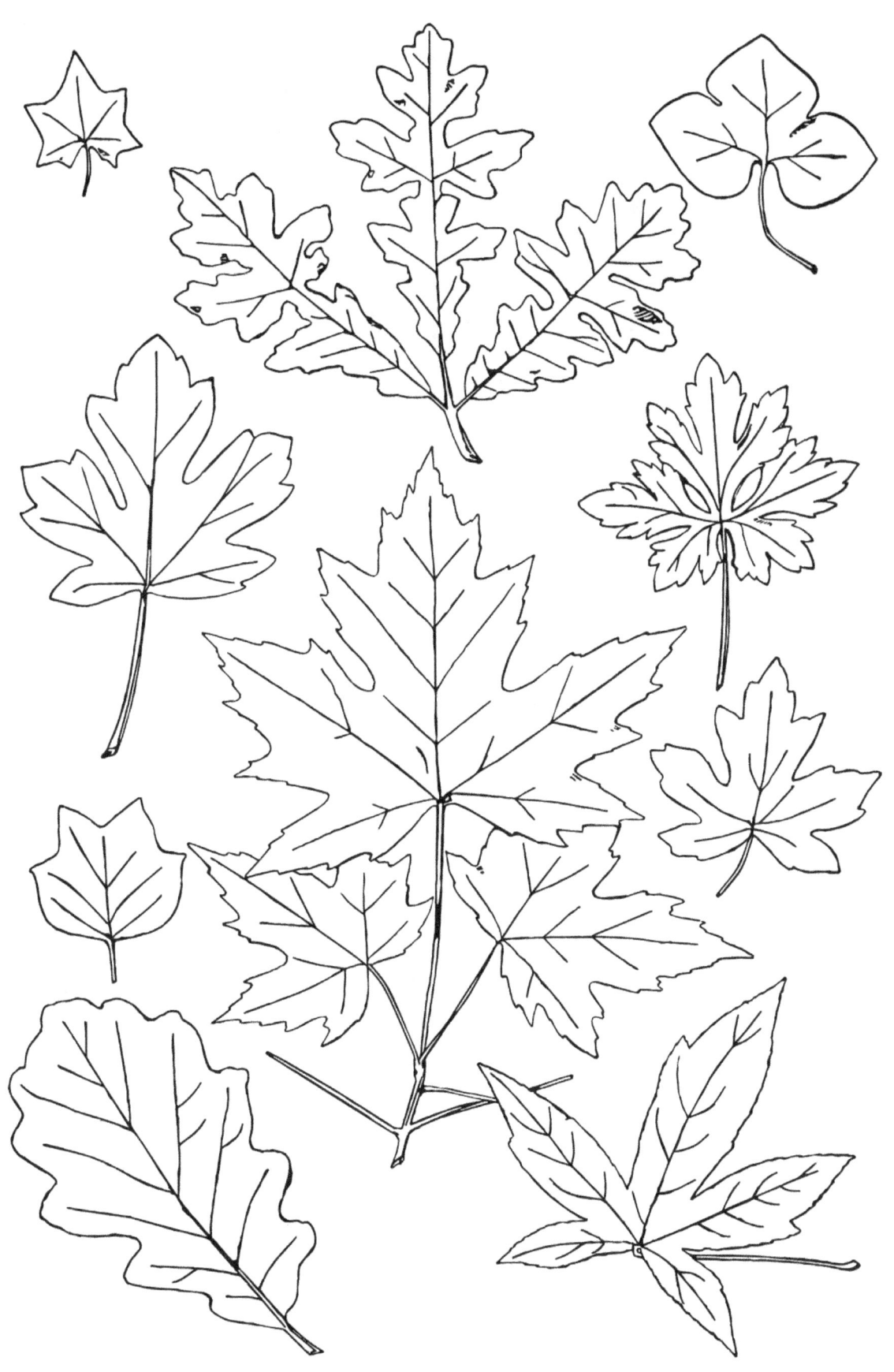

Copyright © 2018 Michael Weiner

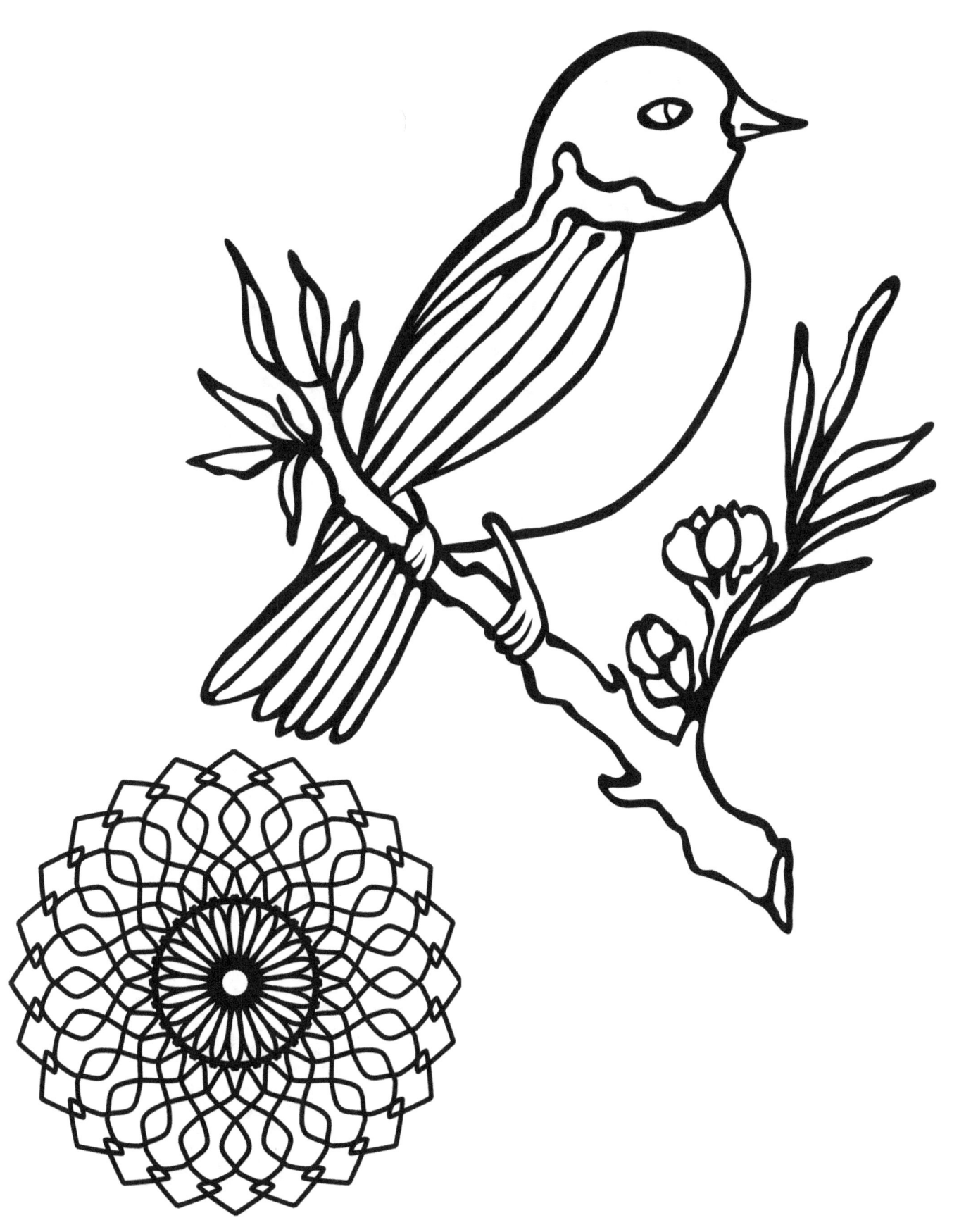

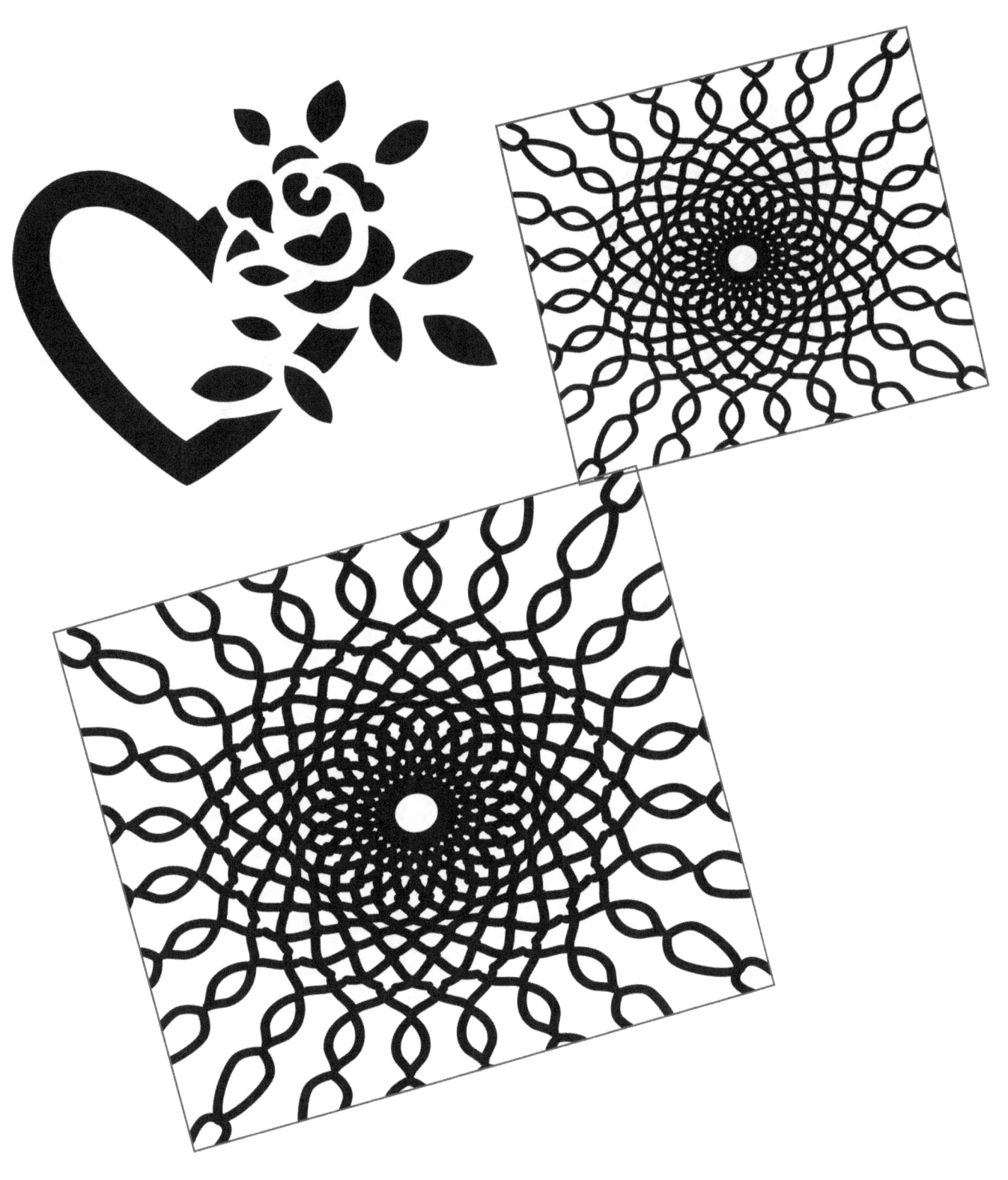

Copyright © 2018 Michael Weiner

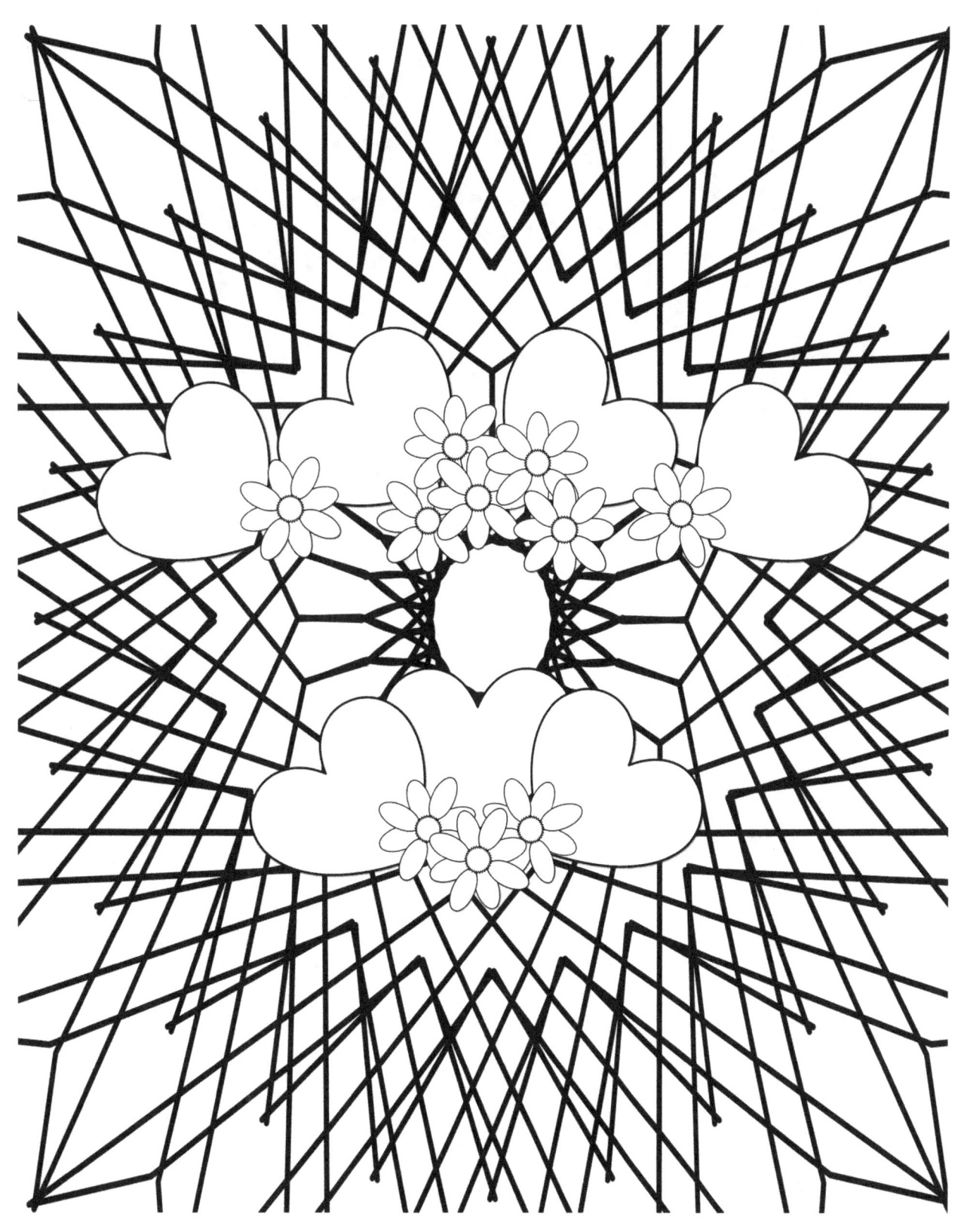

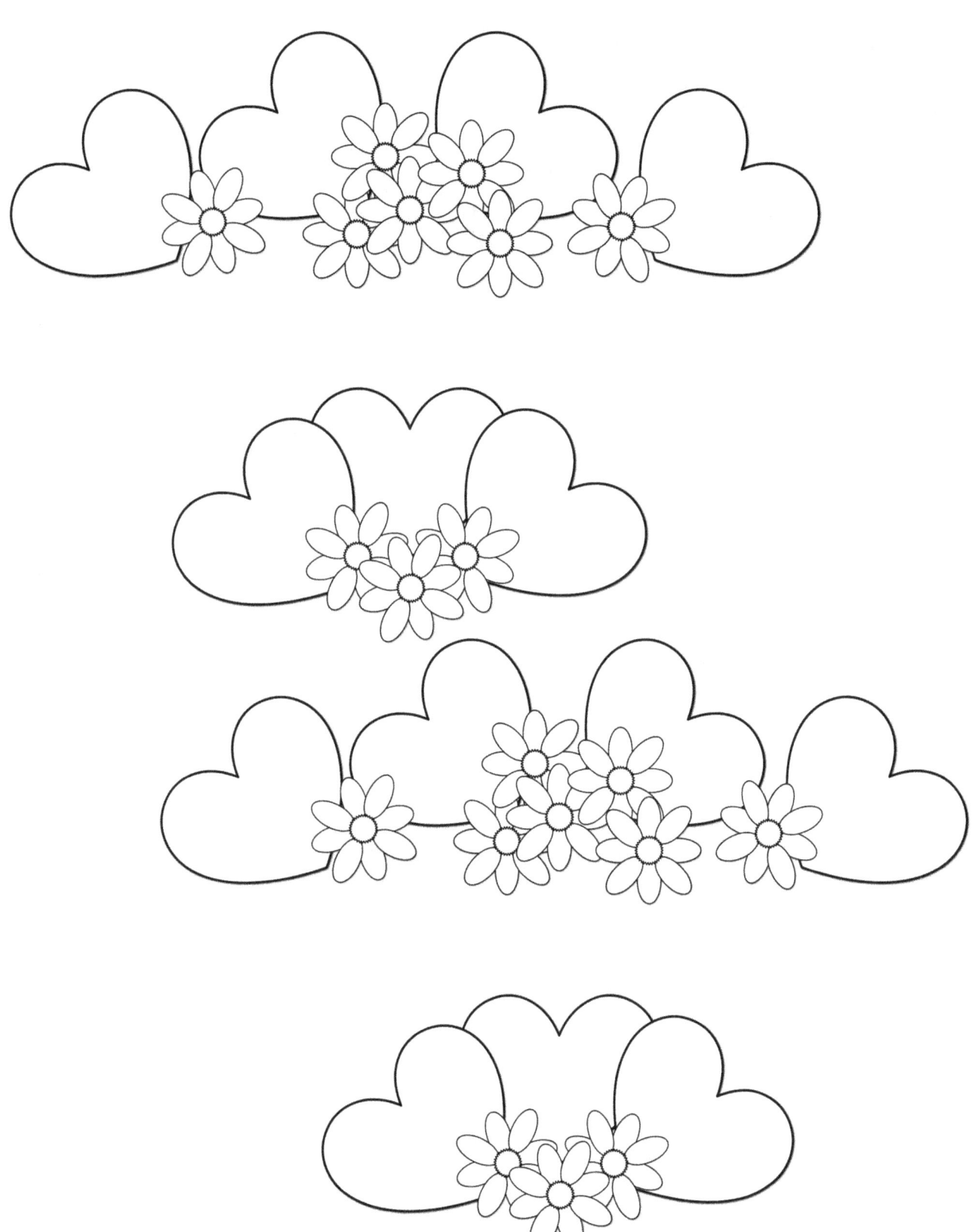

Copyright © 2018 Michael Weiner

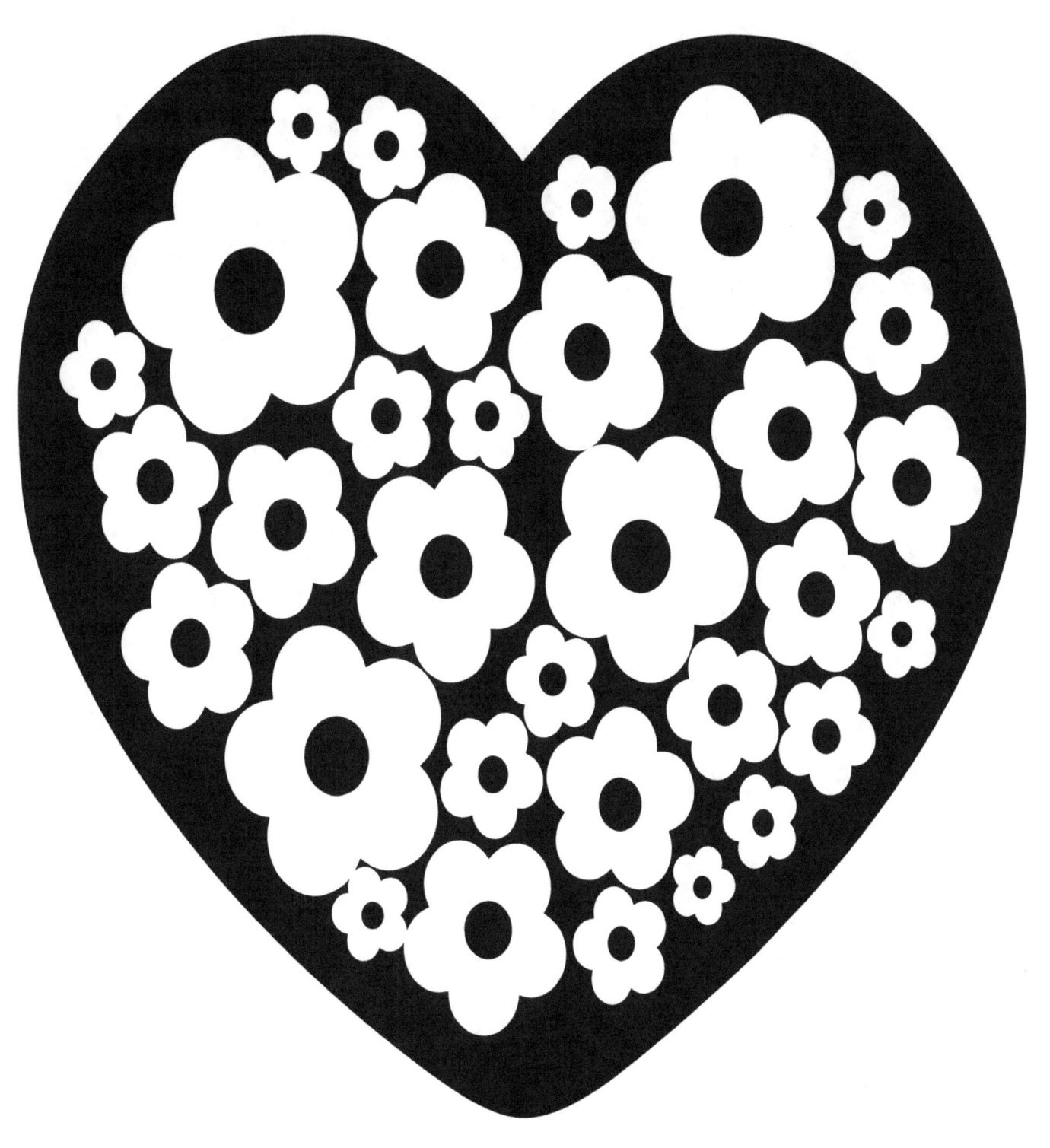

Copyright © 2018 Michael Weiner

Notes

www.ingramcontent.com/pod-product-compliance
Lightning Source LLC
Chambersburg PA
CBHW082245220526
45469CB00009B/2879